ORGANIZED CRIME IN CHICAGO

ORGANIZED CRIME IN CHICAGO

Beyond the Mafia

ROBERT M. LOMBARDO

UNIVERSITY OF ILLINOIS PRESS
Urbana, Chicago, and Springfield

Manufactured in the United States of America
1 2 3 4 5 C P 5 4 3 2 1
This book is printed on acid-free paper.

Segments of this book originally appeared in the following edited volume and journals and are used here with permission: "The Organized Crime Neighborhoods of Chicago," in *Handbook of Organized Crime in the United States,* Greenwood Publishing Group, 1994, reprinted courtesy ABC-CLIO Inc.; "The Social Organization of Organized Crime in Chicago," in the *Journal of Contemporary Criminal Justice* 10, 4 (Dec), reprinted courtesy of SAGE Publications Inc.; "The Black Mafia: African-American Organized Crime in Chicago, 1890–1960," in *Crime, Law and Social Change,* volume 38 (2002), 1, 33–65, reprinted courtesy of Kluwer Academic Publishers - Dordrecht; and "The Forty-Two Gang: The Unpublished Landesco Manuscripts," in the *Journal of Gang Research,* volume 18–1 Fall 2010, pages 19–38, reprinted courtesy of the National Gang Crime Research Center.

Library of Congress Cataloging-in-Publication Data
Lombardo, Robert M.
Organized crime in Chicago : beyond the Mafia / Robert M. Lombardo.
p. cm.
Includes bibliographical references and index.
ISBN 978-0-252-03730-6 (cloth) — ISBN 978-0-252-07878-1 (pbk.)
1. Organized crime—Illinois—Chicago. 2. Criminals—Illinois—Chicago.
3. Gangs—Illinois—Chicago. I. Title.
HV6795.C4L58 2012
364.10609773'11—dc23 2012017778

To Lynda, Tom, and Mike

The view that a secret criminal brotherhood was transplanted to urban America at the end of the nineteenth century produced a formula that lazy, ill-informed journalists would regularly turn to when writing about organized crime that effectively absolved the United States from any responsibility for its drug and crime problems.

—Michael Woodiwiss, *Gangster Capitalism*

CONTENTS

PREFACE

The idea for a study of organized crime in Chicago began when I was in grammar school. As a child, I had a great uncle who was not allowed to visit our home. When I asked my grandfather why we did not associate with Uncle Frank, he only replied that Uncle Frank did not work. I later found out that he was a member of the North Side Crew of the Chicago Outfit, the traditional organized crime group in Chicago. Growing up in the West Side of Chicago, the Outfit was a part of everyday life. I witnessed my first police raid when I was twelve years old as Chicago police rescued a "juice loan" victim who was being held in the basement of a local restaurant by neighborhood gangsters. I also remember being sent home late one evening by Chicago mobster Joseph Lombardo after he "closed the corner" where my friends and I hung out and drank beer long after curfew. As a teenager, I worked in a local grocery store. One of our customers was Ross Prio, head of the North Side Crew. His visits to our store were right out of the movies—bodyguards, black Cadillacs, and five-hundred-dollar suits. Who were these people? Why did the government allow them to exist? What was their relationship to our neighborhood? When I became a university professor and sought a research topic, the choice was easy. I chose to study organized crime in American society.

Research into organized crime presents difficulties not typically encountered in the social sciences. All societies have topics that are considered taboo. The study of organized crime is one of those taboo subjects. Facts and relationships are often uncovered that may be better left hidden. Because organized crime is sustained by collusion, corruption, and complacency, academics have largely ignored this important social problem. In fact, the academic community has been accused of damaging its own credibility by ignoring its moral obligation to remind society of the dangers posed by organized crime.[1]

Sociology and organized crime grew up together in Chicago during the decades that followed World War I. There, sociologists at the University of Chicago were laying the groundwork for criminology as it is known today. Yet these sociologists, whose perspectives focused on life in the streets of Chicago, virtually ignored the phenomenon that became known as organized crime. While Chicagoans and the American public alike were reading about the exploits of Al Capone and other Prohibition-era gangsters in the daily newspapers, only one social scientist, John Landesco, was actively studying the problem of organized crime.

Landesco's book *Organized Crime in Chicago* is the single most important sociological work ever written about this subject. Although completed in 1929, Landesco's study did not receive wide circulation until it was reprinted in 1968. Its marginal status among the works of the Chicago School of sociology has become the subject of some debate. The recommendations regarding the control of organized crime made by Landesco and Ernest Burgess, who contributed to the original edition of the book, were not widely received by the academic community and other reformers of the period. Unlike most of the work of the Chicago School, Landesco's research was critical of the business community and government of Chicago.[2]

Landesco's recommendations focused on the integration of immigrant communities, and in particular the Sicilian community, into mainstream American society; the creation of a system of "boards of conciliation and arbitration" to mediate labor disputes; the removal of politics from the police department; the control of juvenile delinquency; *and the separation of the political machine and organized crime in Chicago*. These recommendations made it clear that organized crime was rooted in the social structure of society itself. The history, economic system, political order, and stratification of Chicago were responsible for organized crime, not immigrant or recalcitrant members of society. Such findings gave rise to a significant number of questions that few people were willing to answer.

Even without the difficulties imposed by researching potentially taboo subjects, finding out about organized crime is very difficult. People do not always agree upon the meaning of the term *organized crime*. Does it denote a specific type of crime, such as violent crime and property crime, or is it a specific group of people? Is organized crime the type of crime that requires organization in its commission, such as gambling, prostitution, and narcotics trafficking; or does it refer to the Mafia or La Cosa Nostra?

Another problem encountered in researching organized crime is that much of what has been published was written for public consumption. Journalists, law enforcement officers, and government officials have written fanciful accounts about organized crime that are not constrained by the rules of careful scientific investigation as are the works of social scientists. In fact, the literature on organized crime contains so many contradictions that the reader can be reduced to a state of complete confusion when reading about this subject. Writers often use the terms Mafia, Camorra, Black Hand, Unione Siciliana, and Cosa Nostra interchangeably even though they denote entirely different groups of people and forms of behavior.

There are also a number of methodological problems involved in researching this topic. Participants do not want to talk about their illegal activities or admit involvement. Information sources, therefore, must often be circumspect and indirect. The ongoing activities of organized criminals simply are not accessible to observation by the ordinary citizen or social scientist. Even to gain access to the observations made by law enforcement and investigative bodies, one must have "connections."

Fortunately, I had these connections. I received cooperation from federal prosecutors and law enforcement agents, municipal police officers, and a number of other people who are knowledgeable about organized crime in Chicago. I worked with many of these people during my twenty-eight-year career as a member of the Chicago Police Department. During my tenure as a police officer, I was assigned to the Organized Crime Division for twelve years, where I worked directly on narcotics and gambling investigations. I also served with the Illinois Bureau of Investigation, the state's organized crime unit, which was disbanded in 1977.

It should be noted, however, that the cooperation received from government agencies did not include access to investigative memoranda unless the reports had been made public through court proceedings. Most material contained in investigative files is derived from secret grand jury transcripts. As a result, this material is unavailable to anyone who is not on the list of those approved by the courts to receive grand jury evidence.

Law enforcement agencies are reluctant to provide access to other data as well. This lack of cooperation is a rational choice made on the part of these agencies because they do not want to jeopardize their position of dominance in the organized crime control effort. The struggle against underworld activities is dominated by federal law enforcement agencies that have been highly successful in investigating organized crime in recent years. As a result, these agencies stand to gain little by allowing access to outside researchers who may raise questions about their operations.

In spite of the difficulties encountered, modern research into organized crime has been accomplished through interviews with law enforcement officials and criminal informants; case studies; the review of investigative reports, published works, and other documents; and direct observation.[3] Information about organized crime in Chicago is widely scattered among various sources and difficult to obtain, and many of these sources were used to provide data for this volume.

Persons interviewed included police officers, federal law enforcement agents, federal prosecutors, college professors, racket subculture residents, associates of organized crime figures, gamblers, bookies, and actual organized crime members themselves. Of the organized crime associates, two were convicted felons who had served time in the penitentiary for various criminal activities. One of the college professors interviewed was personally responsible for coining the phrase "racket subculture" during research that he conducted in the early 1960s. The other pioneered the concept of the "defended neighborhood." One law enforcement official was ninety years of age and had actually met Al Capone.

Experience has shown that often a snowballing effect occurs as qualitative research progresses; each subject interviewed introduces the researcher to another interview subject. That was not the case in this study. People were reluctant to talk about organized crime and even more reluctant to involve other people. In researching organized crime, Francis Ianni found that the nature of the inquiry puts a major strain on interpersonal relationships with informants and may even endanger one's life when it leads to the exploration of information that people do not want made public.[4]

Research conducted by the Illinois Institute of Technology and the Chicago Crime Commission revealed that it is necessary to conceal the identity of informative sources when dealing with organized crime.[5] Further, it was learned that anonymity was only the first step in obtaining cooperation from knowledgeable persons. Some interview subjects requested that all written record of their statements be destroyed after the completion of the final research. Following the experience of these two organizations, confidentially and anonymity were strictly observed throughout my research. In addition, government-mandated guidelines for research on human subjects, which preclude the identification of those interviewed, were strictly followed.

According to Barney Glaser and Anselim Strauss, every book is as good as the anthropologist's informant or the sociologist's interviewee.[6] They argue that published works may even be superior to informants in that they are based on regularized procedures and are more precise than an informant's memory. As such, academic books and government reports have been reviewed for information relevant to this investigation, as well as government documents, investigative memoranda, and court material.

I also reviewed the records of the Chicago History Museum and the Chicago Crime Commission to obtain information relevant to this study. The library at the Chicago History Museum provided much of the historical information used to describe the Chicago neighborhoods reviewed in the following chapters. The archives of the Chicago Crime Commission provided historical information on the activities of organized crime in Chicago. Chicago's business community started the crime commission in 1919 as an independent investigative agency representing the public interest in matters concerning criminal justice in the Chicago area. One of the commission's specialized areas of interest is organized crime. As a result, the commission maintains an extensive library of newspaper clippings and its own investigative memorandum about organized crime in Chicago.

Much of the historical information provided in this volume came from newspaper accounts of the day. Relying solely on newspaper accounts can give a distorted image of what has occurred. Newspaper reporting can reflect the biases and beliefs of those who write the news. Nonetheless, my analysis relies on newspaper accounts because they are often the only source of data available. In fact, I have found that newspaper accounts often provide a more accurate account of the history of organized crime than published books. Much of what nonacademic authors have written conforms to popular beliefs about organized crime, such as the Mafia paradigm, which is not supported by the historical record.

The criminal histories of 191 members of organized crime in Chicago were also examined. While this list was thought to include all the members of the Chicago Outfit at the time it was created, it does not imply that only 191 people have been involved in organized crime activities in the Chicago area. Many other people such as lawyers, bookies, burglars, gamblers, and thieves worked for and with the Chicago Outfit, but they were not members themselves. This fact has been documented in the President's Commission on Law Enforcement and the Administration of Justice, *Task Force Report: Organized Crime.*[7] Their findings showed that beneath the "soldiers" (the lowest level of organized crime member) are large numbers of employees and commissioned agents who do most of the actual work in the various criminal enterprises. They take bets, drive trucks, answer telephones, and work in legitimate businesses.

Fieldwork was conducted whenever possible to document and corroborate information received from other sources. Past research suggests that recruitment into organized crime is facilitated by the presence of the organized crime in select community areas. Five communities in the Chicago area have a reputation of being associated with organized crime. Since I wished to gain a greater understanding of community support for recruitment into organized crime, I visited each of the community areas that organized crime figures were known to frequent. I also gathered data concerning the number of crime syndicate members born and residing in each of these areas. Many, if not most, persons known to be members of organized crime in Chicago can be linked to a select number of city neighborhoods or suburban communities where they have historically frequented certain bars, restaurants, and private social clubs.

The validity of much of the data collected has been tested, to the extent possible, through the triangulation of interview data, direct observation, and published books and records. *Triangulation* refers to the collection of data utilizing different methodologies with respect to a single research question. For example, interviews were used to verify data obtained from published sources. The strength of such a multi-method inquiry stands on what is referred to as the *triad*. Each leg of the triad represents a unique mode of data collection that presents the researcher with a different vantage point from which to study the issues at hand.[8]

The sociological literature demonstrates that recruitment into organized crime is facilitated by a community's social structure. The analyses performed in the following chapters not only tests these earlier findings but also explains how organized crime continues to recruit new members today despite changing social and demographic conditions. The data gathered follows the tradition of the Chicago School, which challenged students to go out into the streets of Chicago and make some sociological sense out of life as they found it. Research methodologies have included social history analysis, interviews, personal observation, and case studies. Social history analysis—that is, explaining why and how things happen—is particularly important to this study. In fact, history is so critical to sociological study that history and sociology are often thought to be one and the same. We simply cannot explain society as it is without studying the historical decisions that have shaped our social world.

Every book is a product of the labor of the author but also a product of the education of the writer. As such, I would like to acknowledge those who provided me with the sociological understanding of our world that enabled me to write this volume. They include professors Howard Abadinsky, William Bridges, John Johnstone, John Koval, Michael Maltz, David Rubenstein, and Charles Suchar. A number of law enforcement professionals also gave of their time to answer my research questions, and I would like to thank them as well. They include Anthony Carduf, Thomas Capparelli, Robert Cody, Donald Herion, John Hinchy, J. Kenneth Lawrie, Nick Levas, Charles Molnar, Thomas Moriarity, Paul Seiler, Gary Shapiro, Thomas Spanos, and Richard Weber. I would also like to recognize Arthur Bilek and Dominick Candeloro, who reviewed the final draft of this book. Many thanks also go to Lisa Bayer, Jill R. Hughes, Laurie Matheson, and all the people at the University of Illinois Press who worked to make this book possible. Members and associates of Chicago's underworld also contributed to this volume. Although they cannot be mentioned by name, I would also like to thank them for the trust they have placed in me by providing the information obtained in this analysis.

ORGANIZED CRIME IN CHICAGO

INTRODUCTION

This book examines organized crime in the city of Chicago from a sociological perspective. The term *organized crime* is used to define the political corruption that afforded protection to gambling, prostitution, and other vice activity in large American cities from the second half of the nineteenth century until the end of the twentieth century. The dominant belief is that organized crime in Chicago, and other American cities, is descendent of the Sicilian Mafia. In fact, the alien conspiracy theory argues that organized crime evolved in a linear fashion beginning with the Mafia in Sicily, emerging in the form of the Black Hand in America's immigrant colonies, and culminating in the development of the Cosa Nostra in America's urban centers. This book challenges the alien conspiracy theory and argues that the development of organized crime in Chicago, and elsewhere, was not related to the emergence of the Sicilian Mafia, but was rooted in the social structure of American society.

Defining Organized Crime

Organized crime is referred to by many names in the United States. Described variously as the Mafia, the Cosa Nostra, the crime syndicate, and the mob, its operations were first officially spelled out in 1951 when Tennessee senator Estes Kefauver launched an investigation into crime before the Special Congressional Committee to Investigate Organized Crime in Interstate Commerce. Kefauver found that there was a nationwide association of criminals, descendent of the Sicilian Mafia, who controlled vice activities and other rackets in many large American cities.[1]

Further evidence of the existence of a nationwide confederation of criminals came in 1957 when the Senate Select Committee on Improper Activities in Labor Management, under the direction of Senator John McClellan of Arkansas, found that there was extensive organized crime involvement in the labor union movement and in legitimate business. Later that same year, seventy-five of the nation's top hoodlums were discovered meeting at the home of Joseph Barbera in Appalachian New York. This event provided evidence of the existence of a nationwide crime syndicate and underscored the need for government action in dealing with organized crime.[2]

The need for government action against organized crime was further highlighted in 1963 when Joseph Valachi, a lifelong member of one of New York's five "crime families," testified before the Permanent Subcommittee on Investigations. Valachi labeled organized crime as the "Cosa Nostra" (literally "our thing"), describing it as a nationwide confederation of criminal groups linked together through a national commission. The federal government subsequently adopted the term Cosa Nostra in an effort to differentiate American organized crime from the Sicilian Mafia. The Kefauver Committee and Valachi's testimony gave rise to the belief that organized crime was an alien conspiracy that was imposed upon American society by recently arrived Italian immigrants.

The 1967 President's Commission on Law Enforcement and the Administration of Justice continued the work of the Kefauver and McClellan Committees. The commission's *Task Force Report: Organized Crime* scientifically explained organized crime for the first time to the American public. Its principal theoretical support came from an accompanying paper, "The Structures and Functions of Criminal Syndicates," written by Donald Cressey, which provided academic authentication for the alien conspiracy theory and its Italian connections.[3]

The commission referred to the Cosa Nostra as twenty-four "crime families," whose membership was exclusively men of Italian descent, working within structures as complex as those of any large corporation to supply gambling, loan sharking, narcotics, and other forms of vice to countless numbers of consumers.[4] Although the task force's estimate of the size and extent of organized crime activity has been questioned, their bureaucratic analogy was given wide circulation by Cressey and Ralph Salerno, both of whom authored popular books on the subject. The work of the President's Task Force carried on what the Kefauver Committee had begun by continuing to equate organized crime with Italian Americans.[5]

A 1964 report by the Federal Bureau of Investigation (FBI) traced the historical development of organized crime in Chicago to the "Unione Siciliano" or "Mafia."[6] According to the FBI, the Unione was strictly made up of Sicilians who specialized in extortion, prostitution, and narcotics. Tony

Lombardo was the head of the Unione. He was sent to Chicago on direct orders from Italy to settle a dispute between the Genna brothers and another Italian group, who controlled the North Side area of the city. Lombardo was eventually killed by the North Side group, the Aiellos. Al Capone then gained control of the Unione. With the ascension of Capone, the FBI reported, the words Mafia and Unione Siciliano lost their significance.

Support for the Italian origins of organized crime continues today. In fact, the alien conspiracy connection between the Mafia, the Black Hand, and American organized crime is the official position of the FBI. The following descriptions of the Cosa Nostra and Italian organized crime were taken from the FBI website in September 2006:

> Since the 1900s, thousands of Italian organized crime figures have come illegally to the United States, most of those being Sicilian Mafiosi. Many of those Mafia members who fled here in the early 1920s helped establish what is known today as the La Cosa Nostra or American Mafia. . . . The American Mafia has undergone many changes. From the Black Hand gangs around 1900; and the Five Points Gang in the 1910s and 1920s in New York City; to Al Capone's Syndicate in 1920s Chicago.[7]

Alien Conspiracy versus Ethnic Succession

Sociologists have offered two competing arguments to explain the emergence of organized crime in American society. The *alien conspiracy theory* argues that organized crime is the result of a foreign criminal conspiracy that was brought to American shores by southern Italian and Sicilian immigrants. Frederic Homer refers to the alien conspiracy theory as the "guns and garlic" approach because of its focus on Italian American criminals. The competing *ethnic succession argument* explains organized crime as the result of conditions inherent in American society that are utilized by successive waves of immigrants to obtain economic mobility. These arguments have two different theoretical foundations. The alien conspiracy formulation is grounded in cultural deviance theory, while the ethnic succession hypothesis is grounded in social disorganization and strain theory. Closely related to ethnic succession theory is the argument that organized crime is functional; it provides not only an avenue of social mobility but also a range of services for which there is a public demand.[8]

The alien conspiracy theory argues that organized crime originated outside of American society. It is viewed as a sinister foreign force that perverts the American system of government. It did not emerge out of American culture, but was thrust upon the United States by alien newcomers. Its roots lie in values that are contrary to the American way of life. These values are tied to the cultures of specific ethnic groups who brought organized crime with them when they immigrated to the United States. Organized crime in the form of the Mafia is viewed as an alien force that uses criminal activity to satisfy a desire for profit and to perpetuate its own wickedness.

The alien conspiracy position was classically summarized by the findings of the Kefauver Committee, which stated:

> There is a sinister criminal organization known as the Mafia operating throughout the country with ties in other nations. . . . The Mafia is the direct descendant of a criminal organization of the same name originating on the island of Sicily. In this country, the Mafia has also been known as the Black Hand and the Unione Siciliano. . . . The Mafia is a loose-knit organization specializing in the sale and distribution of narcotics, the conduct of various gambling enterprises, prostitution, and other rackets based on extortion and violence.[9]

The Kefauver Committee's findings were not without its detractors. In reviewing the work of the committee, William Moore wrote that although the committee played a vital role in orienting both professional and popular opinion toward a conspiracy interpretation of organized crime, it ignored a nascent but promising body of sociological literature.[10] In fact, Moore concluded that after comparing the committee's evidence with its conclusions, he was convinced that its emphasis was wrong, and he viewed its work as a study in "miseducation" and a strengthening of old myths that might better have been laid to rest.

In contrast to the alien conspiracy interpretation, the ethnic succession theory argues that organized crime is the direct result of conditions in American society. This theory posits that criminal groups have played an important part in the social differentiation of American society and that the urban rackets have allowed successive waves of immigrants who are on the bottom rungs of society a means of economic and social mobility that transcends the involvement of any particular ethnic group. The Irish were among the first groups to immigrate to the United States, and as a result they eventually dominated crime as well as big-city political machines. The Irish newcomers of the mid 1800s, with their political protection and tacit police approval, built criminal empires that provided services to urban politicians, gamblers, brothel operators, and saloon keepers alike. By 1920 and Prohibition, however, the Irish had won wealth, power, and respectability and had moved out of organized crime.[11]

Jewish gangsters filled the void left by the upwardly mobile Irish racketeers, particularly in New York City, where they came to dominate gambling and other criminal activities. Arnold Rothstein, probably the most important Jewish gangster of the 1920s, served as the inspiration for one of the major characters in F. Scott Fitzgerald's book *The Great Gatsby*. The Jews, however, quickly moved out of crime as legitimate avenues of opportunity became available. One school of thought attributes the rapid departure of the Jewish gangster to the fact that Jewish families placed a great deal of importance on education.[12] Jewish hoodlums are believed to have used their ill-gotten gains to educate their children, which prepared them for the business and professional world and departure from organized crime.

Italians eventually replaced Jewish gangsters but found it much more difficult to achieve wealth and political influence than earlier immigrant groups.[13] The Italian immigrant found that many of the big-city paths from rags to riches had been preempted. Although this was a period of urban growth and large-scale public works projects, Irish political machines strictly controlled city jobs and contracts. Excluded from public employment and the political ladder by earlier groups, Italian immigrants found fewer routes open to wealth and advancement, leading some to turn to illicit ways and eventual entrance into crime.

The Italians, who had replaced the Jews, who in turn had replaced the Irish in organized crime, are now being replaced by blacks and Hispanics, the most recent urban immigrants. The ethnic succession theory argues that alien conspiracy advocates ignore the social conditions that have given rise to organized crime in this country. Organized crime was not the result of a transplanted Sicilian Mafia, but the product of American society. Many of the Italian and Sicilian immigrants who entered into organized crime did not come to this country as criminals. They were raised in the United States; most were even born here. In fact, Al Capone, himself, was born in Brooklyn, New York.

The roots of the ethnic succession argument lie in the history of machine politics in urban areas. Organized crime began in the neighborhood saloons and gambling halls of the cities of the Northeast and Midwest and is the outcome of an evolutionary process extending nearly a century. The creation of modern-day organized crime is the result of a critical juncture in history in which established interdependencies between machine politicians, vice entrepreneurs, and criminal gangs found new meaning in the provision of illegal alcohol during Prohibition.

During the late 1800s, the saloon keeper, gambling house operator, and politician were often the same person. The saloon was the center of neighborhood life and an important base of political activity. It was the place where ward and municipal politics were openly discussed. This position enabled the saloon keeper to deliver a significant number of votes at election time. In return, saloon keepers were rewarded, by the reigning political party, with protection of their vice activities from the enforcement actions of the local police. This protection led to the development of gambling and prostitution syndicates in many urban areas.

Street corner gangs who frequented the neighborhood saloon were also utilized to bring in the vote. These gangs were usually centered in immigrant areas, where the gangster served as the right arm of the corrupt politician at election time. Gang members were asked to distribute campaign literature, hang posters, and canvass for voters. They were used as "repeaters," who voted early and voted often, and as "sluggers," who employed violence to ensure that others voted in the "right way." In exchange for delivering the vote, gang members were allowed to continue in their criminal activities, the proceeds of which often went to support local political organizations.

Herbert Asbury estimated that in New York City alone there were over thirty thousand men who owed their allegiance to gang leaders and through them to the political leaders of Tammany Hall. To keep gang members busy between elections, machine politicians often found jobs for them in the gambling houses and brothels that were under the patronage of the party organization. Thus, the underworld became an important factor in big-city politics.[14]

The necessities of urban American life also gave big-city political machines control over thousands of jobs. Construction workers, street cleaners, police officers, firemen, and numerous other types of workers were in demand. These jobs were handed out to those who worked to support the machine and would vote only for its candidates. Because immigrants and their offspring comprised more than two-thirds of the population of America's largest cities, such jobs often went to foreigners.[15]

The unorthodox activities of the big-city political machine, and the foreign-born element that comprised it, did not go unnoticed. Early in the twentieth century, Henry Osborn, the president of the American Museum of Natural History, warned American-born citizens of the threat to American institutions posed by the influx of foreigners and their ideas of self-government that held power in America's largest cities. In an attack on machine politics, Osborn stated that in many urban areas the original American element had entirely lost control and that alien foreign-born groups were now in power.[16]

The activities of the political machine, and the culture of the immigrant, often Catholic, urban poor who comprised it, clashed with those of Protestant, rural America. In an attempt to regain control of the city and diminish the power of the corrupt political machines found there, reformers attacked the relationship between the political machine and the neighborhood saloon. In order to destroy the political boss, reformers of the period believed it was necessary to destroy his base of operation—the saloon.[17] The acrimony between rural and urban, Protestant and Catholic, and native and immigrant America reached its pinnacle with the ratification of the Eighteenth Amendment to the Constitution in 1919. Prohibition, as it is commonly referred to, banned the sale of alcoholic beverages in the United States.

The enactment of Prohibition changed the relationship between political machines, vice syndicates, and criminal gangs. This change, however, was not the one foreseen by social reformers. Before Prohibition the local political boss acted as a patron for vice entrepreneurs and gang members, who in return assisted him with financial and voting support. Because of the huge sums of money involved in bootlegging, local vice syndicates and criminal gangs quickly moved into the liquor trade. Struggles to control liquor distribution territories and protection from rival organizations suddenly became more important than protection from the local police. Prohibition unleashed a previously unknown level of competitive violence that changed the nature of organized crime by removing the machine politician and placing the gangster on the top of the criminal hierarchy.

Prohibition acted as a catalyst of opportunity that caused organized crime to blossom into a powerful force in American society. Common crooks were turned into sophisticated gangsters, who worked to provide an otherwise law-abiding American public with alcohol. The gangsters were even admired by some ethnic and working-class Americans because of the diverse ways that their activities influenced local communities.[18] They provided jobs, supported local charities, and helped mediate labor disputes. They were also seen as champions of the poor, as they fought for their community by aiding ethnic politicians in the rough and often violent politics of the slum. They were the success stories of their neighborhoods.

Prohibition also forced cooperation among criminal gangs nationwide in an effort to ensure the uninterrupted flow of alcohol. The liquor business was international in scope. Illegal alcohol was often smuggled into the United States and then shipped to various areas of the country, all of which demanded the cooperation of criminal groups from around the nation. This cooperation, though largely limited to the period of Prohibition, was the foundation of the belief in the existence of a nationwide crime syndicate.

The repeal of Prohibition in 1933 found large, rationally organized criminal organizations in place in many of the nation's largest cities. The end of Prohibition did not mean the end of the newly expanded crime syndicates.

Instead of disappearing, these organizations focused their attention on gambling and utilized their newly established power to carry out other forms of illegal activities, such as loan sharking, labor racketeering, pornography, and narcotics distribution. These activities brought the American gangster into what has been described as the "Golden Age of Organized Crime."[19]

The Racket Subculture

Although sociologists favor the ethnic succession argument, the alien conspiracy theory dominates the literature and is the generally accepted explanation for the emergence of traditional organized crime. This can be explained by the popularity of media portrayals of the Mafia paradigm and the fact that there has never been a comprehensive theoretical explanation for the emergence and continuation of traditional organized crime in American society. Although there is strong support for strain theory, that is using crime to overcome poverty, as the foundation of the ethnic succession argument, strain alone cannot explain the continuation of organized crime. While ethnic succession explains the entrance of poverty-stricken newcomers into vice and crime at the turn of the last century, it cannot explain the continued dominance of organized crime by Italian Americans. This book argues that Italians continued to dominate organized crime after rising out of poverty because of the presence of "racket subcultures" within American society.

A familiar theme running through the sociology literature argues that there is a direct relationship between community areas and organized crime. This argument is grounded in the social disorganization perspective and has been frequently expressed in the delinquency literature. Described as racket subcultures, select community areas have been found to be centers of underworld activities and recruiting grounds for organized crime participation.

In his report on organized crime to the President's Commission on Law Enforcement and the Administration of Justice, Donald Cressey argued that in order to survive, every organization must have an institutionalized process for inducting new members and impressing upon them the values and ways of the organization's social system. Referring to organized crime, he noted that in some neighborhoods all three of the "essential ingredients" of an effective recruiting process are in operation: "inspiring aspiration for membership, training for membership, and selection for membership." Boys growing up in these areas knew it was a good thing to become a member of the "mob" just as boys growing up in other areas knew it was a good thing to join a prestigious club or attend a famous university.[20]

Additional evidence that select neighborhood areas provide recruiting grounds for organized crime was found by Irving Spergel in his study of New York City's "Racketville" community. According to Spergel, the presence of a well-organized criminal system in this community offered a "learning environment, which eventuated in certain types of behavior in preparation for later careers in the rackets." Similar findings were uncovered by Ianni, who described this classic recruiting process: "In ghetto neighborhoods kids still hang around in loosely formed gangs looking for 'action' or a chance to make some money. The local 'hoods' send them on little errands—buying coffee or carrying messages—and as they get older, trust them with more important tasks, such as picking up numbers or delivering number slips. Gradually some youngsters establish increasing degrees of trustworthiness with the 'hoods'."[21] In his testimony before the McClellan Committee, gangster Joseph Valachi stated that local mobsters carefully watched young men from racket communities as they participated in criminal activity.[22] The hoods paid special attention to the behavior of the boys when they were jailed. A boy who subscribed to the underworld code of being a "stand-up guy" and revealed nothing about himself, or his criminal associates, was a potential candidate for membership—other boys were not.

Evidence of community areas providing support for recruitment into organized crime can also be found in Gerald Suttles's conceptualization of the "defended neighborhood." He defined the defended neighborhood as a residential group that seals itself off through the efforts of delinquent gangs, restrictive covenants, sharp boundaries, and a forbidding reputation.[23] These communities have traditionally ensured the continuity of organized crime. In these neighborhoods the conventional and criminal value systems are highly integrated, allowing residents to share collective representations and moral sentiments that allow them to recognize the pursuit of a career in the underworld as a legitimate way of life.

The types of communities described by Ianni, Valachi, and Suttles have provided learning environments for the acquisition of values and skills associated with the performance of criminal roles and entrance into organized crime. Although a person living in a racket area is automatically exposed to criminal attitudes, selection and tutelage are granted to only a few. While the young men who form the pool of applicants are only a tiny portion of the community, they have been sufficient to replenish the ranks of organized crime.

The logic of the ethnic succession argument stresses that the dominant criminal group's hold over the world of vice and crime weakens as its ghettos dissolve and the protection they were afforded from police intrusion disappears. This assertion is based upon the argument that in the early stages of ethnic mobility, illicit upward movement is aided by residential segregation, allowing criminal networks to flourish in ghetto areas. Although the racket neighborhoods that were studied by Cressey, Spergel, Ianni, and others once provided important recruiting grounds for organized crime, many no longer exist today because of changing social and economic conditions. Important structural changes have taken place in large urban areas. Suburbanization, the end of machine politics, the large influx of rural blacks, and the dispersal of Italian American populations away from urban neighborhoods have all altered the social structure of racket areas.[24]

The existence of racket subcultures in American society raises the question of the importance of Mafia traditions to the continued existence of organized crime. Does the fact that post-Prohibition organized crime was often centered in Italian communities lend support to the alien conspiracy theory? Certainly one would think so, but there is an alternative explanation. The ethnic succession argument is grounded in social disorganization and strain theory. Residents of socially disorganized slum neighborhoods have traditionally used crime—and organized crime, in particular—as a mechanism of social advancement. Following the social disorganization tradition, this book argues that these so-called racket subcultures exhibited a "differential" social organization. This differential social order integrated the presence of adult criminality into the social structure of community life, a life that was dominated not by Mafia culture but by corrupt machine politics. From nineteenth-century vice syndicates to the modern-day Outfit, organized crime in Chicago could not have existed without the official blessing of those who controlled municipal, county, and state government. Organized crime was not imported from Sicily, but was bred in the socially disorganized slums of America, where elected officials routinely franchised vice and crime in exchange for money and votes, and it was these differentially organized community areas that allowed Italian-dominated organized crime to continue after Italian Americans achieved middle-class status.

Plan of This Book

This book is an attempt to show the importance of social structural conditions for the emergence and continuation of traditional organized crime in American society. Cultural deviance, social disorganization, anomie, and various economic theories have all been utilized to explain this phenomenon. Yet, no researcher since John Landesco (1929) has directly addressed the importance of social structural contexts for the emergence and, in particular, the continuation of organized crime.[25] Although organized crime serves a functional role in American society by providing the illicit goods and services that the public demands, the original source of the gangster's power lies in the social construction of his own communities and not in his ability to meet these demands. It was in the local community that the line between the underworld and the wider society became obscured as the formal mechanisms of social control were corrupted by an unholy alliance between machine politicians and the organized criminal element allowing for the rationalization of crime.

In the pages that follow, I present a view of organized crime that challenges the alien conspiracy interpretation. Chapter 1, "Explaining Organized Crime," reviews the theoretical underpinnings of the alien conspiracy and ethnic succession arguments as explanations for the emergence and continuation of organized crime in American society. The discussion then moves on to a review of the sociological literature linking community social structure with deviant behavior. The theories of human ecology, cultural transmission, and differential social organization are examined. Delinquency theories and their relation to organized crime are also reviewed with particular attention being paid to recruitment issues. The relationship between Gerald Suttles's conceptualization of the defended neighborhood and racket subcultures is also examined.

Chapter 2, "The Gem of the Prairie," traces the history of vice and crime in Chicago from the Civil War until the beginning of Prohibition. Special attention is given to the rise of machine politics under Michael C. McDonald, organizer of Chicago's first crime syndicate, and the symbiotic relationship between government, vice, and crime. This chapter argues that organized crime in Chicago was not imported from the south of Italy but began because Chicago machine politicians provided political protection to vice syndicates and criminal gangs in exchange for votes and campaign contributions. One vice district played a particularly significant role in the development of organized crime in Chicago—the Levee. This chapter reviews the history of the Levee beginning with the original Custom House Levee and its eventual movement to the "New" Levee in the Near South Side of the city. Special attention is given to the roles of municipal aldermen John Coughlin and Michael Kenna and their roles as protectors of vice and crime in Chicago's First Ward. This chapter also reviews the history of the public outcry against segregated vice and the eventual closing of the Levee vice district.

The historical role of African Americans in organized crime in Chicago is reviewed in chapter 3, "The Black Mafia." The role of black Americans in organized crime has been greatly ignored by the academic community. The research that does exist argues that black Americans played a minor role in the ethnic gambling and vice industries that existed in many American cities at the beginning of the twentieth century. This view is supported by the alien conspiracy theory, which argues that the participation of African Americans and other minorities in syndicated vice and crime followed the decline of traditional Italian American organized crime groups. This chapter argues that sophisticated African American organized crime groups existed in Chicago independent of white organized crime largely because of the segregated nature of American society. The importance of African American organized crime during this period in history cannot be underestimated. Its existence not only challenges the alien conspiracy argument that organized crime was imported from Italy but also qualifies the ethnic succession formulation. African American organized crime did not follow Italian organized crime but existed alongside Irish and Italian groups from the first days of syndicated vice.

Chapter 4, "The Syndicate," reviews the significance of Prohibition for the evolution of organized crime in Chicago. Prohibition provided the opportunity for Chicago's vice entrepreneurs and criminal gangs to extend their activities into bootlegging. Levee district vice mongers such as Johnny Torrio and Al Capone competed with criminal gangs such as the Valley Gang, the O'Banion Gang, the Genna brothers, and others for control of the illegal alcohol racket. The end result was the infamous "beer wars" of the 1920s, which brought a previously unknown level of violence to the streets of Chicago. In the end, the Capone syndicate emerged as the supreme overlord of vice and crime in Chicago. When Prohibition ended in 1933, the Syndicate, as Capone's organization became known, extended its operations to include control of all illegal gambling in Chicago and began an extensive racketeering campaign to seize control of trade associations and labor unions in the Chicago metropolitan area.

The Forty-two Gang is the subject of chapter 5. The Forty-two Gang is one of the most famous groups in gang history, yet we know very little about it. Combining data from published and archival sources, this chapter provides a history of the gang and explores its impact on the emergence of the Outfit, the traditional organized crime group in Chicago. The archival sources used in this chapter come from the unpublished John Landesco manuscript collection. The manuscripts provide not only a rich source of information on the Forty-two Gang but also a fresh look at the diffusion of delinquency subcultures and female participation in gang life during the early years of the twentieth century. This chapter also provides a look at the formation of criminal values among the youth of slum areas. The racket subculture thesis argues that lower-class youth are attracted to adult crime because of the example provided by the presence of adult criminals in slum areas. While the literature provides little other than anecdotal evidence about recruitment into the original Capone syndicate, Landesco's writings on the Forty-two Gang provide a unique opportunity to examine the social conditions that fostered the recruitment of slum youth by the Chicago Outfit.

Chapter 6, "The Outfit," describes the activities of post-1950 organized crime in Chicago. It is during this period that the Torrio-Capone syndicate evolved into the Chicago Outfit as we have come to know it. This chapter also describes the Outfit's takeover of all illegal gambling in Chicago, including the Negro policy racket. Special emphasis is given to the relationship between the Outfit and Chicago mayor Ed Kelly (1933–1947) and the political protection given to vice activities in Chicago. Finally, the often confusing relationship between the Outfit and narcotic trafficking is explicated. This chapter also argues that African Americans played an important role in the activities of the Chicago Outfit, the Italian American organized group in Chicago. African Americans continued to work in the policy racket after its takeover by the Outfit and worked with the Outfit to distribute heroin in the black community. This chapter additionally provides a history of the West Side Bloc, a group of elected public officials who supported the efforts of organized crime in Chicago, and argues that the West Side Bloc contributed directly to the establishment of racket subcultures in Chicago's "street crew" neighborhoods. Finally, this chapter also provides a history of government efforts against organized crime. One of the reasons that organized crime existed was the failure of local municipalities and the national government to take effective enforcement action against it.

The Outfit as a complex organization is described in chapter 7. It is based upon an analysis of interview data collected from persons knowledgeable about the activities of the Outfit in the Chicago area. The Outfit's hierarchical structure, chain of command, and division of labor are explained. This chapter also describes the positions within the criminal organization and discusses the public that the Outfit serves. Accounts of the activities of the Outfit suggest that positions exist for bosses, members, and associates, who are said to be "connected." This chapter also argues that the Chicago Outfit has an organized public, made up of gamblers, thieves, and "wannabes" (people who want to be associated with the Outfit), that has provided a ready source of participants for organized criminal activities as well as recruits for the Outfit itself.

Chapter 8, "Street Crew Neighborhoods," describes the organized crime neighborhoods of Chicago. Five communities in the Chicago metropolitan area have a history of being associated with organized crime. They are commonly referred to as Taylor Street, Grand Avenue, Twenty-sixth Street, the North Side, and the suburb of Chicago Heights. These communities are the locations of the five original "street crews," or branches, of the Chicago Outfit. In addition to these areas, a number of other Chicago communities have a reputation of being associated with organized crime. These communities differ, however, in that they are all descendant from the five original street crew neighborhoods. The groups that have been present in each of these other Chicago communities began because people from the five original street crew neighborhoods relocated there. This chapter explains the history of organized crime in each of these areas and offers a sociological explanation for their emergence in conformance with social organizational theories of crime. Although these areas are Italian communities, this chapter argues that Mafia traditions had no bearing on the existence of racket subcultures in these neighborhoods. I argue that the presence of organized crime in Chicago's street crew neighborhoods was the direct result of machine politics and the differential organization of these Chicago communities.

The concluding chapter argues that social conditions in Chicago bore more responsibility for the development of organized crime than any foreign criminal group. Organized crime in Chicago was not the result of an alien conspiracy or cultural deviance. Political corruption and an ineffective criminal justice system played more of a role in the development of the Capone syndicate and later the Chicago Outfit than any foreign criminal group. This chapter concludes that organized crime in Chicago was not related to the emergence of the Sicilian Mafia but was the product of America's disorganized urban areas. The chapter also stresses the importance of community social structure for recruitment issues and acknowledges the influence of differentially organized community areas for the development and continuation of organized crime in Chicago.

1

EXPLAINING ORGANIZED CRIME

The competing *alien conspiracy* and *ethnic succession* explanations for the emergence of organized crime in America are based upon two separate but related theories of crime: cultural deviance and social disorganization. Although they are both mainstream theories, their classification is often a difficult task. Cultural deviance theory, for example, has been explained at both the micro and macro levels, and there are two variants of social disorganization theory. To add to the confusion, there is also what has come to be known as Clifford Shaw and Henry McKay's "mixed" model of delinquency, combining both social disorganization and cultural deviance.[1] All of these are associated with the Chicago School of sociology, which emerged from the University of Chicago in the early 1920s. This analysis follows the paradigm developed by the Chicago School. Both cultural deviance and social disorganization theory are reviewed in this chapter as possible explanations for organized crime in Chicago and other American cities.

Cultural Deviance

The alien conspiracy argument is based upon cultural deviance theory. If we follow the imagery portrayed in Mario Puzo's book *The Godfather*, we see a picture of a Sicilian immigrant family who brought the traditions of the Mafia to America, which they accepted as a legitimate means of obtaining the fruits of the new world.[2] Young Michael Corleone, the U.S. Marine Corps hero, who at first showed distaste for criminal activity, was celebrated when he turned away from the values of the larger society and joined the "family business." Michael's entrance into organized crime marked his acceptance of the cultural norms to which he had been socialized and, therefore, to which he owed his allegiance.

Cultural deviance is a middle-range theory grouped under the positivist paradigm. Cultural deviance argues that every person is identified with a social group that has developed its own norms of conduct. In cultural deviance theory, norms are never violated. Criminals are well-socialized members of the groups to whose cultural codes they invariably conform. What appears to be deviance is simply a label applied by outsiders to the conforming behavior endorsed by one's own group. People act, for the most part, in accordance with the rules of the group to which they belong.[3] If these rules are in conflict with those of other cultural groups, who have the power to incorporate their values into law, crime occurs. The cause of crime is culture conflict—that is, variation in cultural values defining crime.

Pure cultural deviance theory argues that conflict exists when divergent rules of conduct govern a person's situation in life. There are two types of culture conflict. Primary group conflict occurs when members of one cultural group migrate to another area. Because immigrants often bring divergent religious beliefs, norms, and systems of values, culture conflict is inevitable. For example, William F. Whyte found a discrepancy between middle-class values and immigrant morality in an inner-city Italian community.[4] In the Boston neighborhood of "Cornerville," gambling was seen as normal conduct even though by the standards of the larger society it was considered illegal. Secondary culture conflict occurs with the evolution of different subcultures and value systems within the same society. The secondary culture conflict argument has often been used to explain the development of street gangs in modern society.

Francis Ianni provided a real-life example of cultural deviance theory as it pertains to organized crime in his study of one of New York's five crime families. He states that the members of Italian American organized crime "share a common culture and organize their universe and respond to it in ways which are considered culturally appropriate." This shared culture is internalized as a code of implicit rules of behavior that members learn to use as part of these groups. This code is manifested in their actions, since it defines the equation through which they perceive the objective world and make culturally acceptable decisions about how to behave. Ianni believes that many of the attitudes and values that supported the entry of Italian immigrants into organized crime came with them from their mother country, where Mafia practices have existed since the mid-1800s.[5]

Despite its popularity, support for the alien conspiracy/cultural deviance explanation for organized crime in America is sparse. There is, however, a body of research that focuses on the Sicilian Mafia as a cultural form and a de facto method of social control in the absence of effective state government and not a criminal organization in the American sense of the word. In particular, the historical Mafia was a phenomenon associated with the large agricultural estates of western Sicily and their relationship to the commercial markets in Palermo, the island's capital. The managers of these estates, the *gabellotti*, established a system of control in their own agricultural districts that facilitated cattle rustling, smuggling, and the monopolization of the citrus market, which ultimately extended to the *Conca d'Oro*, the agricultural region that surrounded Palermo. These activities, though illegal, hardly provided the necessary basis for the organization of gambling, prostitution, and labor racketeering in American society.[6]

There is even less support for the existence of the Black Hand. The alien conspiracy view argues that the Black Hand was a transitional step between the Mafia in Sicily and the Cosa Nostra in American society. Modern research, however, has established that the Black Hand was not a criminal organization, but simply a crude method of extortion used to blackmail wealthy Italians and others for money. Blackmailers would simply send a letter stating that the intended victim would come to harm if he did not meet the extortion demands. The term Black Hand came into use because the extortion letters usually contained a drawing of a Black Hand or other evil symbols. The Black Hand was nothing more than a method of crime, like armed robbery or safe cracking. There was no international association. There was no central organization. There was no connection to the Camorra or Mafia. There was, however, the press, which through its Mafia interpretation turned Black Hand crime into an international criminal conspiracy.[7]

Social Disorganization

While little research has been conducted to support the cultural deviance explanation for the emergence of organized crime, a substantial body of inquiry exists to support the social disorganization explanation. Social disorganization theory would have us look at the fictional Corleone family as just another immigrant group who came to America at the turn of the last century looking for the economic benefits provided by the Industrial Revolution. Coincident with this rapidly increasing immigration and industrialization was an assumed increase in the complexity of social life. The proponents of social disorganization theory hypothesized a relationship between this increased social complexity and higher rates of deviance, particularly in urban areas. These theorists, borrowing ecological notions, saw society as a complex whole whose parts—communities, institutions, and associations—were interdependent and maintained some sort of equilibrium in which people agreed with one another about values, and this agreement was reflected in a high degree of social organization. When this consensus became upset and traditional rules of conduct were brought into question, social disorganization occurred.

The basic premise of the social disorganization approach is that deviance is most likely to increase in periods of rapid social change. In explaining deviance it is important to remember that social change disrupts not only routine ways of living but also traditional methods of regulating behavior. As a society becomes more heterogeneous, primary relations are subject to strain, which in turn leads to a decrease in social control. The old forms of control represented by the family and the local community become undermined and their influence greatly diminished. According to social disorganization theory, all members of society are thought to have certain similar basic values. Criminality results from community conditions that prevent these values from being attained. Social disorganization theory can be divided into two variants, strain and control explanations.[8]

Strain theory seeks to explain what happens to people when the controls imposed by social life are relaxed or no longer function, as in periods of great social change. Under ordinary conditions, normative restrictions are clear and most people adhere to them. But when society becomes disorganized, the mechanisms that define these restrictions become weakened and "normlessness" results. Emile Durkheim referred to this social condition as *anomie* and argued that as anomie increased in a society, so would the rate of suicide. Man's activity lacked regulation and, therefore, led to suffering and death.[9]

Robert Merton applied Durkheim's concept of anomie to deviant behavior, arguing that anomie arises from an incongruity in society between emphasis on the importance of attaining valued goals and the availability of legitimate institutionalized means to reach these goals. According to Merton, the most efficient available means to attain socially defined goals, whether legitimate or not, is acceptable. The stress on culturally defined goals in the absence of the necessary means to obtain them invites "exaggerated anxieties, hostilities, neurosis, and antisocial behavior." Strain is overcome, according to Merton, through four types of deviant activities: innovation, ritualism, retreatism, and rebellion. It is innovation that is the major concern of the criminologist. The innovator, not being able to achieve success via conventional or legitimate avenues of opportunity, achieves success through the violation of social norms.[10]

Strain theory explains organized crime as a mechanism by which an individual or group can obtain the socially approved goals of wealth and power through "innovative" or illegal means. In fact, Merton wrote, "Al Capone represents the triumph of amoral intelligence over morally prescribed 'failure' when the channels of vertical mobility are closed or narrowed in a society that places a high premium on economic affluence and social ascent for all its members."[11]

It is because of such normal goals as independence through a business of one's own and such moral aspirations as the desire for social advancement and prestige that Daniel Bell argues that in the complex and ever-shifting structure of urban society the rackets are one of the crooked ladders of social mobility in American life.[12] Strain theory, like cultural deviance theory, assumes that people are religiously devoted to following the dictates of their culture. In cultural deviance theory, crime is normative. In strain theory, crime is the result of exposure to a cultural ideology in which failure to orient oneself upward is regarded as a moral defect and failure to become mobile is proof of it.

Ruth Kornhauser argues that it is ironic that strain theory traces its history to Emile Durkheim, because she believes he is a control theorist. Durkheim stated that when a society is disturbed by some painful crisis or experiences some abrupt transitions, it is momentarily incapable of exercising its influence. It could be argued, therefore, that deviance is the result of an absence of restraint upon aspirations and not the stress caused by an absence of legitimate means to attain these aspirations.[13]

Control theory assumes that deviant acts result when an individual's bond to society is weakened. The strength of this bond is the foundation of social control. Its weakening is the result of the failure of the controlling institutions of society to properly function. This failure is brought about by social disorganization—the weakness or breakdown of established values and norms—that destroys social order and hence social control. Simply put, social disorganization leads to a lack of control, which leads to crime.

Frederic Thrasher developed the first control version of social disorganization theory. Studying gang delinquency, he stated, "Gangs represent the spontaneous efforts of boys to create a society for themselves where none adequate to their needs exists."[14] This effort results from the failure of the normally directing and controlling institutions of society to function efficiently in the boy's own experience and is indicated by disintegration of family life, inefficiency of schools, formalism and externality of religion, corruption and indifference in local politics, low wages and monotony in occupational activities, unemployment, and the lack of opportunity for wholesome recreation. The causal structure of Thrasher's model is as follows: social disorganization leads to a lack of social control, which leads to gang formation and crime.

Following this line of reasoning, weak controls not only account for variation in the occurrence of criminality but also explain the existence of organized crime. Whether those engaged in organized criminality are products of a disorganized area or simply operate there, a weak community will not be able to provide resistance to their activities. The literature provides ample evidence of the inability of communities to combat organized crime. Daniel Bell, Alan Block, and John Gardner all document the existence of organized crime in communities whose elected officials and mechanisms of social control have been corrupted through an established interdependency between machine politics and organized criminality.[15]

The development of social structural explanations for organized crime and other deviant phenomena can be traced to the work of Robert Park, Ernest Burgess, and Roderick McKenzie.[16] These authors were best known for their ecological approach to the study of urban social structure. They hypothesized that human nature and human institutions were related to the spatial relationships of human beings. As these spatial relationships changed, the physical basis of social relations became altered, thereby producing social and political problems. Their studies of Chicago showed that a number of factors, often economic in nature, determined the patterns of land use, which in turn underlay the social structure of the various areas of the city.

The human ecologist saw land as a scarce commodity, with different locations having different values. As a result, land became a market commodity subject to the laws of supply and demand. Because of the cost of land and specific functional needs, different areas became associated with particular human activities.[17] For example, the central focal point of a city, the downtown area, provided the minimum travel distance from all points within the city and, as a result, became the central business district. For industry, large tracts of land located near waterways, railroads, and other means of transportation were often more important than proximity to the city's center, leading manufacturers to set up shop where these resources were available.

Park, Burgess, and McKenzie maintained that the typical process of land use within a city could best be illustrated by a series of concentric circles that may be numbered to designate both the successive zones of urban extension and the types of areas differentiated in the process of expansion.[18] In Chicago this typology located the downtown area in Sector I. Encircling the central business district was an area in transition, which was being invaded by business and light manufacturing (Sector II). Land values were high in this sector because of the expectation of industrial development. As a result, residential buildings expected to be sold were left in a state of disrepair and rented cheaply. This area stretched from the central business district as far west as Halsted Street along the north and south branches of the Chicago River. Rooming houses, unskilled workers, and settlements of foreign-born populations inhabited the resulting slums. Workers who were employed in Sector II and second-generation immigrant settlements inhabited the third area (Sector III). Beyond this zone was a residential area of high-status apartment housing and single-family residential homes (Sector V). Still farther was the commuter zone (Sector VI), the suburban and satellite city area.

Park, Burgess, and McKenzie argued that the growth of the city resulted from the influx of unskilled labor into the second zone, the zone in transition. As these immigrant groups became more fully integrated into the economic structure of the city, they moved progressively outward to more attractive and costly areas. Because of the economic forces at play, each of these zones maintained its own peculiar characteristics despite the influx of various racial and national groups. Because they maintained their characteristics and invariably impressed their effects on those who settled there, they were referred to as "natural areas"—areas that were the result of natural forces and not the result of human intentions.[19]

The works of Park, Burgess, and McKenzie, as well as other early human ecologists, have important implications for the study of deviant behavior. The area closest to the central business district (Zone II) was the least attractive to residents and thus was characterized by high rates of population turnover. Residents moved out as soon as they were economically capable. This rapid transition made it difficult to form strong formal and informal ties among the residents. Anonymity and isolation characterized social relations in the area. No one knew who his neighbors were and no one cared what they thought. Consequently, social control was weakened, resulting in a breakdown of standards of personal behavior and a drifting into unconventionality. Following this line of reasoning, deviant behavior can be seen not as an offshoot of dominant patterns of propriety, but rather as the normal pattern resulting from the social life of certain areas of the city.[20]

Shaw and McKay

Building upon the work of Park, Burgess, and McKenzie, Clifford Shaw and Henry McKay found that regardless of changes in the ethnic makeup of a community, the relative distributional pattern of delinquency remained stable over time. This finding resulted in the formulation of their famous cultural transmission hypothesis. Shaw and McKay argued that the spatial distribution of delinquency in a city is a product of larger economic and social processes characterizing the history and growth of the city and of the local communities that comprise it. They believed that the dynamics of this process give a local community a character that differentiates it from other communities. This character persists in so-called delinquency areas and is assimilated into the life of whatever group is currently dominant in the area.[21]

Shaw and McKay found that the development of divergent systems of values requires a type of situation in which traditional conventional control is either weak or nonexistent. They state that it is a well-known fact that the growth of cities and the increase in devices for transportation and communication have so accelerated the rate of change in our society that the traditional means of social control, which are effective in primitive society and in isolated rural communities, have been weakened everywhere and rendered especially ineffective in large cities. As a result, a special setting is created in socially disorganized areas that leads to the development of a divergent system of values in conflict with conventional norms.[22]

Shaw and McKay's theory stressed the fact that patterns of juvenile delinquency follow the physical structure and social organization of the city. Their research also showed that delinquency is concentrated in areas of physical deterioration and neighborhood disorganization, the types of areas characterized by the inability to deal with the social factors that are highly correlated with crime, such as poverty, disease, education, and family instability. In essence, Shaw and McKay attributed the causes of delinquency in the blighted areas of the city to the ineffectiveness of the community as a unit of social control. Writing for the 1931 National (Wickersham) Commission on Law Observance and Enforcement, Shaw and McKay stressed that the "Zone in Transition" in Chicago was characterized by "immigrant colonies, rooming houses, gambling resorts, sexual vice, and bootlegging."[23]

As a result of these abhorrent conditions, children living in these areas were exposed to a variety of contradictory standards and forms of behavior and to either a system of conventional values or a system of criminal values, or both.[24] Their attitudes and habits, therefore, were formed largely in accordance with the extent to which they participated in and became identified with one or another of these several types of groups. In explaining delinquency, Shaw and McKay not only grant importance to variation in social control but also stress the importance of exposure to delinquent groups and the transmission of delinquent values. In essence, Shaw and McKay's theory states that social disorganization leads to a lack of control, which leads to cultural deviance and crime.

In explaining crime and delinquency, Shaw and McKay stressed the two somewhat divergent theories of social disorganization and social organization. One the one hand, the theory of social disorganization stressed the structural conditions that breed criminal behavior: high population mobility, divorce and desertion, unemployment and poverty, deteriorated housing, and the failure of neighborhood institutions like schools and the church to impart moral values. On the other hand, their theory stressed that crime and delinquency are rooted in the social organization of urban neighborhoods.

Edwin Sutherland and Donald Cressey illustrated the consonance of these two theories.[25] Sutherland stated that the areas of concentration of delinquents in large American cities, and especially Chicago, are areas of "physical deterioration, congested population, economic dependency, rented homes, foreign and Negro populations, and few institutions supported by local residents." At the same time, he maintained that in these communities, "lawlessness has become traditional" and adult criminals are frequently seen and have great prestige. Gangs have continued to exist, with changing personnel, for fifty years, and at any particular time the gang may have a "senior, junior, and midget" branch where the "techniques, codes, and standards" for committing crime are transmitted from older to younger offenders.

The emphasis placed upon poverty by the research of Shaw and McKay focused much of the attention of sociology upon slum areas. It was there that researchers found the most striking manifestations of social disorganization. What was often overlooked by early social scientists, however, was the existence of other indigenous social organizations in urban slum areas.

Differential Social Organization

Because some communities were in fact organized, sociologists began using the term *differential social organization* in order to avoid the confusion that results from characterizing a community as disorganized. As originally coined by Sutherland, the term referred solely to the fact that the social structure (poverty, unemployment, etc.) of a community contributes to its crime rate. Both the terms *differential social organization* and *differential group organization,* however, later came to be used to describe communities whose social structures facilitate not only delinquency but also other types of identifiable activity. For example, there were Jewish "ghettos," Little Italys, and Chinatowns in most large American cities. These immigrant sections of the city were highly organized and served an important role. In the foreword to Louis Wirth's study *The Ghetto,* Park states that these areas performed important social functions and, as a result, were among the so-called natural areas of the city.[26] Jewish ghettos and other ethnic neighborhoods were social institutions that allowed immigrant groups to maintain their own cultural heritage in diverse surroundings. These areas allowed newcomers to settle among their fellow countrymen, who understood their cultural habits and shared their views on life. They also provided a place of transition for first-generation immigrants, whose children, more often than not, were assimilated into mainstream American culture.

Just as certain communities provided a place of transition for newly arriving immigrants, other communities also served functional roles within the total organization of the city. Most large cities had experience with delinquency areas, "bright light" entertainment districts, Bohemias, and skid row areas. These neighborhoods provided opportunities for crime, specialized areas for entertainment, locations for the exchange of ideas among artists, and low-income housing for homeless men. They were also described as natural areas because they were the result of the economic and social organization of the city, each serving their own unique function within the total urban scheme.

Delinquency areas and other specialized areas of vice and crime were referred to as *moral regions.* Park defines a moral region as a place where a divergent moral code prevails. Thrasher applied the concept of the moral region to his study of gang delinquency in Chicago. He found that the seriousness of modern crime grew largely from the fact that it had ceased to be sporadic and occasional and had become organized and continuous. Thrasher observed that in Chicago, as in other large American cities, there was an underworld, a criminal community. This community was a moral region that could be identified by the hangouts of gang members, such as street corners, saloons, poolrooms (gambling parlors), cabarets, roadhouses, club rooms, and so on. The underworld was not a specific group of people but the environment and social world of the adolescent gang member, the adult gangster, and the racketeer.[27]

Thrasher was part of the Chicago School of sociology, which recognized that deviance was not an offshoot of the dominant pattern of behavior in certain areas of the city but the normal pattern of social life in select community areas. These authors all rejected the commonsense view of the day that criminality could be explained by the personal or ethnic traits of immigrants that were brought with them to the New World. They stressed that it was not ethnic or racial groups that were criminal, but it was the disorganized—or if you will, differentially organized—urban slums that led to crime.

The Racket Subculture

The emphasis upon differential group organization as an explanation for organized crime is well documented in the sociology literature. In 1929 John Landesco conducted research into organized crime in Chicago as part of the Illinois Crime Survey. This study, funded by the Illinois Association for Criminal Justice, a private foundation supported by prestigious civic leaders of the period, sought to understand the lawlessness of the Prohibition era. The main theme of Landesco's book was that organized crime had its roots in the culture and social structure of the neighborhoods in which the gangster was raised. He found that gangsters came from neighborhoods where "the gang tradition is old" and where the residents could absorb the attitudes and skills necessary to enter into the world of crime.[28] Landesco argued, "The gangster is a product of his surroundings in much the same way that the good citizen is a product of his. The good citizen grows up in an atmosphere of obedience to law and of respect for it. The gangster has lived his life in a region of 'law breaking, graft, and fixing.'" The importance of Landesco's work is that it clearly pointed out that gangsters did not come from Sicily or the south of Italy, but that they came from the slums of American cities.

Studying Chicago's Near West Side Italian community, Landesco found that the only role models available to the children were the successful gangster and the politician.[29] There were big-shot liquor and beer bosses with their flashy cars, and there were elected officials who fixed cases for the criminal underworld. Together with their gangster followings, these big-shot politicians ruled the civic life of the neighborhood.

The importance of Landesco's work is that it clearly established that every criminal career had its beginning. In the preface to Landesco's book, Andrew Bruce wrote that the problem of crime is the problem of youth.[30] Landesco's work not only described the operations of the adult racketeer but also revealed that neighborhood environment and social philosophy started many young boys upon careers of crime and made it possible for them to obtain political power and immunity from punishment.

Support for the social organizational explanation for organized crime can also be found in the work of William F. Whyte. His classic study, *Street Corner Society: The Social Structure of the Italian Slum*, analyzed the Old North End of Boston, which by many criteria appeared to be highly disorganized. Although the conventional institutions of the larger Boston society appeared to be ineffective in preventing poverty, physical deterioration, crime, delinquency, corruption, and vice, the neighborhood, which Whyte referred to as Cornerville, had a complex and well-established organization of its own. Street-corner groups, the rackets (gambling), police, politics, the church, and old-country ties all contributed to the social organization of the Cornerville area.

Whyte concluded that the "problem" in the Cornerville district was not a lack of social organization but the failure of the community's social organization to mesh with the structure of the larger society.[31] The differential organization of the community became apparent when one examined the channels through which the Cornerville man gained advancement and recognition in his neighborhood and the society around it. To get ahead, the Cornerville man had to move either into Republican politics and the world of business or into Democratic politics and the world of the rackets. Other avenues of social mobility were closed to the Cornerville resident because of his immigrant status and his association with the Cornerville area.

Whyte's research led him to conclude that the sociologist who fails to analyze the role of racket and political organizations within urban areas neglects two of the major elements of slum life.[32] He contends that both have provided important avenues of social mobility for those who were blocked from advancement in other ways. As a result, large numbers of young men have participated in a social world dominated by the corner gang, politics, and the rackets.

Additional evidence of societal support for the pursuit of a career in organized crime can be found in the delinquency literature. In fact, most theoretical research involving organized crime is a by-product of work directed primarily at the relationship between social structure and juvenile delinquency. What makes the delinquency literature especially significant is that past research has shown the importance of the integration of youthful offenders and adult criminality for the acceptance of criminal values. For example, Shaw and McKay found that the presence of large numbers of adult criminals in select community areas meant that children living there were in contact with crime as a career and with "organized crime" as a way of life.[33]

Following Shaw and McKay, Solomon Kobrin found that specific group patterns of delinquency are determined in large part by the "character of the interaction between the conventional and the criminal value systems." This position suggests the existence of a typology of delinquency areas based upon variations in the relationship between the two. Kobrin identified the two polar types of this typology as the presence or absence of "systematic and organized adult activity in violation of law" and argues that the stable position of an illicit enterprise within a community is reflected in the nature of delinquent conduct on the part of the children. He writes:

> In a general way, therefore, delinquent activity in these areas constitutes a training ground for the acquisition of skill in the use of violence, concealment of offense, evasion of detection and arrest, and the purchase of immunity from punishment. Those who come to excel in these respects are frequently noted and valued by adult leaders in the rackets who are confronted, as are the leaders of all income-producing enterprises, with the problem of the recruitment of competent personnel.[34]

In their seminal work, *Delinquency and Opportunity*, Richard Cloward and Lloyd Ohlin also tie delinquent behavior to the social structure of community areas.[35] They state that the form of delinquency that is adopted in a particular area is conditioned by the social organization of that area. As such, their study uncovered three types of criminal subcultures: the criminal, the conflict, and the retreatist. Among the various criminal subcultures described by Cloward and Ohlin was one that tied delinquency to organized crime in select neighborhood areas.

Irving Spergel proposed a major modification to the Cloward and Ohlin formulation by dividing the criminal subculture into racket and theft adaptations. The central hypothesis of Spergel's work was that delinquent subcultures develop as a result of the varying nature and extent of criminal opportunities available to youth in lower-class neighborhoods. According to Spergel, each neighborhood seemed to provide social pressures and different opportunities for the development of distinctive and characteristic types of delinquent subcultures. In one area the presence of an integrated and well-organized criminal system offered a learning environment that eventuated in certain types of behavior in preparation for later careers in the "rackets."[36]

This delinquent racket subculture was found in an Italian lower-class East Harlem neighborhood. As would be expected, Spergel determined that the indexes of social breakdown—poverty, infant mortality, disease, and delinquency—were high in this New York City community. In addition, criminal and conventional adult activities were also highly integrated. Spergel explains:

> The racketeer played a variety of significant economic and social roles in the neighborhood. He was the sponsor and subsidizer of legitimate and illegitimate business enterprise. He was helpful when others were in trouble by raising bail money and making the appropriate payoffs. He was a parent surrogate for recalcitrant youth. He could establish direct controls over certain types of

> undesirable deviant behavior such as prolonged or violent gang fighting, and drug selling to local neighborhood youth.[37]

It should be noted, however, that the type of criminal subculture described above is not prevalent in American society. For example, in their study of gang behavior, James Short and Frank Strodtbeck attempted to locate criminal, conflict, and retreatist subcultures in Chicago. Although criminal activity was found in nearly all groups, criminally oriented gangs like those hypothesized by Cloward and Ohlin were difficult to locate. Instead, Short and Strodtbeck's data indicate that gang activity was consistent with descriptions of semiprofessional theft within the context of the parent delinquent subculture as developed by Albert Cohen. This failure to locate a criminal group led the authors to conclude that community areas where carriers of criminal and conventional values are integrated in such a way as to produce adolescent criminal subcultures occur relatively infrequently.[38]

Short and Strodtbeck's findings highlight the point that access to illegitimate opportunity is not freely available to everyone. There is "differential opportunity." Only in those neighborhoods where crime flourishes as a stable, indigenous institution do fertile criminal learning environments for the young exist. It is in this type of neighborhood that institutionalized criminal careers become available. There, the delinquent youth may rise above petty crime and aspire to a permanent position in some form of organized criminal activity and, according to Cloward and Ohlin, look forward to acceptance by the local community, both criminal and conventional alike.[39]

In a recent update of the racket subculture hypothesis, Mary Pattillo found that black middle-class areas in Chicago have created unique forms of social organization resulting from the desire of street gang members within their community to live in a safe environment.[40] The resulting ties promote neighborhood-level familiarity, integrate disparate social networks, and facilitate informal and formal social control. These ties also thwart efforts to totally rid the neighborhood of gangs and drugs. The end result is that the criminal minority, part of kin and neighborhood networks, is given a degree of latitude to operate freely in the neighborhood.

Another example of a modern-day update of the racket subculture hypothesis is provided by Sudhir Venkatesh. In his study of Chicago's Robert Taylor Homes, Venkatesh found that gang leaders had weekly meetings with clergy and community leaders in order to address community problems like gang crime and after-school use of parks by children, and to settle disputes with community residents—an ad hoc form of community policing.[41] Following the example of earlier criminal groups, Venkatesh found that members of the Gangster Disciple street gang had tried to regulate the underground economy in their neighborhoods by extorting burglars, prostitutes, and car thieves. They even ran card games and provided usurious "juice loans."

Both Pattillo and Venkatesh provide recent examples of differential social organization and the stable position of an illicit enterprise in adult society that prepared young people for a life in crime, and the integration of the carriers of conventional and deviant values—all without Italians! These findings highlight the fact that racket subcultures are not restricted to the presence of traditional organized crime and speak to the durability of the racket subculture hypothesis.

The Defended Neighborhood

Evidence of the existence of community structures that support entrance into organized crime was also found by Gerald Suttles in his study of the Addams area of Chicago and by Donald Tricarico in his study of New York's Greenwich Village. Both the Addams area and the Greenwich Village area have been described as *defended neighborhoods*. The conceptualization of the defended neighborhood was first published in Suttles's 1972 work, *The Social Construction of Communities*. There he defined the defended neighborhood as a residential group that sealed itself off through the efforts of delinquent gangs, restrictive covenants, sharp boundaries, and a forbidding reputation.[42]

Tricarico describes the defended neighborhood as a "safe moral world that kept the city at arm's length," and notes:

> While the city may have been threatening and noted for crime, the defended neighborhood was a different world. Although there were exceptions, people were trustworthy and crime was infrequent. Doors and windows were left open, and there was no fear of the streets, even at night. Neighbors were watchful and solicitous and closely monitored the movements of strangers. A careful scrutiny of outsiders and a toughness with interlopers earned the South Village Italian neighborhood a reputation that residents believed would frighten predators away.[43]

The defended neighborhood, just as criminality itself, is the result of weak social controls. Given the inability of formal procedures of social control to detect and forestall all or even most forms of urban disorder, a set of rules has developed in the form of a cognitive map that is used to regulate spatial movement in order to avoid conflict between antagonistic groups. This cognitive map gives birth to the defended neighborhood as an additional basis for social differentiation and social cohesion. The necessity for this additional basis of social organization of cities lies in their very nature, since cities inevitably bring together populations that are too large and composed of too many conflicting elements for their residents to find cultural solutions to the problems of social control.[44]

The roots of the defended neighborhood lie in social disorganization. Immigration, industrialization, and urbanization have fostered individual variability and population diversity, which has had an effect upon mechanisms of social control. Park, Burgess, and McKenzie point out that the general nature of this change is indicated by the fact that the growth of the city has been accompanied by the substitution of indirect secondary relations for direct primary (face-to-face) relations in the association of individuals in the community.[45] This is because the city is too diversified and heterogeneous to provide a single normative order that is shared sufficiently by its citizens to maintain order. The shift of social control to the formal sections of society has not been entirely successful, as is evidenced by the persistence of organized crime and other forms of aberrant conduct.

The defended neighborhood differs from other neighborhood areas because of certain distinctive structural characteristics. Perhaps the most important of these is the identity of the neighborhood itself. Suttles states that a neighborhood may be known as snobbish, trashy, tough, exclusive, dangerous, and so on, or it may simply lack an identity altogether.[46] Obviously, the main lines of differentiation between neighborhoods are the divisions of stratification that are pervasive in the larger society: race, ethnicity, income, education, and so forth. The content of a neighborhood's identity, however, does not stop here. The defended neighborhood in particular is apt to have a large part of its identity ascribed by its differences from adjacent neighborhood areas, especially those threatening it with invasion.

It must be remembered that the defended neighborhood is a mechanism of social control that provides residents with a means for the segregation of conflicting populations. As such, it exists in opposition to adjoining neighborhoods, and it is this opposition that gives the defended neighborhood its homogeneity and identity. It is also here that contrasts of ethnicity, race, pedigree, and ascribed background become relevant to the identity of a defended neighborhood and provide residents with an additional means of differentiation from surrounding populations. Such self-description not only conveys a distinctive role for the community but also provides its residents with a sense of sharing in a special, even privileged knowledge. Such sources of prideful exclusiveness, according to Suttles, are present in neighborhoods that claim an exceptional familiarity with famous people, such as Hollywood stars, political figures, and Mafia members![47]

A second structural characteristic of the defended neighborhood is that its residents often share a common fate at the hands of city planners, realtors, industry, and politicians. For example, large portions of the Addams area studied by Suttles have been cleared for public housing and the construction of the University of Illinois, both without the support of community residents. In Emmett Buell's study of a defended neighborhood in South Boston, busing was forced upon neighborhood residents in an effort to desegregate the public school system. Buell states that when assigned a common fate by powerful external groups or city government, residents of the defended neighborhood will interpret such plans as threats to their entire community way of life, and resistance through protest is a probable response, which in turn adds to the cohesion of the residents of the neighborhood.[48]

Perhaps the most subtle structural feature of the defended neighborhood is its shared knowledge of what might be called the community's "underlife." People who share a residential identity are privy to a variety of secrets that range from the assured truths of gossip to the collective myths of rumor. Taken to their full extreme, these local truths may add up to a sort of subculture where a private existential world takes hold and overshadows beliefs provided by the wider society. The possession of these bits and pieces of knowledge contributes to the collective identity of the neighborhood and acts to further separate insiders from outsiders. Those who share a residential identity have a special right to such knowledge, and this "inside dope" may lead them to aberrant or provincial ways of behaving.[49]

Another structural characteristic of the defended neighborhood is that it may be divided into levels or orbits that radiate from an "egocentric to a sociocentric" frame of reference.[50] Suttles states that when a person speaks of "*my* neighborhood," he may be referring to a small area that centers on him and is different for any two individuals. When a person speaks of "*our* neighborhood," on the other hand, he tends to refer to some localized group that can also be identified by other structural boundaries like ethnicity or income. "The neighborhood," however, has a more fixed referent and usually possesses a name and some sort of reputation known to persons other than the residents.

While each of these structural characteristics may be found in other types of neighborhoods, it is their combination in a single place that establishes the defended neighborhood. What is unique about organized crime is that community efforts at social control, in the form of the establishment of the defended neighborhood, have actually acted to support this deviant phenomenon. In New York's Greenwich Village, a substantial part of neighborhood life was organized for defense against strangers. Male street-corner groups were the self-appointed enforcers of local order. Their job was to make sure that the streets were safe. The Mafia reinforced this control function. Tricarico describes the scene:

> The Italian neighborhood was a field for syndicate activities: extra-legal activities were coordinated from local clubs and bookies serviced accounts on the street corners. Therefore, it was necessary to restrict access to persons who were not trustworthy. There was a special concern that strangers might turn out to be undercover policemen. The syndicate also exercised control over troublemakers, and generally sought to keep the neighborhood quiet in order to deflect attention from its activities and personnel. Toward this end, it backed up corner boys with something more formidable—the reputation for total violence. This reputation was a valuable resource for a defended neighborhood.[51]

The very essence of the defended neighborhood is its ability to create cohesive groupings. The most common type of cohesion said to exist in all types of neighborhoods is a positive and sentimental attachment to neighbors, local establishments, and local traditions to the exclusion of other persons, establishments, and traditions.[52] If these local traditions favor criminality because it stabilizes the environment, the community will certainly not organize itself against it.

In its traditional application, the term *neighborhood* stood for rather definite group sentiments that were the products of intimate personal relations among the members of small, isolated communities of which society was formerly composed. Although this definition suggests that the urban neighborhood is a remnant of an earlier rural community, neighborhood sentiment can take on the characteristics and qualities of current inhabitants. Just as this sentiment reflects lines of religion, language, and ethnic tradition, it may also reflect subcultural and normative acceptance of criminal or deviant values.[53]

Suttles's research has shown that residents of select neighborhood areas share collective representations and moral sentiments that allow them to be privileged to a diversity of knowledge regarding the community's underlife. In his study *The Social Order of the Slum*, Suttles found that in the Addams area of Chicago, many residents valued the fact that they shared, or believed they shared, associations with members of the Outfit, as they called organized crime. Within the Addams area is a section called Taylor Street. Above anything else, Suttles found that this street name implied a connection with organized crime.[54]

Even though Taylor Street's reputation did not identify a lifestyle that was acceptable to the larger society, it did offer for some neighborhood residents a certain honor and for others a way of defining people. Thus, persons embraced the images of gangster, hood, and tough guy that were provided, because it gave them a sense of power, which few were willing to question. Those who rejected these labels themselves assumed their truth for the wider community. To show how far the residents carried their belief in organized crime, Suttles gave an example of young boys referring to Frank "The Enforcer" Nitti (onetime leader of the Outfit) as casually as other boys might mention current baseball heroes.[55]

Spergel had similar findings.[56] He found that the racketeer was more than a person who shared a residential identity and knowledge of the underworld. The racketeer was actually the standard-bearer of the neighborhood and the acknowledged source of norms and values. These racketeers were sought out to settle family and neighborhood arguments. For those who claimed their association, they were even used as a shroud of protection against threatening groups from outside the community.

The studies of both Suttles and Spergel indicate that the concerned communities developed values that were sympathetic to the criminal underworld and that the residents drew upon in orienting themselves to the community. A major source of social control is the community and its institutions. Criminality results when there is a relative absence of, or conflict in, social rules or techniques for enforcing behavior in the social groups or institutions of which a person is a member. There is obviously a conflict in normative values in any community that embraces the gangster image or acknowledges the racketeer as a source of norms and values. Such conflict may be viewed as a consequence of the failure of the primary group to properly define organized criminal activity as deviant or aberrant conduct. Once such a failure occurs, a specialized social structure is created that provides for the integration of conventional and deviant lifestyles and will support the pursuit of a life in the underworld.

Nicholas Pileggi classically describes the social organization of this type of area:

> In Brownsville–East New York, wiseguys were more than accepted—they were protected. Even legitimate members of the community—the merchants, teachers, phone repairmen, garbage collectors, bus depot dispatchers, housewives, and old-timers sunning themselves along the Conduit Drive—all seemed to keep an eye out to protect their local hoods. The majority of the residents, even those not directly related by birth or marriage to wiseguys, had certainly known the local rogues most of their lives. There was the nodding familiarity of the

> neighborhood. In the area it was impossible to betray old friends, even those old friends who had grown up to be racketeers. The extraordinary insularity of these old-world mob-controlled sections, whether Brownsville–East New York, the South Side of Chicago, or Federal Hill in Providence, Rhode Island, unquestionably helped to nurture the mob.[57]

Suttles also provides a unique explanation for adolescent street gangs and their relationship to organized crime within the defended neighborhood.[58] He states that social order is made possible by limiting interactions to safe relationships such as those based on similar age, sex, ethnicity, and territory. This process of limiting social relationships is called *ordered segmentation*. There is also a sequential order in which these groupings can be combined through a process of accretion when the social order is threatened. Suttles found that an integral part of a slum neighborhood's ordered segmentation is its named adolescent street-corner groups or youth gangs. The gang, therefore, can be seen as an elementary group formed in a quest for order, and not a highly structured unit organized by values and norms or a unit that is functionally specialized in the pursuit of delinquency.

Suttles dismisses subcultural and lower class explanations for the existence of gangs. Instead, he argues that they are the result of a quest for safety. Suttles states that people in the inner city perceive one another as untrustworthy and dangerous. Unlike middle-class people, they are unable to evaluate one another in terms of educational attainment, job status, and financial success. As a result, the moral order, which is based on individual judgment, is tenuous and lacks applicability to real people. Social order is maintained primarily through the retreat of individuals to their own ethnic, territorial, gender, and age groups, including the adolescent street-corner gang. The gang thus becomes one unit in the segmentary social organization of inner-city neighborhoods. The gang provides a way of ordering people into a manageably small number of aggregates. The function of the named street-corner group is rudimentary and primitive. It defines groups of people so that they can be seen as representatives rather than as individuals. Like Thrasher, Suttles states that the function of the gang is to create order where none is provided by the larger society.[59]

Through the process of ordered segmentation, Suttles traced some of the youth gangs in the Addams area to organized crime.[60] Adolescent street-corner groups were building blocks out of which the older and more powerful Social Athletic Clubs (SACs) originated. Some of these SACs had members who belonged to the Outfit. These SACs provided a mechanism for the association of street-corner groups with organized crime. Anthony Sorrentino, working with the Chicago Area (delinquency prevention) Project, also tied the SACs in the Addams area to machine politics describing how local precinct captains would provide help through their political contacts whenever a club member was in trouble. Politicians were also boosters of the club and provided sweaters and jackets for the club's ball teams, all in an effort to ensure their support at election time.[61]

Tricarico echoed Suttles's findings in his study of Greenwich Village.[62] He found that street-corner boys frequented "Mafia clubs" and "horse-rooms" (betting parlors), which functioned as outposts for the administration of syndicate business and control. These clubs and gambling parlors supported a convivial atmosphere, allowing members to hang out, play cards, and watch television. The clubs also served as centers for the consumption of syndicate services such as gambling and the recruitment and socialization of syndicate personnel.

This review has demonstrated that the existence of organized crime has been influenced in crucial ways by the social organization of the communities in which it emerged. Park wrote that though the sources of our actions are in the "organic impulses" of the individual man, actual conduct is determined, more or less, by public opinion, by custom, and by a code that exists outside of us "in the family, in the neighborhood, and in the community." As stated by Frank Tannenbaum: "It is the community that provides the attitudes, the point of view, the philosophy of life, the example, the motive, the contacts, the friendships, and incentives. No child brings these into the world. He finds them here and available for use and elaboration. The community gives the criminal his materials and habits, just as it gives the doctor, the lawyer, the teacher, and the candlestick maker theirs."[63]

2

THE GEM OF THE PRAIRIE

In 1670 French trader Pierre Moreau built a cabin on the site where the Chicago River empties into Lake Michigan.[1] The area was called *chickagou* (bad smell) by the Potawatomi Indians because of the aroma of the skunk cabbage that choked the bogs draining into the river. It was not until one hundred years later that Chicago's first permanent settler arrived. In 1779 Jean Baptiste Point du Sable established residency at the intersection of the north and south branches of the Chicago River. The area, however, continued to be controlled by local Indians until 1794, when army general "Mad Anthony" Wayne won a six-square-mile tract of land at the mouth of the Chicago River in the Battle of Fallen Timbers. In 1803 Fort Dearborn was established there and a settlement grew up around the fort.

By 1837 the Fort Dearborn settlement had grown to 4,000 people. It was incorporated as the city of Chicago in March of that year. Chicago's real growth began in 1848 with the completion of the Illinois and Michigan Canal. The canal, connecting the Illinois River and the south branch of the Chicago River, provided Midwest farmers with access to Great Lakes shipping and eastern markets. The Illinois River also provided a direct route to the Mississippi River and the cities of Saint Louis and New Orleans. Chicago's first railroad, the Galena and Chicago Union, also began operating in 1848. By the time of the Civil War, Chicago was the rail crossroads of the nation. It was the terminal for ten railroads and boasted a network of track that stretched four thousand miles. In 1860 Chicago's population grew to 109,000 people, making it the largest city in Illinois.[2]

Chicago's central location made it an important transportation and shipping center in the country's westward expansion. During the 1860s more than thirteen thousand ships a year docked at the Chicago harbor. In addition, more than two million bushels of grain passed through Chicago annually. Packet boats that had traveled the Erie Canal and the Great Lakes unloaded settlers at the Chicago port. For $1.25 an acre, pioneers could buy land in Iowa, Nebraska, Minnesota, Kansas, and the Dakotas. Not all those who came to Chicago left. The grain trade, industrialization, and the growth of the Union Stock Yards created jobs. The demand for meat by the Union Army during the Civil War made Chicago's meatpacking industry the largest in the world. Soon European immigrants began to arrive to fill the demand for labor. By 1870 nearly three hundred thousand people lived in the city of Chicago.[3]

Chicago's ecological position as the gateway to the unsettled lands of the West also contributed to its involvement in crime. Many young bachelors spent their last nights in Chicago before heading out to make their fortunes in the vast western wilderness. Chicago was often their final chance for supplies and other needed items. Saloons, gambling parlors, and brothels quickly sprang up around the city to make these pioneers' last night in "civilization" memorable. Dwight Moody, founder of Chicago's Moody Bible Institute, commenting on the times, remarked, "If the Angel Gabriel came to Chicago, he would lose his character within a week."[4]

One of Chicago's earliest vice districts was an area known as the Sands. Located just north of the Chicago River and extending to Lake Michigan, the Sands was filled with gambling dens, brothels, and rooming houses. The *Chicago Daily Tribune* described the Sands as "the vilest and most dangerous place in Chicago" and "the hiding place of all sorts of criminals." On April 20, 1857, newly elected Chicago mayor "Long John" Wentworth led a column of police and firefighters in a raid on the Sands. (Mayor Wentworth was referred to as "Long John" and "His Highness" because of his six-foot, six-inch height.) Former mayor William B. Ogden had obtained a legal interest in the property resulting in a court order to eject the inmates of the "Sand Houses" as the disorderly properties were called. This early crackdown on crime resulted in the eviction of a number of gamblers and prostitutes and the demolition of nine buildings and the burning of six others.[5]

Another of Chicago's early vice districts was named the Willows. The Willows flourished during the Civil War and was the headquarters of one of Chicago's first crime czars, Roger Plant. Plant ran a saloon at Monroe and Wells Streets known as the Barracks. The Barracks was an around-the-clock gambling den and bordello. Like most of downtown Chicago, it was built upon the wetlands that surrounded the Chicago River's entrance into Lake Michigan. As a result, the streets surrounding the Barracks, and much of downtown Chicago, were notorious for their muddy conditions. In an effort to combat this quagmire, the city decided to raise the level of many

Chicago streets, making it necessary to raise the foundations of the buildings along the newly upgraded roadways. In some cases whole blocks were elevated as much as ten feet. The result was the creation of underground passages, alleys, and earthen rooms. One subterranean area was controlled by Plant and became home to the many thieves, pickpockets, and muggers who frequented his saloon. It is said that the many underground rooms that existed beneath the Barracks gave rise to the term *underworld* as a description of the segment of society who engaged in organized criminal activity.[6]

In spite of its underworld, Chicago was still a "greenhorn" town when compared to places like New York and New Orleans. It took the Civil War to bring the professional gambler to Chicago. Because of the outbreak of the war, the economy of the South could no longer support the gentleman gambler. As a result, the smart gambler moved north to Chicago, where fortunes were being made during the war years. As the supply center for the Union Army of the West, men and money poured into the city to furnish the needs of the armed forces.[7]

These professional gamblers, or so-called southern gentlemen, could be seen strolling on Randolph Street and were the subject of much esteem. So extensive was gambling in Chicago's center that the two-block stretch of Randolph between Clark and State Streets became known as Hair-Trigger Block, so named because of the large number of shootings that occurred there stemming from disagreements in the gambling houses. The area of Clark Street from Randolph to Monroe was dubbed Gamblers Row.[8]

By the 1870s there were so many vice districts in Chicago that a directory was published to enable visitors to find their way to such areas as Little Cheyenne, Satan's Mile, Whiskey Row, and the Levee. One of the more notable saloon proprietors of the day was Mickey Finn. Finn operated two saloons, the Lone Star and the Palm Garden, at the southern end of Whiskey Row and was famous for one of the drinks that he offered in his saloon, the "Mickey Finn Special." This drink was allegedly made from a secret powder that Finn had obtained from a voodoo witch doctor. A Mickey Finn Special would render the drinker unconscious, giving Finn the opportunity to rifle the unsuspecting patron's pockets. Because of his activities, today Mickey Finn's name can be found in most dictionaries, denoting "any of several powerful drugs, especially chloral hydrate, that are secretly put into alcoholic drinks to produce unconsciousness."[9]

Another vice district, Gambler's Alley, ran from Dearborn Street to La Salle Street between Madison and Washington Streets. In these two blocks were seven gambling halls, disguised as "poolrooms," where the card game faro, roulette, and other hazards tempted the unwise to risk their money. One could bet a few pennies or thousands of dollars on horse races, baseball games, walking and rowing matches, and elections at home or around the country. Each "poolroom" had its own telegraph operator, who was in direct contact with racetracks and other events to be wagered on around the country. The *Chicago Daily Tribune* reported in 1887 that the rooms in Gambler's Alley were visited by three thousand to five thousand people a day.[10]

On October 8, 1871, a small fire broke out in the barn of Patrick O'Leary at 558 West DeKoven Street. Because of an unseasonably dry summer and the wooden nature of most Chicago buildings of that time, the fire soon spread throughout the city. It was twenty-five hours before the "Great Chicago Fire" was extinguished. The fire killed more than three hundred people, destroyed 3.3 square miles of the city, and left ninety thousand people homeless. The destruction was comparable only to the great fires of London and Moscow. Although it is commonly believed that the O'Leary cow kicked over the lantern that started the fire, the Northwestern University school of journalism has provided a different story. On September 30, 1944, the dean announced that Louis M. Cohn, a benefactor to the school, had acknowledged that he and several other young men, who were playing dice in the barn with the O'Leary boys, had accidentally knocked over the lantern during the excitement of the game and started the conflagration.[11]

Criminals from many localities poured into Chicago to take advantage of the fire disaster. Businesses were robbed and everything in sight was stolen. Conditions were so bad that the city was placed under martial law. Less than a month after the fire, Chicago elected Joseph Medill as mayor. Medill was elected on the "Union Fire-Proof" ticket, promising to prevent the misappropriation of fire relief funds. Chicago was so demoralized after the Great Fire that public drunkenness became a major social problem. Conditions were so bad that a group of leading citizens and clergymen formed the Committee of Seventy to battle crime and the liquor trade. Another group, the Committee of Twenty-five, was formed to improve the moral fabric of the city. Their efforts were entirely supported by reform-minded mayor Joseph Medill, who welcomed Sunday saloon-closing laws and worked to close the gambling houses. This effort at reform, however, may have set the stage for the eventual development of organized crime in Chicago.[12]

Organized crime in Chicago had its beginning in the 1870s with the activities of Michael Cassius McDonald. McDonald owned a tavern at Clark and Monroe Streets known as the Store, which reportedly was the largest liquor and gambling house in downtown Chicago. (Taverns differed from saloons because they also sold food.) It is said that it was McDonald, not P. T. Barnum, who coined the phrase "there's a sucker born every minute."

McDonald reportedly made this statement when one of his employees expressed fear that the Store was too big and that there would not be enough customers to make it profitable. McDonald was also interested in boxing. It was McDonald who gave John L. Sullivan the backing that enabled him to make his bid for the world's heavyweight boxing championship in 1892.[13]

McDonald was also active in politics and headed what was commonly referred to as the "gamblers' trust." In an effort to overcome the reform activities of Mayor Medill, McDonald organized Chicago's saloon and gambling interests. "Mike McDonald's Democrats," as they were called, elected their own candidate, Harvey Colvin, as mayor of Chicago in 1873. With Colvin in office, McDonald organized the first criminal syndicate in Chicago composed of both gamblers and compliant politicians. After suffering a temporary setback at the polls in 1876, when Chicago elected reform mayor Monroe Heath, Mike McDonald's Democrats elected Carter Harrison as mayor in 1879.[14]

More than any one person, McDonald played a key role in organizing Chicago's criminals and laid the foundation of Chicago's Democratic Party. At the height of his power, "King Mike" boasted that he "ran the town" and that the police were "under his thumb." He controlled political offices, while his faro banks and his "skin" and "brace" games fleeced unsuspecting gamblers. McDonald also owned the short-lived *Chicago Globe* newspaper and built Chicago's first elevated rail line, the Lake Street "L," which was known in gambling circles as "Mike's Upstairs Railroad."[15]

The alliance between the gambling interests and politicians in Chicago proved to be successful. Harrison served four consecutive terms as mayor from 1879 to 1887. Noted evangelist William T. Stead commented that the peculiar thing about the Chicago plan of dealing with illegal gambling was not that the houses were allowed to run but how gaming was used as an engine of party finance. "Chicago taught the world how to make the dice box, wheel of fortune, and pack of cards a resource of partisan finance." Gambling houses were charged fifty dollars and up per month; panel and badger houses (brothels where the client was robbed) were charged thirty-five to fifty dollars; music halls and saloons where prostitution was solicited, one hundred dollars; cigar store and barbershop bookies, ten dollars; blind pigs (unlicensed saloons), ten to thirty dollars; dice games, ten to twenty-five dollars; and opium dens, ten to twenty-five dollars.[16]

Mike McDonald remained in politics until his death in 1907. Control of gambling in Chicago then passed on to a number of different people, the most prominent of whom were James "Big Jim" O'Leary, Jacob "Mont" Tennes, and First Ward aldermen John Coughlin and Michael Kenna (each

Chicago ward had two aldermen at that time). Both Coughlin and Kenna were part of McDonald's organization. Gambler, politician, and warden of the county insane asylum "Prince Hal" Harry Varnell had recruited Coughlin, who in turn recruited Kenna to fill the second aldermanic seat. Coughlin and Kenna retained control of gambling in downtown Chicago, while the gambling activity that existed in the Southwest Side, around the Union Stock Yards, went to Big Jim O'Leary, son of Mrs. Catherine O'Leary, whose cow had allegedly started the Great Chicago Fire.[17]

Because of the unwanted attention caused by the fire, the O'Learys sold their cottage (which, surprisingly, survived the blaze) and moved to the stockyards district, where nobody knew them and they could live out their lives in peace. Jim O'Leary grew to manhood in the area. Neighbors called him Big Jim because of his gigantic frame and physical prowess. He never attended school, but despite his being nearly illiterate, he showed great promise with numbers. As a teenager, he went to work in the stockyards, and it was there that his fascination with gambling began. He opened his first saloon in the 1890s on South Halsted Street and soon added a "handbook" (a bookie) for off-track betting. Eventually expanding into bookmaking and other gambling enterprises, he quickly made friends with political powerhouses John Coughlin and Michael Kenna. Big Jim O'Leary is best known for his saloon at 4183 South Halsted Street, which combined a Turkish bath, bowling alley, poolroom, and billiard parlor, all of them legal enterprises. Next door to the saloon, however, was O'Leary's two-story "Palace of Vice." Described as "fireproof, bombproof, burglarproof, and police proof," O'Leary's gambling emporium was separated from his saloon by two steel doors and included any number of gambling rooms, trap doors, and even a fake chimney to facilitate escape in the event of a police raid.[18]

Responding to municipal reform efforts in 1904, Big Jim O'Leary opened a poolroom in Birneyville, Illinois, eighteen miles west of Chicago along the Santa Fe rail line in DuPage County. Called the "Stockade," this gambling resort resembled a frontier fort. A tight board fence, 14 feet high, enclosed the Stockade. Between the outer barricade and the main building was a space of 50 feet, and this was divided into all sorts of yards and runways by high fences. Scattered through the enclosures were approximately twenty dog kennels. The poolroom was 150 feet long and 120 feet wide. At the west end were a lunch counter and bar. At the east end, 10 feet above the floor and running the length of the room, was a blackboard that was divided into five sections to correspond with five local racetracks. A crier used a megaphone to announce the progress of each race. As many as eight hundred people occupied the poolroom at any given time. DuPage County officials closed the Stockade in March 1905 after it was discovered that illegal gambling and liquor sales were going on there.[19]

Mont Tennes inherited McDonald's activities in the North Side of the city and was one of the first to recognize the important changes that were taking place in the gambling arena. The traditional games of the riverboat gambler—poker, faro, and craps—had been replaced in popularity by horse racing. The astonishing popularity of horse racing at the turn of the century was due to two important factors: (1) betting at the tracks was legal and race handicapping offered a better chance of winning, and (2) new advances in communications, such as the telegraph, allowed bettors to place bets from local bars and poolrooms.[20]

In 1907 John Payne of Cincinnati established a telegraph service that provided results from racetracks around the country. Payne granted Tennes the exclusive right to his service in the Chicago area. Tennes then sold race results to Chicago gamblers for 50 percent of their daily take, for which they were also provided protection from the police. Tennes's monopoly over the wire service gave him absolute control over all of Chicago's bookies and handbooks. His wire service, the General News Bureau, soon began expanding into areas outside of Chicago, which resulted in both a legal war as well as a shooting war with the competing Payne News Agency. Tennes eventually drove the Payne agency out of business, which made him the undisputed boss of racetrack gambling in the United States.[21]

"Bathhouse" John Coughlin (also known as "the Bath") and "Hinky Dink" Michael Kenna, controlled politics and vice in Chicago's downtown area and Near South Side, which included an area commonly referred to as the Levee. Coughlin was elected alderman of Chicago's First Ward in 1894, Kenna in 1897.

Coughlin began his adult life as a rubber (masseur) in the Palmer House Baths and eventually opened his own bathhouse, which is how he received his nickname. Coughlin also operated the Silver Dollar Buffet Saloon at 169 East Madison Street, whose patrons included the Levee's prostitutes, gamblers, and thieves. Chicago mayor Carter Harrison II described Coughlin as flighty, pompous, temperamental, easily embarrassed, ambitious, addicted to a strange kind of eloquence, perhaps a bit of a caricature, and a would-be Beau Brummel in his attire. Carter Harrison II was elected to the mayor's office in 1897 after succeeding George Bell Swift. The return of another Harrison to the mayor's office caused such an uproar in the Levee district that hundreds of men armed with horns and banners paraded through the streets shouting for Harrison and Mike Kenna.[22]

Kenna was reportedly nicknamed after the waterhole he swam in as a young boy. He began his working career as a newsboy and eventually became a successful saloonkeeper and politician. Kenna's saloon at 120 East Van Buren Street was called the Workingman's Exchange.[23] Its second floor was home to unemployed vagrants, panhandlers, tramps, cardsharps, and down-on-their-luck gamblers who formed a well-disciplined army of voters on Election Day. There Kenna also served a free lunch to anyone, whether they bought a beer or not, as part of his efforts to build a loyal following of voters. Kenna spent campaign money feeding his hungry army and satisfying their thirst. When a French writer asked him why he did this, Hinky Dink replied that politics was his business and this was how he made votes.

Kenna demonstrated a marvelous finesse at organizing what Carter Harrison II called the strange "flotsam and jetsam" who were gathered in the First Ward by the tides of life. Harrison wrote:

> From all sides it washed, from the ship decks of the Great Lakes, the harvest fields of the Far West, the railroad construction works of a dozen states; with this great army came tramps, panhandlers, cardsharps, tricksters, mountebanks, circus and side-show hangers-on, human derelicts of all kinds and descriptions, the weirdest, most fantastic accumulation of beings in human semblance imaginable. The barrelhouse saloons, the ten-cent "flop" lodging houses of the ward served as the magnet to draw them together in one squirming mass. Fifty cents a vote became the established rate of exchange. The keen brain of Hinky Dink schemed out ways and means of organizing this unthinking mass into a cohort of obedient political freebooters ready to do the master's bidding at the right time, which was according to his estimate those elections in which the aldermen of the ward were to make personal appeal to this travesty of an intelligent constituency.[24]

Coughlin and Kenna organized this remarkable collection of voters into the First Ward Democratic Club. Each member was given an identification card that entitled him or her to assistance in time of sickness or distress. Dying with the card on their person even entitled the holder to a decent burial. In 1893 the aldermen formed an organization selling protection to gambling house and brothel operators working in the First Ward and, in particular, the Levee district. They also established a defense fund, placing two lawyers on retainer to appear in court anytime one of their clients was arrested. When police arrested two of their flophouse voters for burglarizing a local wholesale merchant, Coughlin and Kenna pressured the police department to stop arresting their constituents until after the upcoming election. As a result, an order came down from police headquarters directing the Harrison Street and

Des Plaines Street stations to allow criminals to run wild until after Election Day so long as they stopped short of committing murder.[25]

Kenna also enlisted the help of the Quincy Street Gang when Coughlin faced a tough election challenge in 1894 from First Ward regular Billy Skakel. No one wearing a Skakel button was immune from attack by the Quincy Street boys. Some bore six-shooters, others baseball bats, which were frequently used to prevent Skakel's followers from casting their votes. The Quincy Street Gang consisted of some two hundred pickpockets and house robbers from twelve to thirty years of age. Although the members of the gang came from many parts of the city, their activities were centered along Quincy Street in the First Ward.[26]

Criminals like the Quincy Street Gang played an important part in ward politics in Chicago during this period in history. A criminal who was prominent at ward meetings and fought for the candidates of his party received political protection from the authorities when needed. Pickpocket Eddie Jackson is a good example. Jackson worked to elect Coughlin and Kenna to their positions as First Ward aldermen. His political strength was based on the fact that he led a group of repeat voters. Jackson's reward was immunity to carry out his trade. If arrested and brought to court, Jackson could count on First Ward committeeman Al Connolly to seek leniency from the judge assigned to the case, who was also likely a member of the same political party. The only time a case could not be fixed was when Jackson had worked against the political party of the sitting criminal court judge.[27]

Before 1890 the Levee occupied the blocks between Harrison and Polk Streets from Dearborn to Clark. The Levee encompassed the Nineteenth Precinct of the First Ward. Within the precinct there were forty-six saloons, thirty-seven houses of ill fame, and eleven pawnbrokers. The saloons facilitated the prostitution trade as their proprietors opened upstairs vice resorts for the convenience of the free-spending men who had come to Chicago with carloads of cattle and hogs and shiploads of grain. The area was also referred to as the "Custom House Levee" because of its proximity to Chicago's first federal building at 500 South Dearborn. The name Levee resulted from the influx of southern gamblers to the area. The Levee was reportedly the raunchiest part of most southern river towns. The growth of the Levee, and in particular its "red-light district" prostitution trade, can be attributed to the fact that four of Chicago's six railroad depots were centered in the area. The term *red-light district* originated from the use of railroad lanterns. Railroad workers, stopping for a visit, often left their lanterns hanging outside the bordello, thus causing the red lights to become associated with these bawdy houses. The *Chicago Daily Tribune* reported that the area was the basis of Mayor Carter Harrison's political power. Its precincts provided the votes Harrison needed to hold office. In fact, Harrison owned six lots in the district along Clark Street in the heart of the Levee, which he purchased upon moving to Chicago from Kentucky in 1885.[28]

Baptist missionary Viva Divers wrote in her 1891 memoir that the vice district extended from Van Buren to Twelfth Street and from State Street to the Chicago River. The area, which she described as the "Black Hole," contained hundreds of saloons, houses of prostitution, and unlicensed dives of all sorts. On Fourth Street alone she counted forty-four saloons and seventy-eight bawdy houses. Just one block west on Clark Street were another ninety-seven saloons as well as gambling parlors and Chinese opium dens. The most pitiable sight was the children who were being reared in the lap of the vice district. She observed youth of no more than ten and twelve years of age become "beastly drunk" after drinking in the local saloons. Divers described the heart of the district as the "Devil's Four Acres."[29]

The block on Clark Street from Harrison to Polk was notorious for its panel houses. No less than twenty-seven such places were found operating during the 1893 World's Fair. Clark Street from Taylor to Twelfth was known as the Bad Lands, where half-clad females wearing short scarlet dresses and colored stockings could be seen loitering in the doorways.[30]

Centered along Clark Street from Van Buren to Harrison, just north of the Custom House Levee, was Chicago's first Chinese settlement. Like the Levee, Chinatown had its share of vice activity. A Chinese syndicate headed by a local merchant named Hop Lung controlled gambling in the district. Each Saturday night a sum ranging from one hundred to three hundred dollars was collected from each gambling house. The graft money went to the First Ward political organization of aldermen Kenna and Coughlin. Each Sunday at least two hundred laundrymen would come to the gambling dens to be "skinned" (cheated) out of their money. Sunday was the one day that the men had off from work. Although local merchants denied the existence of opium dens in Chinatown, many local stores sold opium and had at least one bench in the rear of their store where the opium smokers could recline. Policy gambling was also popular in Chinatown. Policy (lottery) gambling, Fan Tan (also called Sevens), and Bung Loo card games were so prevalent that members of the local Chinese Christian Union undertook a running battle with the gambling dens in the area.[31]

There was also a great diversity of business in the Levee. Besides the vice resorts were drugstores, blacksmith shops, oyster bars, barrelhouse saloons, livery stables, Chinese laundries, pawnshops, policy shops, flophouses, barber shops, dime museums, tintype galleries, secondhand stores, undertaking parlors, and restaurants. "Coke fiends" openly congregated in drugstores and publicly used hypodermic needles. Drugstores also sold a narcotic called "luck" that was a favorite of the African American prostitutes of the Levee. There were also "immoral dives" that sold pictures of nude women in every kind of posture and "Turkish baths" with lady attendants.[32]

After 1890, because of the growth of Chicago's downtown business district, Mayor Harrison forced the relocation of the Levee to the area between Nineteenth and Twenty-second Streets, from State to Clark. Harrison wrote in his autobiography that he had forced the Custom House Levee to move in order to protect the passengers on streetcars headed downtown from the Englewood and Stockyards districts. The activities of the red-light district exposed women and children riders to embarrassing behavior. Additionally forty thousand to fifty thousand people a day passed through the Levee. Two of Chicago's most important railroad depots, the Wisconsin Central and Northern Pacific terminal and the Polk Street station, were located in the heart of the vice district. The closing of the Custom House Levee did not happen over night; it took nearly ten years to close the whole district.[33]

The new Levee was in the Second Ward. This troubled Hinky Dink and "the Bath." In order to regain control of the Levee, Coughlin, Kenna, and their supporters proposed a redistricting ordinance that would return the Levee to the First Ward.[34] Second Ward alderman William Hale Thompson supported the passage of the ordinance. What was troubling about Thompson's support of the ordinance was that the area ceded to the First Ward also contained the Second Ward's most important business district. The return of the Levee to the First Ward was the beginning of a long association between Coughlin, Kenna, and Thompson that eventually culminated in Thompson's election as mayor of Chicago.

Chicago's Second Ward also contained the fashionable Prairie Avenue and Grand Boulevard residential districts, which were home to such Chicago notables as Marshall Field and George Pullman. The coming of the 1893 World's Fair prompted Chicago's teeming vice district to expand into the Second Ward, encroaching on these wealthy communities. Troubled by the expansion of the Levee and the recent opening of the Everleigh Club, Second Ward citizens sought an aldermanic candidate who could protect their interests. Thompson—millionaire real estate developer; member of the Chicago Athletic Association; and roommate of Gene Pike, the other Second Ward alderman—answered the call. Thompson was no ordinary upper-class gentleman. He had been a real-life cowboy in Nebraska and was just as at home in Levee saloons as in the silk-stocking precincts of the Second Ward.[35]

The "New Levee," as it was called, became home to many of Chicago's saloons and gambling houses. Within its borders were located more than two hundred houses of prostitution: the House of All Nations, the Little Green House, the Bucket of Blood, Ed Weiss's Capital, Vic Shaw's place, Freiberg's Dance Hall, and the Everleigh Club were among its principal attractions. South of Nineteenth Street stood Bed Bug Row, a collection of brothels inhabited by African American girls. A gentleman and his guests could be assured of a good time "going down the line" visiting the various establishments.

The social center of the New Levee was Freiberg's Dance Hall. Freiberg's was located on Twenty-second Street between State and Wabash. It provided dancing and a number of back rooms for activities with the "ladies." Freiberg's was also the command post of the Levee. Aldermen Coughlin and Kenna made their headquarters there while conducting important Levee business. Its owner, Isaac Gitelson—better known to Levee regulars as Ike Bloom—took a leading part in Democratic politics, always delivering his precinct by pluralities of two hundred to three hundred votes, seldom allowing the opposition to rack up any significant tallies.[36]

The pride of the Levee was the famous Everleigh Club at 2131 South Dearborn. Originally designed to accommodate the many visitors to the 1893 Columbian Exposition, the bordello was a three-story double building containing nearly fifty rooms. Two young women, Ada and Minna Everleigh, who had earlier operated a bordello in Omaha, Nebraska, ran the club. The elite patrons of the Everleigh Club were entertained genteelly in one of a number of elegantly decorated parlors. There was the Japanese Room, the Turkish Room, the Persian Room, and the Room of a Thousand Mirrors. The sisters became so famous that in 1902, while touring the United States, Prince Henry of Prussia asked to visit the Everleigh Club. Legend has it that the prince drank champagne from the shoe of one of the girls, who had lost it while dancing on his table, thus creating a new tradition. The fame of the Everleigh Club led to its eventual downfall. While attending a Saint Louis convention, Mayor Carter Harrison II obtained a brochure prepared by the Everleigh sisters describing the pleasures found at their club. The pamphlet caused such an outcry from Chicago's growing reform element that the police closed the Everleigh Club for good in October 1911.[37]

In spite of their dubious activities, the denizens of the First Ward apparently had a heart. Each year a benefit was held for "Lame Jimmy" (some called him Jonny), the crippled pianist at Carrie Watson's brothel. The event was so successful that Bathhouse John Coughlin got the idea to hold a First Ward fund-raising event. The First Ward Democratic Club held its first annual reception in 1896 at the Seventh Regiment Armory. It was such a success that it was moved to the Chicago Coliseum in later years. In 1907 an estimated twenty thousand guests drank ten thousand quarts of champagne and thirty-five thousand quarts of beer at the event. Two hundred waiters and one hundred policemen attended to the crowd, which consisted of such a "bedlam of thieves, robbers, plug-uglies, dips, dope fiends, porch climbers, and chronic bums and drunks as had never been gathered together since the days when the rabble of Rome was feted at the circuses." At the stroke of midnight, flanked by the Everleigh sisters, Bathhouse John Coughlin led the grand march. Every strumpet, ward heeler, madam, and procurer in the First Ward joined the parade. The event was such a grotesque exhibition that Chicago civic leaders, including Walter Sumner, dean of the Cathedral of Saints Peter and Paul, and Arthur Burrage Farwell, president of the Chicago Law and Order League, convinced then Chicago Mayor Fred Bussee to order the end of the event. The last First Ward Ball was held on December 14, 1908.[38]

The 1893 World's Columbian Exposition brought William T. Stead, noted English reformer and editor of the *Review of Reviews* magazine, to Chicago. Stead was appalled by conditions in the Levee and the politics of the city. One year after his arrival, he published a startling exposé of vice conditions titled *If Christ Came to Chicago*. Stead collected much of the information for his book while he was a resident of the Saint Lawrence Hotel at Clark and Polk Streets in the Custom House Levee. Stead argued that political corruption created the conditions in the Levee and that "the religion of the church in Chicago had been replaced by that of the Democratic Party." The furor created by the publication of Stead's book traveled nationwide, and his revelations led to the formation of the Civic Federation, Chicago's first important reform movement. Stead did not live to see the end of the Levee. He died while crossing the Atlantic Ocean on the steamship *Titanic* on April 15, 1912.[39]

Another English reformer, Rodney "Gypsy" Smith arrived in Chicago in October 1909. An illiterate gypsy boy who had found salvation through the gospels, Smith had become a noted evangelist. Backed by sixty Chicago churches, Smith planned to invade the Levee on the night of October 18. Leading a crowd of nearly twenty thousand people, Smith marched through the streets of the Levee preaching the gospel and singing religious hymns. Although he did not remain in Chicago long, he had raised the conscience of the city. On January 31, 1910, the Church Federation of Chicago, composed of more than six hundred religious congregations, passed a resolution urging Mayor Fred Bussee to appoint a commission to investigate vice conditions in the city.[40]

Walter Sumner chaired the commission to investigate the social evil in Chicago. Commission members included Julius Rosenwald, the Reverend Frank Gunsaulus, Graham Taylor, Justice Harry Olson, Dr. W. A. Evans, and U.S. Attorney Edwin Sims. The commission reported in 1911 that there were 506 vice resorts in Chicago employing at least 1,880 prostitutes. The Chicago Vice Commission's report was so sordid in detail that the U.S. Postal Service barred it from the mail. Most of these women worked in the Levee vice district located in the First Ward. The commission's report went on to state that prostitution destroyed the souls of five thousand young women each year and called for an end to vice in the First Ward and the extermination of the Levee.[41]

Many police officers and politicians, including the mayor, however, were in favor of maintaining the Levee as a segregated vice district. They believed that closing the Levee would scatter vice throughout the city and make it more difficult to control. They also believed that respectable women were safer from sexual assault and other crimes if open prostitution were maintained in an orderly fashion as an outlet for the lusts of men. While not exactly supporting the segregated vice concept, social reformer Lincoln Steffens actually wrote in 1902 that vice in Chicago was "honest," saying, "Though the city has an extra-legal system of controlling vice and crime, which is so effective that the mayor has been able to stop any practices against which he has turned his face—the 'panel game,' the 'hat game,' 'wine rooms,' 'safe blowing'—though gambling is limited, regulated and fair, and prostitution orderly; though, in short, through the power of certain political and criminal leaders—the mayor has been able to make Chicago, criminally speaking, 'honest'."[42]

More importantly, the political strength of the First Ward depended on the revenue it obtained from the red-light district and from gambling. These revenues allowed Coughlin and Kenna to buy flophouse votes in large quantities and help ensure the election of office seekers endorsed by the First Ward organization. Chicago was not alone in its efforts against segregated vice: at least twenty-nine other American cities reported closing their red-light districts in the years between 1912 and 1917.[43]

The vice commission's report, however, directly challenged the segregated vice argument. Segregated vice had not kept prostitution in the Levee. Although the Levee was Chicago's main attraction, all the "river wards" had open vice districts. Segregated vice existed in the Near West Side around Halsted and Madison Streets, led by Mike "de Pike" Heitler, and in the Near North Side on Clark Street, both operating with the tacit approval of the city. In fact, Mayor Harrison had sought to have these areas designated as segregated vice districts upon his closing of the Custom House Levee. In addition, a number of massage parlors, manicure establishments, dance halls, and Turkish baths, especially in the downtown area, were nothing more than houses of ill fame. The commission found that nearly five thousand people in Chicago devoted their efforts to the business of prostitution.[44]

Tales of white slavery further fueled the rising sentiment against the Levee. Thousands of young women came to Chicago and other big cities at the turn of the nineteenth century looking for work. Some, not being able to find employment, turned to prostitution. Others were actually kidnapped, drugged, and forced into the trade. The federal government's White Slave Traffic Committee reported that during a two-month period in 1907 authorities had rescued 278 girls under the age of fifteen from Levee dens. Most women who entered prostitution in Chicago, however, probably did so voluntarily. The vice commission found that those who engaged in the trade came principally from the ranks of domestic workers, waitresses, department store clerks, and saleswomen, who could not survive on their paltry salaries. However, even the hint of white slavery was so appalling that Chicago's religious community exerted direct pressure on the federal government to act. As a result, Chicago congressman James Mann sponsored new legislation making the interstate transportation of women for the purpose of prostitution a violation of federal law.[45]

Following the vice commission report, Mayor Harrison began closing the most notorious vice resorts in the Levee. He did suggest, however, that the city hold a popular referendum on the question of segregated vice. (Harrison's stand against vice resulted in his losing the support of Coughlin and Kenna in the 1915 Democratic primary.) The more politically connected resorts, such as Ed Weiss's Capital, ignored the mayor's order and remained open. Finally, State's Attorney John Wayman swore out warrants for the arrest of several hundred resort keepers in an effort to enforce Mayor Harrison's orders.[46]

One of the reasons that it was difficult to close the Levee was the political setup in the First Ward. Police Captain Michael Ryan was in charge of the Twenty-second Street Station. He was the "chief of police" of the First Ward and reported directly to Coughlin and Kenna. Even the commissioner of police could not transfer Captain Ryan without their blessing. With Coughlin and Kenna in charge, Ryan ignored the mayor's pronouncements to close the Levee. In fact, Ryan was the hub of Chicago's vice ring. His plainclothes policemen, or "confidential men," were the spokes, and the sections of the rim were three dive owners and keepers who controlled strings of saloons and bordellos. The first of these rings, and the biggest, was run by James

Colosimo; Julius and Charlie Maibaum headed another; and Joe Marshall and his brothers led the third. This was a different group from the one that headed the Custom House Levee.[47]

Colosimo had immigrated to Chicago from Cosenza, Italy, in 1895 at the age of eighteen. He earned a position as a precinct captain in the Democratic Party by organizing fellow street sweepers into a voting bloc. He also controlled the vote in the Italian settlement centered at Polk and Clark Streets within the First Ward. "Big Jim," as he was referred to, was also involved in prostitution. Colosimo married Victoria Moresco, the operator of a Levee bordello. Soon he himself was operating three Levee houses of prostitution. Colosimo prospered. He wore so many diamonds that he was often referred to as "Diamond Jim." He also opened a restaurant at 2126 South Wabash named Colosimo's Café. His restaurant became the center of social life in Chicago. Enrico Caruso, the famous opera star, was known to frequent Colosimo's whenever he visited Chicago. Entertainer Sophie Tucker was reportedly arrested there for performing a lewd dance called the "Angle Worm Wiggle."[48]

Like many other successful Italians of the time, Colosimo became the target of Black Hand extortion. In order to deal with the Black Hand threat, Colosimo sent for a New York relative, Johnny Torrio. Torrio had been a member of New York's Five Points Gang. His usefulness eventually extended beyond protecting Colosimo from extortion to overseeing his bordellos.[49]

Citing pressure from reform elements, the police department created the office of Second Deputy Superintendent and a Morals Division under its supervision in 1913. Metellus L. Funkhouser, a major in the Illinois National Guard, was appointed to the post. Funkhouser selected William C. Dannenberg to be his chief investigator in charge of the newly created Morals Division. The Morals Division would act independently of the regular district police and of aldermen Coughlin and Kenna, resulting in an ongoing battle against vice in the Levee district.[50]

On July 16, 1914, while conducting a raid in the Levee, two of Dannenberg's men, Fred Amort and Joseph Merrill, were set upon by a group of Levee regulars. Behind the crowd were three cars belonging to Colosimo's assistant Johnny Torrio, white slaver Maurice Van Bever, and Charlie Maibaum. Two local detectives, Stanley Birns and John Sloop, were also in the area. When a man in a gray suit, later identified as Torrio's cousin Roxie Vanille, fired three shots at the Morals Division officers, Birns and Sloop responded with their guns drawn. Thinking that Birns and Sloop were the source of the gunfire, Amort and Merrill returned fire, fatally shooting Birns and wounding Merrill. Two bystanders were also struck by gunfire. The gun battle between the police officers was the straw that broke the camel's back. Enraged by the killing of one of his men, Police Chief Gleason removed Captain Ryan, ending Coughlin and Kenna's rule of the Levee district.[51]

By 1915 the last bordello had shuttered its doors and the Levee was officially closed. However, the end of the Levee did not mean the end of prostitution and gambling in Chicago. Many Levee brothel keepers moved across the Chicago River and resumed their trade in the Near North Side under the protection of Arthur Quinn, son of city oil inspector James Aloysius "Hot Stove Jimmy" Quinn, the onetime political power in the area. Others scattered throughout the South Side, moving into residential districts. Some left the city. The scattering of prostitution also led an increasing number of taxicab drivers to act as panderers and procurers as they steered customers to hidden vice resorts.[52]

The election of William Hale Thompson to the mayor's office in 1915 brought new hope to Levee regulars. "Big Bill," as he was fondly referred to, advocated a wide-open town policy and quickly moved to curtail the power of the Morals Division. In spite of the mayor's personal position on vice, the reform movement had gained enough momentum to prevent the reopening of the Levee as it had been known. The Committee of Fifteen, created to combat the problem of the Levee, and other citizens' groups were ever watchful. There would be vice in Chicago under Thompson, but it would be less flashy as Levee brothels reopened camouflaged as hotels, saloons, and cabarets under the control of the mayor, not the First Ward. Coughlin and Kenna had opposed the Republican Thompson in his bid for mayor and as a result had lost their power. This void was filled by Colosimo, who had become the new power in what was left of the old Levee district.[53]

The closing of the Levee ushered in the era of the "roadhouse." Located in the nearby towns of Posen, Stickney, Calumet City, and others, these roadhouses provided all the comforts of the Levee: prostitution, gambling, and liquor. Colosimo and the enterprising Johnny Torrio reached an agreement with Johnny Patton, the "boy mayor" of Burnham, to move many of Colosimo's illicit enterprises to that suburban town when the Levee finally closed. It was the age of the automobile. Burnham was only fifteen miles directly south of the Levee, a short distance by car. Probably the most famous of the Colosimo roadhouses was the Arrowhead Inn, which he purchased from Ike Bloom, who could not make a go of it. The Arrowhead Inn was not your usual roadhouse; it served up not only wine, women, and song but also gourmet dinners and opera music.[54]

Colosimo, however, eventually lost interest in vice activities. He began spending less and less time attending to business after he married a young singer named Dale Winter. In fact, Colosimo had resisted Torrio's efforts at building a liquor syndicate after the onset of Prohibition. While other gangs were already dividing sections of the city into liquor distribution territories, Colosimo was content to remain with what he had. He not only controlled vice in the Levee district and Burnham, Illinois, but he also ruled the street laborer's union and the city street repairs union, which were under the supervision of his protégé "Dago" Mike Carrozzo. This was not acceptable to Torrio, who recognized the potential of bootlegging. On May 11, 1920, while waiting for two truckloads of liquor from Jim O'Leary at Colosimo's Cafe, Big Jim Colosimo was murdered. He was found shot in the head. The suspect in the killing was Frankie Yale (sometimes spelled Uale) of the Five Points Gang, at the behest of Johnny Torrio.[55]

Nothing could sum up the alliance of politics and crime in Chicago more than the list of pallbearers at Colosimo's funeral. The "active" pallbearers included Alderman John Coughlin, former Cook County Commissioner John Budinger, State Representative John Griffin, and seven other less notable friends of Colosimo. The list of "honorary" pallbearers was no less than astonishing. It included thirty-six men, including three judges, eight aldermen, two former assistant U.S. attorneys, and no less than six Levee gambling house and saloon operators.[56]

The alliance between politics and crime in Chicago was further highlighted by the 1917 indictment of Chicago police chief Charles Healy.[57] State's Attorney Maclay Hoyne accused Healy of taking graft payments to allow vice to operate in Chicago. Healy's graft collector, Tom Costello, testified that he had paid Healy a total of $13,900 to allow vice to flourish. Costello also named ten police captains who had profited from the illegal vice and gambling taxation. Those vice entrepreneurs who failed to pay were the subject of police enforcement directed by the chief himself. The graft ring was so deliberate that commanding officers who were friendly with Costello were put in control of the police districts where vice resorts tended to flourish. Despite the sheer audacity of public corruption in Chicago, the crime situation would get even worse with the restriction of alcohol consumption in the United States.

Although the era of the gangster in Chicago is often attributed to Prohibition, the genesis of the gangsters' power can be traced back long before the enactment of the Volstead Act. From the beginning of Chicago's history, the underworld has been inextricably interwoven with the social and political structure of the city. Beginning with gambling king Mike McDonald, Chicago's criminal underworld constituted the most powerful political force in the city. The vice lords, saloon keepers, and common criminals who had achieved an alliance with politicians and police ultimately assumed a quasi-legitimate function. The gangs provided services that the law prohibited but that, nevertheless, human appetites craved. Organized crime existed to regulate conduct in areas where official and legally sanctioned control had failed or did not exist.

3

THE BLACK MAFIA

This chapter studies the participation of African Americans in organized crime in Chicago. The history of African American involvement in organized crime is confusing, to say the least. Although a number of authors have recognized black participation in the policy (lottery) gambling racket, they also argue that African Americans lacked the political associations and organizational skills necessary to participate in criminal activity on the same level as the once-prominent Italian American crime syndicates. For example, St. Claire Drake and Horace Clayton reported in 1945 that Negroes never got more than "petty cuts" from gambling and vice protection. In their more recent book, *African-American Organized Crime,* Rufus Schatzberg and Robert Kelly add: "Throughout the early period of white gang development, African Americans were not visible in the structure of any significant organized criminal process. Indeed, African-American criminals who entered the twentieth century had no documented history of a leadership role or any significant active affiliation with any organized crime group."[1] In a related article, Kelly goes on to state:

> There was in effect no "Mafia" or syndicate structure among these minority groups. They did not evolve around a common code of behavior or rules governing relationships between and among various groups; the protection they paid to operate illicit goods and services was not of a magnitude that would have significant political impact; and there were no examples of networks influencing an election, delivering a vote, funding a political candidate, or dabbling in union affairs. The scale of corruption was modest, highly localized, and tied to the particular criminal activity involved.[2]

It was not until 1974 that Francis Ianni predicted the emergence of a sophisticated "Black Mafia." Ianni argued that traditional Italian American organized crime was being displaced by African Americans and in some cases

Puerto Ricans. Ianni's argument was rooted in ethnic succession theory. Ethnic succession is the process by which different immigrant groups have used the provision of illegal vice activity, such as prostitution, gambling, and narcotics, as a means of social mobility. The Italians, just like the Irish before them, had found jobs, educated their children, and moved to the suburbs. The ethnic vice industry that they had dominated for so long was now the prerogative of America's newest urban immigrants—minority Americans.[3]

Ethnic succession theory, coupled with the almost complete absence of any published account of African American criminal groups, has led to the popular belief that black Americans did not participate in what came to be known as organized crime in America's urban centers. This chapter will explore the participation of Chicago blacks in organized criminal activity during the period between 1890 and 1950. This analysis will also demonstrate that African American vice syndicates existed in the South Side of Chicago, just as Irish and Italian vice syndicates flourished in other areas of the city. Although they did not participate in bootlegging, African American criminal syndicates ran speakeasies and after-hour nightclubs and participated in illegal casino and policy gambling for almost fifty years. African American organized crime groups differed from other criminal groups only in the fact that they continued to independently exist long after Chicago's other ethnic-based criminal syndicates fell under the dominance of Italian mobsters.

The Black Metropolis

The reason for the lack of a common understanding of African American organized crime can best be attributed to the segregated nature of Chicago's black community during this period in history. Chicago's South Side was a "black metropolis" that had its own elected officials, business community, and underworld, all of whom had little interaction with "white" Chicago. Following the example of Chicago School researchers, this chapter begins with a brief review of black migration and settlement in Chicago. Understanding the establishment of Chicago's black community and its relationship to the larger political, economic, and social organization of the city is critical to understanding the development of organized crime among Chicago's black population. The discussion then centers on the history of the ethnic vice industry that flourished in Chicago's African American community during the first half of the twentieth century. Explaining the social history of black involvement in vice activity is essential to establishing the fact that African Americans formed sophisticated criminal organizations rivaling those of other ethnic groups.

Although Chicago's first permanent resident, Jean Baptiste Point du Sable, was a Negro (from Haiti), there were few other blacks in Chicago until 1840 when large numbers of runaway slaves began arriving in the Windy City. By the time the Civil War began in 1861, there were approximately one thousand African Americans living in Chicago. The first blacks to settle there were concentrated in the center of the city along the banks of the Chicago River. From the center of Chicago, the African American population expanded in all possible directions. Blacks moved southward along State Street in a narrow corridor of land between the Rock Island Railroad and the South Side elevated train. Blacks also moved westward along Lake Street and into the Near North Side's Sicilian community. The majority of Chicago's black population moved south, where rents were cheapest, near the railroad terminals and Chicago's segregated vice district.[4]

The outbreak of World War I increased African American migration to Chicago. The war had stopped the flow of European immigrants to the United States. In addition, many immigrants had returned home to fight for their native lands, increasing the need for workers in war-related industries. In order to fill this need, northern industrialists sent labor recruiters to the South, inviting African American workers to come north. More than fifty thousand Negroes poured into Chicago between 1916 and 1920 to fill the need for labor. By 1920, 90 percent of Chicago's black population was concentrated in the South Side in an area bound by Twelfth and Thirty-ninth Streets from Wentworth Avenue to Lake Michigan.[5]

Chicago was the midwestern focal point of a great African American migration. As the terminus of the Illinois Central Railroad, Chicago was the North's most accessible city for southern job seekers from the Mississippi Delta region. The Illinois Central Railroad station, located at Twelfth and Michigan, was the anchor of Chicago's new and expanding South Side black community. Just as Italian immigrants had settled around the Polk Street station, where the railroad brought Italian immigrants from Eastern ports, black migrants sought housing in the area surrounding the Illinois Central terminal.[6]

Chicago was also attractive to southern blacks because of the activities of the *Chicago Defender* newspaper. The *Defender* was widely read throughout the South and portrayed Chicago as a progressive city that supported a growing African American community. In addition, Chicago exhibited other "pull" forces that drew southern migrants, including higher-paying jobs, better schools, and an African American "bright light" (entertainment) district. Coupled with the "push" forces existing in the South, such as discrimination, economic hardship, and a depressed cotton market, Chicago became an attractive alternative for southern blacks who were seeking a place in the industrial economy.[7]

Chicago's South Side "black belt" grew to be the second largest Negro community in the world; only New York's Harlem exceeded it in size. This black metropolis was a city within a city, seven miles in length and one and one-half miles wide, where more than three hundred thousand African Americans lived, including policemen, firemen, precinct captains, aldermen, state representatives, doctors, lawyers, and teachers. In 1928 Chicago's black community even elected an African American to Congress. Just as other immigrants before them, blacks moving to Chicago settled among their own kind. Unlike other immigrants, however, segregation prevented second-generation blacks from moving from Chicago's African American communities. Despite racial prejudice, Chicago was truly a "house for all people," where each ethnic group could find advancement through political mobilization, even African Americans. Chicago's highly organized "machine" politicians were willing to work with anyone who could deliver the vote and contribute financially to the reigning political party.[8]

Chicago probably boasted a greater degree of black participation in politics than any other city in the nation. In the early days of machine politics, the reward for supporting a successful candidate was jobs and graft. The historical record shows that this applied to the African American community just as it applied to any other ethnic group. Early Chicago blacks were incorporated into both the First Ward political machine of "Bathhouse" John Coughlin and "Hinky Dink" Mike Kenna and the Second Ward organization of Republican alderman William Hale Thompson. African Americans at this time in history were staunch supporters of the Republican Party—the party of Abraham Lincoln. Later the expanding African American community in Chicago's South Side developed into an independent political force whose endorsement was sought by both Republicans and Democrats alike. Chicago blacks learned early that the political life of the community was powerfully allied with the world of the saloon and the gambling house. And just as in other ethnic communities, an African American underworld developed in Chicago's black community to regulate vice activity.[9]

Black Gamblers and Vice Syndicates

The black community's first vice lord was John "Mushmouth" Johnson. Born in Saint Louis, Johnson migrated to Chicago in 1875. After working as a waiter in the Palmer House Hotel and as a "floor man" in a downtown gambling hall, Johnson opened his own saloon and gambling house in 1890. Johnson's saloon was located in the heart of Whiskey Row, which ran for two blocks along the west side of State Street, Chicago's main thoroughfare. His gambling place was said to be unique because the players did not gamble against the house. They gambled against one another, with the game keeper taking a part of every "pot." In 1906 Johnson opened yet another gambling hall, the Frontenac, near Chicago's infamous Levee red-light district. Described as the "Negro Gambling King of Chicago," Johnson himself never gambled. He believed that "a man who gambled had no business with money."[10]

Part of Johnson's secret of success was that he contributed to both the Republican and Democrat parties. This arrangement continued until Coughlin and Kenna took control of the First Ward. Through the usual formula of payoffs and delivering votes, Johnson rose to the position of "Negro political boss" in the First Ward organization of Hinky Dink and the Bath, thus ensuring immunity for his gambling operations. Johnson not only was the patron of black gamblers but also held the distinction of being "the man to see" in Chicago's Chinese quarter. Representing Coughlin and Kenna, he sold protection to more than twenty Chinatown opium dens and gambling halls where Fan Tan and Bung Loo card games were played.[11]

In 1903 Chicago mayor Carter Harrison revoked the license of Johnson's saloon in Whiskey Row. Evidence collected by the city council's "graft committee" described Johnson as a "card cheat" who robbed patrons "stone blind" at his craps (dice), hand faro, and draw poker tables. Witnesses told the committee that it was impossible to win at Johnson's gambling tables. Even when a patron did win a pot, every effort was made to "skin" him of his winnings at another game before he left the resort. In spite of an unsavory reputation, Johnson began what became a long-standing tradition among African American gangsters of contributing to blacks in need. His mother contributed money on his behalf to the Baptist church and to help establish a home for African American seniors.[12]

Pony Moore was another early black gambler and saloon operator. Moore owned the Turf Exchange Saloon and the Hotel De Moore resort in the Levee district. A member of the National Negro Business League, Moore was often referred to as the "Mayor of the Tenderloin." Fond of wearing diamonds, including one padlocked to the front of his shirt, Moore was the "boss colored gambler and saloon keeper on 21st Street." Although Moore was a colorful figure who had some influence over the black vote, he never rose to a position of political prominence. He is best known for his involvement in one of the Levee's most remembered incidents. Moore was involved in a scheme to charge Chicago's infamous Everleigh sisters with the death of Marshall Field Jr., heir to the department store fortune. Although it was commonly believed that Field was killed at the Everleigh Club, the Everleigh sisters steadfastly denied any involvement in his death.[13]

During this same period, Robert T. Motts, Samuel Snowden, and William Beasley also opened a tavern and gambling hall on Whiskey Row. In a very short time their saloon became the resort of choice for black sporting men from Chicago and those visiting from other parts of the country. In 1890 Motts, who had been a porter in Mushmouth Johnson's saloon, followed the migration of Chicago's black community and opened a tavern and gambling hall farther south on State Street in the Second Ward. Bob Motts not only became known as a good "pay-off" for the police but also worked to organize the black vote.[14]

Motts reportedly paid saloon patrons and local women five dollars a day to assist in political canvassing. In return for his activities, Motts was able to place some forty black women in jobs at Chicago's city hall. He also ran a theater named the Pekin in connection with his saloon. The Pekin Theater provided family entertainment and was the only black-owned theater of its kind. In return for his political activities, Motts was able to help elect his protégé Edward Green to the Illinois legislature. Motts remained a political power in Chicago until his death in 1911.[15]

Another saloonkeeper involved in politics at this time was Henry "Teenan" Jones. Born a slave in Alabama, Jones had been in the gambling business in Chicago since 1876. In 1895 he opened a gambling house in Chicago's prestigious Hyde Park community that included dice, roulette, and poker. His Lakeside Club, as it was called, catered primarily to white Chicagoans. Jones also ran two other gambling houses that catered primarily to blacks. One was located in the Windermere House hotel in Hyde Park and the other at the Chicago Beach Hotel. In 1910 a community organization called the Hyde Park Protective Association, fearing that social resorts that catered to blacks would cast blight on the entire community, forced Jones to close both his saloon and gambling halls.[16]

After leaving Hyde Park, Jones opened two clubs in the black Second Ward known as the Elite #1 and the Elite #2. The Elite #1, at 3030 South State Street, was believed to be the first cabaret in Chicago to feature jazz music. The Elite #2, at 3445 South State, was also well known. It became infamous as one of Chicago's most notorious "black-and-tan" resorts. During the mayoral administration of Carter Harrison II (1911–1915), an order was issued to close all gambling houses in Chicago except those in black communities. As a result, many whites began to frequent black taverns, including those owned by Jones. Additionally, Jones ran a column in Chicago's African American *Defender* newspaper titled "Reminiscences from an Old-Timer's Scrapbook."[17]

While Jones was in the Second Ward, he became involved with black Second Ward alderman Oscar De Priest. In 1916 De Priest organized a "colored voters club" that demanded contributions from local gamblers in order to support upcoming elections. "King Oscar," as the *Chicago Daily Tribune* referred to De Priest, ran what was described as his "Tammany Club" from a real estate office at Thirty-fifth and State. In 1917 De Priest was charged with conspiracy to permit gambling in the Second Ward by Cook County state's attorney Maclay Hoyne. Under pressure from Hoyne, Jones became one of the chief witnesses against De Priest.[18]

Jones told investigators that De Priest received a monthly tribute of thousands of dollars from gambling houses that he protected in the "black belt." Jones also testified that he had personally paid twenty-eight hundred dollars in bribes to De Priest during a four-month period to protect his gambling clubs. Represented by none other than the famous attorney Clarence Darrow, De Priest responded that the money he had received from Jones represented campaign contributions and not graft. Chicago's black population resented De Priest's indictment and held a prayer meeting in protest on Chicago's courthouse steps. Because vice and corruption were common throughout Chicago, blacks felt that enforcement targeted at the African American community was unfair.[19]

The trial of city councilman De Priest clearly demonstrated that an African American vice syndicate existed in Chicago and that payoffs from vice entrepreneurs to public officials were just as common in the black community as they were in other parts of Chicago. Black officials followed the pattern established by earlier machine politicians of collecting money from illegal vice operations in order to fund their political activities. De Priest himself testified that he had fought the opening of the Beaux-Arts black-and-tan club because his political enemy Dan Jackson owned it. De Priest feared that Jackson would use the gambling proceeds from the club to fight him in his reelection bid.[20]

The onset of Prohibition in 1920 further intensified vice activity in Chicago's South Side just as it did in other parts of the city. Thirty-fifth Street, between State and Calumet, the bright-light area of the black community, became a congestion of sawdust-floored gin mills fuming with jazz music. Here were found cabarets, nightclubs, gambling halls, prostitution, policy kings, and black-and-tan clubs. Black-and-tan clubs provided locations for the intimate association of blacks and whites. Black men could be seen with white women and white men with black women. Although the Chicago

Commission on Race Relations reported that mixed couples accounted for only 10 percent of the patronage, the mingling of the races was used to characterize all associations there.[21]

The popularity of black nightclubs among all racial groups grew during Prohibition because of the onset of the jazz age. In fact, Chicago residents could often be heard saying they were "going slumming"—visiting bars and nightclubs in the black community. Imported from New Orleans, the new "jass" music was renamed *jazz* when it was introduced in Chicago. This new name was reportedly derived from a slang term that was used to describe fornication in Chicago's Twenty-second Street brothels. The popularity of jazz was a by-product of Prohibition. The underworld's speakeasies, together with legitimate dance halls, thrived on customers with whiskey flasks in their hip pockets and provided a booming market for the new music.[22]

Jazz music began in the South following the Civil War. Emancipated blacks leaving the plantations carried their music with them, including work songs that were developed to ease their labor on hot summer days; Scottish and English hymns that were transformed into spirituals; and the "blues," developed by slaves to help ease their misery. In New Orleans former slaves bought musical instruments left behind by the Confederate Army. Because they could not read music, they played their instruments as they thought the music should sound, carrying the notes in their heads.[23]

In 1896 New Orleans decided to confine prostitution to a red-light district within the French Quarter known as Storyville, so named for the alderman who had introduced the regulating ordinance.[24] The area was home to gambling halls, cabarets, honky-tonks, and an endless number of bordellos that employed black musicians and their new "hot" music. Jazz replaced ragtime and became the music of choice in Storyville, which led to jazz being described as "whorehouse" music by the better elements of society.

In 1917, at the request of the United States Navy, the mayor of New Orleans decided to close down Storyville.[25] While prostitution quietly resumed elsewhere, the local jazz musicians who had played their music in the local honky-tonks and bordellos were out of work. As the red lights went out in Storyville, jazz musicians joined fellow African Americans in their movement to the industrialized cities of the North, many of whom moved to Chicago. Chicago was the rail crossroads of the nation and had an expanding industrial base, and jobs were available to blacks. Thus, the jazzmen of New Orleans found an audience in Chicago that was hungry for southern music and able to pay for it.

South State Street was lined with cafés where jazz music was played—the Elite, the Pekin, the Dreamland, the Panama, the Rose Garden, the Edelweiss, the Open Air Gardens, and the Verdome and Lincoln Theaters. State Street from Twenty-sixth to Thirty-ninth was referred to as "The Stroll."[26] African American poet Langston Hughes described South State Street as: "A teeming Negro street with crowded theatres, restaurants, and cabarets. And excitement from noon to noon. Midnight was like day. The street was full of workers and gamblers, prostitutes and pimps, church folks and sinners. The tenements on either side were very congested. For neither love nor money could you find a decent place to live. Profiteers, thugs, and gangsters were coming into their own."[27]

In his study of African American organized crime, Robert Kelly argued that white gangsters ran the better-known nightclubs in many African American communities. This was not the case in Chicago. A few of Chicago's South Side clubs were owned by whites who hoped to attract a primarily white audience with African American entertainment. However, the leading clubs where the famous black jazz musicians played were owned and managed by black Republican Party organizers, who used the music to attract the attention of potential black voters.[28]

Using Burgess's concentric circle theory as a model, black scholar E. Franklin Frazier argued that Chicago's South Side black community expanded southward and that, through a process of residential selection, different elements tended to become segregated in different zones within the community. As such, Frazier divided Chicago's black community into seven zones. He found that vice activity was centered on Thirty-fifth and State Streets in the heart of Zone 3. The area attracted the bohemian, the disorganized, and the vicious elements of the black race and had a major impact on community life. African American community leaders argued that the attractions of South State Street were a threat to the moral fiber of the black community. They also argued that the "gay life" (hanging out on street corners, throwing loud parties, dressing in the latest risqué fashions, and enjoying the bright lights of the city's nightlife) was giving Chicago blacks a bad name.[29]

Many South Side Chicago blacks lived in close proximity to the Levee district, which also contributed to vice conditions in the area. After the breakup of the segregated vice district in 1912, many prostitutes continued to operate clandestinely in the Near South Side, which was predominantly black by this time. The *Chicago Daily News* reported that almost three thousand women engaged in prostitution in the area between Sixteenth and Twenty-sixth Streets, from Stewart Avenue to Lake Michigan as a small number of Levee regulars reestablished their saloons in the area. Both vice entrepreneurs and the poor alike were attracted to slum areas where the rent was cheap and the community was not organized against criminal activity.

In addition, the corrupt power of the Second Ward allowed vice operations to continue unmolested. As a result, Chicago's black population became increasingly associated with vice activity.[30]

By 1921 Chicago's South Side black community was struggling with an epidemic of gambling and commercialized vice. An exposé by the *Chicago Daily News* revealed that gambling houses, disorderly resorts, booze-selling cabarets, and saloons flourished in many parts of the Second Ward and were overflowing into parts of the Third Ward and other neighboring districts.[31] The *Daily News* reported that all were operating under the protection of political leaders allied with city hall and that Dan Jackson was the "general manager" of Chicago's South Side black vice syndicate.

Daniel McKee Jackson was the most powerful African American vice king that the black community in Chicago has ever known. Jackson, a college graduate, came to Chicago from Pittsburgh in 1892.[32] Working with his father, Emanuel, and brother, Charles, he opened a funeral home in the Second Ward. Jackson, a friend of Bob Motts, married Motts's sister, Lucy, and inherited Bob's estate after his death. Ostensibly an undertaker, Jackson ran several gambling halls, including one in his undertaking parlor and another in the Pekin Theater building. At one time Jackson was also a candidate for state representative, but he was never elected to the office.

Jackson's vice syndicate collected an estimated five hundred thousand dollars a year from gamblers and booze sellers in the Second Ward alone.[33] Graft from the neighboring Third Ward and the adjoining districts was placed at an additional two hundred thousand dollars. Carter Hayes, Jackson's secretary, collected the protection money, which was reportedly 40 percent of the net proceeds of each illicit game. In addition, many poolrooms, saloons, and South Side cabarets were operating craps games, poker games, and blackjack tables while selling illegal whiskey and gin, and their proprietors were expected to contribute to Jackson's syndicate.

As a result of the *Daily News* exposé, Jackson was summoned to Chicago's city hall and ordered to close all of his South Side gambling houses. Within two months, however, he had returned to making his rounds and assuring players and operators that business was getting back to normal. In fact, many of the gambling houses that were listed in the *Daily News* exposé were already back in business. When questioned about the crackdown, Jackson reportedly told a crowd on a South Side street that "The Daily News nor anybody else will ever stop my handbooks from operating."[34]

The *Chicago Daily News* exposé proved the strength of black organized crime in Chicago and revealed intimate details about the connection between vice and politics. Dan Jackson told his followers that if Mayor Thompson paid any attention to the *Daily News* stories, he would quit politics. Jackson's Third Ward lieutenant, Sam Elliot, told police detectives who had raided the Lorraine Gardens that he had "kicked in" thirty-two hundred dollars to Mayor Thompson's last campaign with the understanding that he could run "wide open" if Thompson was elected. Elliot threatened the arresting officers with transfers "out in the sticks" because he was "strong down in city hall."[35]

On June 5, 1922, Dan Jackson opened what was described as the "biggest gambling house" in Chicago. The opening of this gambling hall marked the return of Jackson to power. In addition, there were at least twelve other gambling houses operating under Jackson's supervision that paid as much as 50 percent of their profits to Jackson's vice syndicate. The lawless days of the famous (Levee) red-light district, where the professional gambler prospered under the approving eye of the police, had been restored in Chicago's South Side black belt by Thompson and the political machine headed by Fred Lundin.[36]

One of the major reasons for the success of Chicago blacks in controlling vice and gambling in their community was their political connection with William Hale Thompson, Republican mayor of Chicago. Thompson had a long history of involvement with the black community. Thompson gained his first political office in 1900 when he was elected alderman of the Second Ward . Located directly south of Chicago's central business district, the Second Ward contained the largest concentration of blacks in the city. Blacks in 1900 comprised 16.6 percent of the ward's population and 1.9 percent of the city's total. By 1919 the area was more than 70 percent black, 72 percent of whom were eligible to vote. Citywide, Thompson received 78 percent of the African American vote in the 1919 mayoral election.[37]

Thompson treated blacks more equitably than any other mayor of the era and delivered jobs to African Americans in return for their political support. In fact, so many black Chicagoans were appointed to city jobs during his first term as mayor that Thompson's opponents began referring to Chicago's city hall as "Uncle Tom's Cabin."[38] Chicago blacks hailed Thompson as the "Second Abraham Lincoln." Deprived of the vote in the South, Chicago's black immigrants saw the ballot box as a symbol of their new life in the North and rushed to support the Second Ward politician who had treated them in a respectable fashion. Thompson recognized the right of blacks to self-determination and assisted them in electing African Americans to local offices. He also recognized that local gamblers supported black political officials just as their white counterparts in other areas of the city were supported by the underworld in their wards.

At the prodding of the Chicago Juvenile Protective Association, the Cook County state's attorney began an investigation of vice conditions in Chicago's South Side in 1923.[39] Once again the word was passed down from city hall to close all disorderly resorts, illegal cabarets, and gambling houses. The only one found to openly disobey the edict was Dan Jackson. His Racetrack resort on South State Street continued to operate without interference.

The rest of Jackson's vice syndicate did not remain out of business for long. There was an election looming. William Bass, the operator of two gambling houses, complained to the press that the upcoming 1923 mayoral election had made the hand of the "graft collector" weigh heavily on his business. Bass stated that he was normally required to surrender 20 percent of his profits as graft. The approach of the mayoral election had raised the toll to 25 percent. The stakes were so high in the 1923 election that Jackson was accused of invading several Second Ward polling places and intimidating voters, election judges, and police officers alike.[40]

William Hale Thompson did not seek reelection in 1923. As a result, Jackson had supported William Dever against the Republican candidate at the urging of Democratic politicians who believed they could intercede with Dever to protect Jackson's gambling operations. The resulting election of Dever, however, brought Jackson's protection syndicate to an end. Despite the efforts of Democratic leaders, who had sought Jackson's political support, he was not allowed to conduct his rackets as long as Dever was mayor. When his advances were spurned by the Dever administration, Jackson and his supporters threatened to "put the politicians out of business," which in fact they did when South Side blacks helped defeat Dever in 1927 and returned Thompson to the mayor's office.[41]

The reelection of Thompson was the signal for the reopening of Chicago's South Side gambling dens. Dr. R. A. Williams, opponent of Oscar De Priest for the position of Republican committeeman in the Third Ward, charged that gambling and the policy racket had become a plague on the black community. Men and women who were hardly able to support their families spent their last dimes on policy gambling. The epidemic of policy gambling that was the scourge of Chicago's black belt was the result of a political deal in which Dan Jackson overwhelmingly delivered the African American vote to William Hale Thompson. In the 1927 mayoral election, 91.7 percent of all blacks in the Second Ward supported him for mayor.[42]

Jackson had proven the power of the black vote. He had swung the last two elections for mayor. The price Jackson demanded was the privilege of operating gambling in the Second and Third Wards. Chicago's black belt gamblers, however, were not happy with Jackson's return. Under Jackson, the district had been financially drained. Although gamblers were allowed to operate openly, under Jackson's heel they were compelled to pay out more for political and police protection than they had taken in. Much of the money was used to support Thompson's "America First" candidates who were running in the April 1928 primary elections. One report indicated that as much as one million dollars was collected.[43]

The return of Thompson to the mayor's office in 1927 brought back his "wide-open town" policy and Dan Jackson back to the height of power. In fact, Thompson had appointed Jackson to the post of acting Republican committeeman of the Second Ward. He was formally elected to this position in 1928. Governor Len Small also appointed Jackson to the Illinois Commerce Commission. After Jackson's death in 1929, he was remembered as being "close mouthed and canny in politics and open handed and generous to the less fortunate among his fellow Negroes"; he had donated money to the NAACP and other charities. After Jackson, no one man ever again rose to be the leader of Chicago's African American underworld.[44]

At the time of Jackson's death, an indictment charging his involvement in gambling and political fraud was pending against him. Dan Jackson and Oscar De Priest, described as the "Thompson leaders" in the Second and Third Wards, were charged with accepting tribute from vice resorts in order to fund the primary campaign of State's Attorney Robert Crowe. Two members of Jackson's political organization were also charged with altering ballots in the Sixtieth Precinct of the Second Ward in favor of Thompson's candidates. According to the grand jury report, blame for the gambling ring was to be placed on the Thompson regime.[45]

By 1931 most Chicagoans had lost their faith in Big Bill Thompson. Many Chicago communities had become rampant with prostitution, gambling, murder, and flagrant lawlessness because of the mayor's acceptance of protected vice. Harry Lewis, Republican state central committeeman from the First Congressional District, declared that Jackson and his supporters had strangled the financial life out of the black community through their merciless methods of syndicating vice. Although Thompson treated his black followers more fairly than they had ever been treated before, he had allowed the African American community to be corrupted and placed blacks who were connected to the underworld of vice and gambling into power. Even so, he did not lose African American support in the 1931 election. Thompson lost forty-five of fifty Chicago wards to Anton Cermak. The five wards Thompson won all had large African American populations.[46]

Cermak spared no time retaliating against Chicago's South Side black Republican stronghold. On taking office he fired 2,260 temporary city employees, many of whom were black. Recognizing that the black gambling overlords were the source of the money that greased the South Side Republican machine, Cermak also instructed the city police force to attack black-controlled gambling and policy operations. In addition, Cermak increased police pressure against the illegal activities of the Capone mob. Capone also had been a major supporter of Thompson.[47]

The pressure was kept on South Side gamblers until they saw the error of their ways and left the Republican Party to join Cermak's Democratic fold. The new setup called for graft to be paid to Cermak's personal representative William R. "Billy" Skidmore.[48] An investigation conducted by George Lambert of the Property Owners Improvement Association, which represented sixteen hundred African American taxpayers, revealed that every Friday Ily Kelly, representing gamblers and the policy wheel syndicate, delivered ninety-five hundred dollars to Skidmore. The graft payments were made at the Lawndale Scrap Iron and Metal Company, a junkyard in Chicago's Near West Side.

Cermak traveled to Miami in February 1933 to confer with president-elect Franklin D. Roosevelt. When an attempt on the life of the president was made during a brief address in the city's Bayfront Park, Cermak, who was nearby, was left mortally wounded. After the death of Cermak, Edward Kelly became the mayor of Chicago. Kelly took a different approach to Chicago's black community and allowed a return to gambling and vice in the city's South Side. Evidence that the leading figures of the black underworld were supporting the Democratic Party surfaced when the Jones brothers—Edward, George, and McKissick—who were major policy gamblers, began to actively participate in Third Ward Democratic politics. In fact, one gambling organization dispatched fifteen hundred policy writers to canvass for the Democratic ticket. Kelly treated the black community much like Thompson had. "Big Red," as Chicago blacks called the mayor, appointed African Americans to city jobs and public office and was generally known as a "friend of the race."[49]

The development of black gambling in Chicago passed through three stages that reflected the development of African American politics in the city.[50] During the first stage, blacks worked within existing political structures such as in the First and Second Wards. During the second stage, blacks gained control of the Republican Party in the Second and Third Wards and ran their own political organizations. The third stage of black politics began with the election of Cermak and the eventual migration of black political organizations into the Democratic Party in Chicago.

The historical record suggests that the nature of vice activities also changed during each of these periods. During the first period, saloon gambling was the most important type of vice activity. Black dominance of the Second and Third Wards during the second period coincided with Prohibition and the jazz age. Speakeasies and jazz clubs were added to the already existing gambling racket. During the third and final period, policy gambling eclipsed the importance of all other forms of vice. Because of its popularity, policy gambling became the most important form of vice activity in Chicago's black South Side.

Policy

Policy is the name given a lottery gambling system that was once common in black communities in which players wagered a small sum of money on a combination of three numbers. Various schemes were used to choose the numbers. Some used the text references to their favorite Sunday sermons; others used the badge numbers of the police officers who had arrested them earlier for playing policy. A drum or "wheel" was used in which seventy to eighty capsules containing numbers from one to seventy-eight were whirled about rapidly. A blindfolded person selected twelve numbers at each of the drawings, which were held as often as three times a day. If the holder of a ten-cent ticket found that all three of his numbers were drawn, he had a "gig" and won ten dollars. If only two of the three numbers appeared, he had a "saddle," paying forty cents or higher in ratio to the amount bet. The odds of winning were estimated to be 7,878 to 1.[51]

Three men are generally credited with bringing policy to Chicago: Patsy King, an Asian named King Foo, and Sam Young. While little is known about King Foo, Patsy King, the owner of the Bucket Shop Saloon, was believed to be a Mississippi riverboat gambler who had migrated to Chicago at the time of the 1893 World's Fair. He was a genius gambler who invented his own games of chance and had grown rich on the proceeds. Patsy King reportedly gave the idea for policy to a porter in his saloon named Sam Young. With King's financial backing, Young opened a small policy wheel in downtown Chicago. Young also became a bail bondsman and developed strong political ties. His ability to aid minor gamblers led to his acquiring a reputation as a political "fixer" throughout the black community.[52]

John "Mushmouth" Johnson was probably the first important black gambler to see the potential of policy. In the late 1890s Johnson entered the policy racket in partnership with Patsy King and King Foo. By 1903 Johnson and another man, named Tom McGinnis, owned two policy companies, the Phoenix and the Union, which were headquartered at Johnson's Tavern. McGinnis, a former potato peddler, also owned a saloon and gambling hall on South State Street called the Berlin Café.[53]

Johnson earned the disfavor of gambler Bob Motts by refusing to cut Motts into the policy game. In retaliation, Motts used his association with Illinois congressman Edward Green to pass anti-policy legislation in 1905. This law was viewed to be exceedingly drastic in that it targeted all persons involved in the game, from the policy racketeer to the caretaker of the building in which the gambling was conducted. The new pressure on policy forced Young and others to temporarily withdraw from the game.[54]

In 1915 Young reentered the game by introducing policy gambling along South State Street in the black community. His betting slips bore the name "policy," and he was his own "runner" (collector of bets). A waitress from the Pullman Restaurant at Thirty-first and State Streets pulled the numbers out of a derby hat while standing under the elevated train station at that location. Sam Young is remembered as the "father of the game." His policy wheel was named the Frankfort, Henry, and Kentucky. "Policy Sam," as Young became known, later explained the idea of the numbers game to tavern owners Julius and Caesar Benvenuti, who then formed Chicago's first well-regulated policy wheel, called the Blue Racer, and installed Policy Sam as its headman. Sam Young supplemented his policy income by supervising games of chance at street carnivals held on vacant lots and back streets in the Second Ward and at picnics at Golden Gate Park in Robbins, Illinois.[55]

Julius Benvenuti was somewhat of a favorite in Chicago's predominantly black Second Ward. Described as a "millionaire who looked like a bum," the congenial Sicilian emigrant moved freely throughout the district. Notwithstanding race or background, people were glad to have Benvenuti's acquaintance, and First District congressman Arthur Wergs Mitchell counted him among his closest friends. Benvenuti's popularity may have stemmed from the fact that he happily bankrolled the entire ward operation. Additionally, the Syndicate ignored his policy operations, as Benvenuti was a friend of Al Capone.[56]

The success of policy attracted others to the game, but policy remained a small business until the beginning of the First World War.[57] Sam Preer, who operated the De Luxe Café; William "Bill" Bottoms, owner of the Dreamland Café; and Virgil Williams, the owner of the Royal Gardens, all took a fling at operating the game. Williams was somewhat of a showman and the most successful of the three. He advertised his big payouts, which caught the attention of housewives who began trying their hand at the numbers game. The game soon caught on, and wheels were springing up everywhere throughout the South and West Sides of Chicago.

In 1923, with the financial backing of Julius Benvenuti, Sam Young began another wheel, titled the Interstate Springfield Policy Company, which became one of the largest policy operations in Chicago. The Interstate Springfield lottery employed more than two hundred policy writers and solicitors who collected bets from ten cents to one hundred dollars throughout the South Side. In 1923 the *Chicago Daily News* reported that Dan Jackson, "chief graft collector" of Chicago's South Side black district, had attempted to gain a monopoly on policy gambling and that Jackson had become a partner in the gambling business with Sam Young.[58]

By 1928 it was estimated that twenty independent policy operators were required to pay Jackson three hundred dollars a week for the privilege of operating their wheels.[59] William Dawson, a black candidate for congress and a vigorous opponent of Mayor Thompson, estimated that one million dollars a month was being wagered with the policy barons, with less than one percent of the sum being returned to players in the form of winnings. Some of the largest policy wheels operating openly without police interference in Chicago's South Side were the Kentucky Derby, the East and West, the Monte Carlo, the Interstate Springfield, the Black Gold, the Oriental, the Iowa and Wisconsin, and the Tia Juana.

Walter Kelly, owner of the Tia Juana policy wheel, was especially important to the policy racket, having taken over the position of chief graft collector after the death of Dan Jackson. Kelly maintained an office on South State Street under the auspicious name of Kelly and Washington Brokers. Policy drawings were held there three times a day. Traffic was so congested at noon in the vicinity of Kelly's office that a police officer was stationed directly in front of the building to direct traffic. Passing through the front room of the building, one recognized a normal business office. Stepping into a rear office, however, one observed a row of slot machines, a short-order restaurant, and rows of desks where policy writers made out their reports.[60]

Sometime around 1935 Walter Kelly extended his policy operations to East Chicago and Gary, Indiana. He later attempted to further extend his activities to Hammond and planned to go into the slot machine business. He also became involved in Lake County, Indiana, politics and had donated more than two hundred thousand dollars to local political campaigns. Kelly's rising importance placed him in direct competition with the Capone syndicate, which also had a presence in these areas. On January 6, 1939, Kelly was murdered in Chicago. The suspect was a Capone gangster known only as "Cicero Steve." More than five thousand people turned out for Kelly's funeral. He was eulogized, following the tradition of earlier black gamblers, as a "man who had fed the hungry and clothed the needy," having given away over fifteen thousand dollars to those in need at Christmas time.[61]

Ily Kelly, the brother of the murdered Walter Kelly, became the new link between the political bosses and the policy fraternity.[62] It was now Ily Kelly's job to collect the graft from policy operators before each election. For his efforts, he was also given the privilege of operating his famous keno (similar to bingo) game in the Royal Circle Building at Fifty-first Street and Michigan Avenue. Keno, as his emporium was called, was among the most extravagant gambling palaces ever to grace the South Side of Chicago. In addition to keno, Kelly's gambling hall hosted roulette wheels, blackjack tables, and a dice pavilion.

From his office at the Keno Club, Ily Kelly reportedly gave nightly handouts to police officers, who stood in line waiting for their payoffs. He also gave generously to ward bosses and toured voting precincts with political leaders on Election Day to see how the vote was going. Kelly remained policy's chief graft collector until his health gave out, at which time the mantle was passed to "Big Ed" Jones, owner of the Harlem, Bronx, and Rio Grande policy wheel. Jones also operated the Golden Tavern at 504 East Forty-seventh Street, where he ran a racehorse book, a craps game, and a keno operation.[63]

A gambler by the name of Ezra Leake had sold the idea of policy to Jones and his brothers. The Jones brothers owned a taxicab stand in Evanston, Illinois. They had moved to Evanston from Vicksburg, Mississippi, with their father, who was the pastor of a Baptist church in Evanston. It was Ed Jones who greatly popularized the game. Jones, a Howard University graduate, hired a vast army of pickup men and beautiful girls to operate his policy stations. His Bronx wheel lured as many as a thousand people to its drawings. Blackjack, chuck-a-luck, craps, and other forms of gambling served as added attractions at these events.[64]

Big Ed Jones eventually became the spokesman for twelve policy wheels operating in Chicago's South Side. The protection fee was $250 per week, per wheel. The more than two hundred handbooks operating in the area also had to pay $150 a month. Police officers were given a printed slip listing the "Favored Few," a group of policy wheels that were not to be disturbed. Vice activity had migrated south along State Street. Kelly's Keno club and Jones's Golden Tavern were not in Big Bill Thompson's old Second Ward, but in the Fourth. In 1933 Chicago's South Side was described as a veritable Monte Carlo of graft, vice, and corruption. A headline in the *Chicago Defender* on September 24, 1932, read, "Rackets Now Flourish in All Quarters."[65]

In 1938 the *Chicago Daily News* named the kings of policy in Chicago.[66] They included Julius Benvenuti, who owned the Red Devil and Goldmine wheels in addition to the Interstate Springfield lottery. Also named were the Jones brothers, who owned twelve gaming halls plus their policy wheels. Ily Kelly was named as the owner of the Lucky Strike, Green Dragon, Old Reliable, Streamline, Cyclone, and the Black and White policy wheels in addition to the Tia Juana. Charles Farrell was listed as owning the Gold Shore and North Shore wheels, and Julian Black the North and South and the East and West policy companies. Other wheels owned and operated by members of the policy syndicate included the Cremo, the Prince Albert, the Airplane, the Old Gold, and the Black Gold.

The press estimated that $18 million a year was being bet with Chicago's thirty-eight policy wheels. The source of these funds was believed to be salary, welfare, and pension money destined for thousands of Works Progress Administration (WPA) workers and their children. A survey conducted by the *Chicago Daily News* of South Side businesses estimated that 20 percent of all relief money was being spent on policy. Instead of buying food, clothing, and other necessities of life, the poor were gambling away their money.[67]

In 1942 twenty-six key figures in Chicago's policy racket were indicted.[68] Among them were Ily Kelly, the Jones brothers, Julius Benvenuti, and West Side policy baron James "Big Jim" Martin. Just before the case was brought to trial, the Cook County state's attorney declared that city officials would not cooperate in the investigation. The policy syndicate was critical for maintaining control over the black vote by Ed Kelly's political machine. Policy was a source of patronage for ward politicians. Untold numbers of people were given jobs as policy writers at the request of ward leaders, and graft money rolled steadily into the coffers of the Democratic ward organizations.

Policy had become important to the black community and to black politicians in particular. An interview quoted in Harold Gosnell's *Negro Politicians* regarding policy gambling describes the relationship: "It is a prize to the political party to be able to dictate to them and form a syndicate, which will support them politically. They also derive a tariff which supports the political organization." This tariff was estimated to be $250,000 a month in 1927.[69]

According to the records of the Illinois Writers Project, many members of the policy syndicate were assigned precincts that they were required to deliver at election time. "Walking writers," the persons who went from door to door collecting policy wagers, knew the constituency and could be used to canvass for votes. In 1928 Walter Kelly instructed three hundred of his Tia Juana policy writers to boost the Thompson ticket while making their house-to-house calls. Kelly had instructed his people to support white congressman Martin B. Madden against William Dawson, who was likely to be favored by black voters.[70]

The typical attitude among policy players was that people like to gamble and that policy gave the poor man the same opportunity to test his fate that the rich man had.[71] In addition, it was argued that the money played stayed in the black community. It was estimated that policy employed as many as seven thousand people, who otherwise would be out of work. The money earned was used to support legitimate business in the black community. The paper and ink used to print policy slips was purchased from African American companies. A burial insurance company known as the Metropolitan Funeral System Association was supported. Automobiles were purchased. Black-owned taverns, restaurants, and department stores were patronized. The Chicago Crime Commission reported that policy operators even contributed regularly to black churches.

One of the reasons the policy racket was so important was that policy bankers were often the only members of the black community with money to invest. Nineteen policy wheel operators owned at least twenty-nine different businesses in the black community. For example, the Jones brothers owned the Ben Franklin Department Store, four hotels, and several large apartment buildings. Policy operator Dan Gaines owned the only black Ford automobile dealership in Chicago. Policy banker King Cole invested in the Metropolitan Funeral System. Julian Black, owner of the East and West Policy Company, was the manager of world heavyweight boxing champion Joe Louis. Matt Bivens, owner of the Alabam-Georgia, the Whirlaway, and the Jackpot policy wheels, also owned Bivens Van Lines. It was rumored that his moving vans were excellent places to print policy slips because they were always moving, which made them difficult for the police to detect.[72]

In addition, numerous shoeshine parlors, candy stores, barbershops, beauty parlors, coal and wood stations, cleaners, taverns, groceries, and laundries all benefited from increased traffic from policy customers.[73] There were fifty-nine policy stations alone in the area between Thirty-first and Thirty-ninth Streets and State Street to South Park. Unless the "heat" was on, there was no effort made to conceal policy gambling. Policy shops openly displayed signs reading "doing business," "all books," and the policy gig "4–11–44," a number with a long history in black culture and music referring to the combination of the width and length of a penis.

The policy racket was also responsible for the establishment of a fair number of quasi-legitimate but colorful enterprises such as the sale of "policy players dream books," "lucky number candles," "lucky number incense," and "sure-fire gigs," which were all used to create good luck. The dream book told a policy player what number to bet based on a player's dreams. For example, dreaming of hiding in the woods was a signal of danger, and the "gig" number for such a dream was 4–43–58. Lucky number candles came with a piece of paper containing three lucky numbers, one to seventy-eight. The paper was placed under the candle, which was burned for ten minutes daily until the lucky numbers were drawn. Sure-fire gigs were purchased from "professors" who guaranteed that they produced winning numbers.[74]

As this chapter has shown, African Americans have always been part of organized crime in Chicago. They controlled gambling in black areas and formed vice syndicates that helped to organize the vote for a period of almost fifty years. African American organized crime in Chicago followed the same stages of development experienced by other ethnic groups, differing only in the fact that they were more successful than other groups in resisting the overtures of traditional organized crime. As will be seen in chapter 6, it took the Chicago Outfit an additional twenty years to gain control of the black underworld, which included a ten-year struggle to control policy gambling.

Part of the confusion over African American participation in organized crime has been society's fixation with the so-called American Mafia. If we ignore the alien conspiracy argument that organized crime was brought to America by southern Italian and Sicilian immigrants and instead concentrate on the historical record, we find that at the beginning of the twentieth century Chicago was home to a number of ethnically based organized crime groups made up of local gamblers, brothel keepers, and politicians. The activities of Dan Jackson and his supporters in the Second Ward were no different from the activities of Big Jim Colosimo and Johnny Torrio and their Italian gangsters in the First Ward, or Dion O'Banion and his Irish mobsters in the Forty-second Ward. They all participated in the "Big Fix," in which tribute was collected by the ruling political party from crime and vice in exchange for money and immunity from the enforcement actions of the police. This is what organized crime was in America! Sure, the Chicago Outfit eventually consolidated all vice activity and became the supreme mediator between Chicago's underworld and the political structure, but they had to defeat Irish, African American, and other Italian groups first.

It has been argued that African American organized crime has not been the subject of serious inquiry by the academic community and that any new investigation has to consider the question of race in determining the lack of scholarly interest.[75] Although this research has not uncovered any evidence of racism on the part of academic researchers, it is apparent that the existing literature, like much of the literature on organized crime, suffers from a lack of empirical research. This chapter has attempted to examine African American participation in organized crime by examining the historical record in light of what is known about other ethnic-based criminal groups. Once viewed from this perspective, it becomes clear that black gamblers in Chicago were once among the most powerful criminal groups ever to exist in America. These findings also have important implications for the alien conspiracy theory. Sophisticated organized crime existed in Chicago's African American South Side without the presence of the Mafia or Italian gangsters.

4

THE SYNDICATE

The National Prohibition Enforcement Act ended the sale of alcoholic beverages in the United States. The enactment of Prohibition in 1920 was the result of a one-hundred-year struggle to curtail the use of alcohol by the American public. At the time of the American Revolution, alcohol was seen as the "good creature of god," an indispensable part of clean and healthy living. It was a regular part of the daily diet and was thought to prevent many diseases. In fact, workmen often received part of their pay in rum or other spirits, and alcohol consumption was common at business and government meetings as well as festive occasions.[1]

Eventually, however, people began to develop an increased awareness of the consequences of the misuse of ardent spirits. Drunkenness was soon recognized as a community problem, and temperance was a common subject of religious sermons. In 1785 Dr. Benjamin Rush, surgeon general of the Continental Army and a signer of the Declaration of Independence, published America's first scientific inquiry into the use of alcohol. Rush concluded that alcohol had no food value and that it not only aggravated common diseases but was also the direct cause of many.[2]

The emerging temperance movement welcomed Rush's conclusions. In 1808 the first temperance society in the United States was begun in the state of New York by a young physician named William Clark. Within a decade, a number of temperance societies were established throughout the Northeast. By 1836 eight thousand temperance societies had been formed with an overall membership of more than a million and a half people who openly advocated total abstinence from alcohol. The impact of the temperance movement was also felt in Chicago. By 1844 nineteen hundred Chicagoans belonged to various temperance societies.[3]

Temperance became a means of distinguishing different ethnic groups. Cultural consumption habits pitted "blue-nosed teetotalers" against European immigrants, who regularly consumed alcohol as part of their diet. Germans drank beer; Italians and Jews drank wine. The New England Federalist aristocracy actively used the temperance movement to bolster their declining leadership role. The native American reformers of the mid-1800s saw the curtailment of alcohol consumption as a way of solving the problems of the immigrant urban poor, whose culture often clashed with American Protestantism. The temperance movement became a struggle between rural Protestant society and the developing urban industrial order. Henry Ford, Prohibition's prime industrial protagonist, saw Prohibition as a great force for the "comfort and prosperity" of America, because it would prevent the wages of his workers from being taken away by the saloon.[4]

With Prohibition came a demand for illegal alcohol, which the Torrio vice syndicate and other similar groups around the city were in a position to supply. They were well organized and had the political connections to prevent interference from the police. All the concealed agreements made with local politicians over the years, as well as the experience gained through years of struggle against reform elements, were brought into service in organizing the production and distribution of beer and whiskey. Johnny Torrio ran his criminal organization from the Four Deuces Café at 2222 South Wabash Avenue. Torrio is widely believed to have been a no-nonsense businessman who excelled as a master strategist and quickly built an empire that far exceeded Big Jim Colosimo's.

Torrio's syndicate was an organization of professional gangsters. It differed from other criminal groups, such as the Valley Gang, in that it was not an outgrowth of a neighborhood play group; its members were from different areas. The gang was formed by adult criminals for the administration of vice, gambling, and illicit liquor. Many of Torrio's henchmen were seasoned veterans recruited from the various segments of the criminal community. For example, Torrio gangster Marcus Looney, an arsonist and labor slugger, had been a member of the Gilhooley Gang. Anthony "Tough Tony" Capezio and Claude Maddox were recruited from the Circus Café Gang. And James "Fur" Sammons was a former member of the Klondike O'Donnell Gang.[5]

Realizing there was enough money to be made by all, Torrio approached the leaders of Chicago's other top gangs and suggested they give up burglary, robbery, and crimes of violence in favor of bootlegging. (For personal use, illegal alcohol was poured into a flask and hidden in one's boot, thus the term *bootleg booze*.) The return from these traditional practices, he contended, did not justify the risks taken when compared to the profits to be made from smuggling alcohol. The key to success during Prohibition was territorial sovereignty. Each gang would control liquor distribution in its own area and not encroach upon the territory of the others. Many gang leaders agreed to Torrio's plan, and the system functioned well—for a while.[6]

In 1923 Chicago elected reform mayor William Dever. Dever was a firm believer in the rule of law and quickly ordered the police department to enforce Prohibition. Within weeks of taking office, Dever's police shut down seven thousand soft-drink parlors and restaurants operating as "speakeasies." (The word *speakeasy* referred to speaking softly when ordering.) Dever's reforms prompted Torrio to move his headquarters to nearby Cicero, Illinois. While Torrio was vacationing in Italy, his assistant, Alphonse "Al" Capone, chose the Hawthorne Inn at 4823 West Twenty-second Street as the gang's Cicero headquarters. Torrio had brought Capone from New York to work in the Colosimo syndicate. Fearing the spread of the reform wave that had taken control of Chicago, Cicero's local Republican leader asked Capone to assist the party in the 1924 election.[7]

In return for helping the Republicans maintain control, Torrio and Capone were given a free hand in Cicero. On Election Day two hundred Syndicate gunmen descended on Cicero to ensure that people voted the "right way." Conditions were so bad that Cook County judge Edmund Jarecki deputized seventy Chicago police officers to go into Cicero and engage the Capone gang. Frank Capone, Al's brother, was killed in a gun battle with police at a polling station at the intersection of Twenty-second Street and Cicero Avenue. After winning the election, Cicero Republicans kept their side of the bargain. The number of liquor and gambling establishments controlled by Torrio and Capone in Cicero soon grew to 161.[8]

Outside the area of the First Ward and the Torrio organization, a number of other gangs were also working in collusion with local politicians and police to support vice activities and violate Prohibition laws. Dion O'Banion and his followers controlled Chicago's Near North Side. Klondike O'Donnell and his brothers controlled the Near Northwest Side. Roger Toughy, who claimed to be only a bootlegger and not involved in vice, controlled the Far Northwest Side. The "Terrible Genna brothers" controlled the Near West Side Taylor Street area. Terry Druggan and Frankie Lake and their Valley Gang controlled the Far West Side. On the Southwest Side, the Irish O'Donnell brothers, the Ralph Sheldon Gang, and the Saltis-McErland Gang were all active in bootlegging.[9]

These gangs were largely centered in immigrant areas where the gangster often served as the right arm of the corrupt politician at election time. In exchange for delivering the vote, gang members were allowed to continue in their criminal activities, the proceeds of which often went to support local political organizations. Take the example of the Ragen Colts. The Colts were members of the Ragen Athletic Club, which fulfilled the multiple functions of running football and baseball teams, training boxers and wrestlers, and operating as the ward center for the Democratic Party. The club was sponsored by Frank Ragen, a member of the Cook County Board of Commissioners. Ragen provided these important community services in an effort to influence the young men of his district to support the Democratic ticket. The Ragen Colts played a prominent role in the 1919 Chicago race riot that resulted in the deaths of twenty-three black Chicagoans. Their territory extended from Cottage Grove Avenue to Ashland and from Forty-third Street to Sixty-third Street. They also supplied the manpower for the Ralph Sheldon Gang.[10]

Chief among Torrio's rivals were Dion O'Banion and the six Genna brothers—Angelo, Sam, Jim, Pete, Tony, and Mike. O'Banion was raised in the Irish shantytown of Kilgubbin in Chicago's Near North Side and was a product of the Market Street Gang, which operated in the area around Chestnut and Orleans Streets. The Market Street Gang had been organized by local Republican leaders to help get out the vote at election time. Known to his friends as Dion, Dean, or Deany, O'Banion sold newspapers as a child. When he was twelve, he was hit by a streetcar in the LaSalle Street tunnel under the Chicago River. One of his legs was so badly injured by the accident that he limped when he walked. O'Banion had attended Saint Dominick's School and served as an altar boy at Holy Name Cathedral. Later he became a singing waiter at McGovern's Saloon (later renamed the Liberty Inn) at Erie and Clark Streets. O'Banion was never known to drink alcohol but was rumored to have killed at least eight people. In spite of his potential for violence, he was also known for his compassion, having sent a neighborhood cripple for treatment to the Mayo brothers' clinic in Rochester, Minnesota.[11]

O'Banion and his followers George "Bugs" Moran, Earl "Hymie" Weiss, and Vincent "Schemer" Drucci were also known to the police as accomplished burglars, safecrackers, and truck hijackers. ("Hi, Jack," you call to the trucker. When he stops, you pull a gun and climb in behind the wheel.) Weiss reportedly invented one of gangland's favorite murder methods, coining the phrase "taking him for a ride"—a one-way ride. With the advent of Prohibition, O'Banion and his gang quickly moved to control most of the illegal liquor distribution in the Near North Side except for the Little Sicily area, which remained outside of his control. His glory years in crime extended from 1920 to 1924, or from the time he was twenty-eight until his death at the age of thirty-two.[12]

O'Banion's borough encompassed the Forty-second and Forty-third Wards. His ability to deliver the Irish vote made him an important political figure in ward politics. When asked who would carry the Forty-second and Forty-third Wards at election time, the response often heard was "O'Banion in his pistol pockets." It is said that O'Banion would go into saloons on Election Day and shoot the doorknobs off the entrances to the toilets in order to remind people to vote Republican. In one 1924 election he reportedly lined up two hundred gangsters to work the Republican ticket in the Forty-second Ward. O'Banion was so important to ward politics that he once was honored with a diamond-studded platinum watch at a testimonial dinner given by the theater janitors union at the Webster Hotel, attended by Albert Sprague, the Chicago Commissioner of Public Works, and Cook County Clerk Robert Schweitzer. O'Banion began his political career under the patronage of ward boss James Aloysius Quinn, an ally of gambling boss Mont Tennes. Quinn was better known to his constituents as "Hot Stove" Jimmy because of his use of the aphorism "he would steal a hot stove."[13]

The "Terrible Gennas" held a government license for processing industrial alcohol at their plant located at 1022 West Taylor, where they produced illegal whiskey as well. They also built a fifty-gallon distillery in the rear of the Near West Side Marsala Club, whose members were recently arrived Sicilian immigrants from the Gennas' home village. The Genna brothers also organized large numbers of Italian immigrants from their Near West Side Taylor Street neighborhood in the home production of alcohol. Commenting on the Gennas, Jane Addams, a noted social reformer of the period, wrote, "They put stills in the home of every Sicilian whom they were able to dominate." Many Italian and Sicilian immigrants traditionally made their own wine. With the advent of Prohibition, Italians continued making their wine at home. What they could do with grapes and sugar in making wine they could also do with corn and sugar in producing grain alcohol. So extensive was bootlegging in Chicago's Near West Side that the intersection of Roosevelt and Halsted Streets was referred to as Bootleggers' Square.[14]

In June 1925 Chicago police conducted fifty raids on Genna stills, arresting 320 people and seizing more than ten thousand barrels of illegal alcohol and scores of shotguns and revolvers. The raid was prompted by the killing of police officers Raymond Walsh and Harold Olson, who had been shot in a gunfight with Mike Genna and Genna gangsters Albert Anselmi and John Scalise. Until the killing of their officers, Chicago police were happy to leave the Gennas alone. Three hundred policemen were said to receive payoffs each month from the Gennas' Taylor Street plant. The Chicago Police Department also responded to the death of its officers by transferring one-third of the men assigned to the Maxwell Street district, citing collusion with local bootleggers. All total, three lieutenants, four sergeants, and twenty-nine patrolmen were transferred to duty in other stations.[15]

The Genna brothers were also active in the Unione Siciliana. In fact, Angelo Genna had ascended to the presidency of the Unione in 1924 upon the death of its founder, Mike Merlo.

The Unione Siciliana began in 1895 as a lawful fraternal society designed to advance the interests of Sicilian immigrants. The Unione provided life insurance and was active in Italian American civic affairs. The president of the Unione controlled many Italian votes in Chicago and was therefore a powerful man. Most Chicago Sicilians resided in two neighborhoods: the Sicilian colony centered on Sedgwick Street in the Near North Side, and the Near West Side Taylor Street area. In addition to being a benevolent association, the Unione also acted as an intermediary in the settlement of personal feuds that the members of Chicago's Sicilian community were reluctant to bring to the attention of the police.[16]

It was only a matter of time before O'Banion clashed with the Genna forces. Stepped-up pressure by the Dever administration had forced liquor sales to dwindle, resulting in greater competition among Chicago's bootleggers. For example, the Genna brothers had been selling liquor in O'Banion territory, and there were reports that O'Banion had been hijacking the Gennas' trucks. O'Banion also is said to have made many enemies among the Italians, often calling them "grease balls" and "spic pimps," the latter being a reference to the Torrio-Capone involvement in prostitution. O'Banion had also quarreled with the Gloriana Gang, the Italian and Sicilian hoodlums in his own Near North Side community, during the 1924 municipal elections. The Glorianas supported Forty-second Ward Democratic candidates who were running against the Republicans supported by O'Banion and the Irish.[17]

O'Banion appealed to Torrio to intercede in his quarrel with the Gennas but was not satisfied with the response. As a result, he offered to sell Torrio his share in Sieben's Brewery at 1464 North Larrabee, which he knew was soon to be raided. On the morning of May 19, 1924, Chicago police raided the brewery, arresting thirty-one bootleggers, including Torrio, and recovered 128,500 gallons of illegal beer. O'Banion had set up Torrio! This was inexcusable. At noon on November 10, 1924, O'Banion was gunned down in his floral shop (whose trucks specialized in delivering alcohol along with flowers) at 738 North State Street. The suspects were none other than the Genna brothers, who were working at the direction of Torrio and Capone. Despite the fact that O'Banion had been an altar boy at Holy Name Cathedral, he was denied funeral services by the Catholic Church. This was standard practice for the Church, which steadfastly refused to allow gangsters to be buried in consecrated ground. Even so, O'Banion's funeral nearly equaled that of Big Jim Colosimo. Some forty thousand people viewed his body. His funeral procession, which was a mile long, included twenty-six truckloads of flowers.[18]

On January 24, 1925, Torrio himself was shot, presumably by members of the rival O'Banion gang, but he survived. A short time later he entered the Lake County jail to serve out his nine-month sentence stemming from the Sieben's Brewery raid. (The Lake County jail was used as a federal lockup at the time.) Upon his release, Torrio retired to New York, where he once again became involved in bootlegging and worked as a bail bondsman. When Torrio left Chicago, he transferred control of the syndicate to Al Capone. Capone was now the lord of the Levee and much of Chicago's underworld. With the disintegration of the Torrio coalition, however, Capone faced a war with many of Chicago's criminal gangs. The intense competition that resulted led to Chicago's infamous "beer wars" during the late 1920s. The gangs mainly aligned themselves along ethnic ties. The Irish, Polish, and Jewish gangsters, such as the West Side O'Donnells and the Saltis-McErlane Gang, joined behind O'Banion's successor, Hymie Weiss. The Sicilians, notably the Gennas and most other Italians, stuck with Capone. So did Terry Druggan and Frankie Lake, whose Valley Gang was headquartered in the Near West Side Maxwell Street area adjacent to the Taylor Street Italian stronghold.[19]

Among the first casualties of the war was Angelo Genna. He died at the hands of Weiss, Moran, and Drucci on May 26, 1925, in retaliation for the killing of O'Banion. One month later the police killed Mike Genna after he ambushed Moran and Drucci at the corner of Sangamon and Congress Streets. On July 8 Anthony Genna was also killed, some suspecting "Schemer" Drucci. The surviving Gennas fled Chicago. Upon the death of Angelo Genna, Sam "Samoots" Amatuna ascended to the presidency of the Unione Siciliana, but he too was soon murdered, while sitting in his favorite barbershop.[20]

Under the guidance of Angelo Genna, the Unione Siciliana had placed its mantle of authority over the home production of alcohol in the city's Near West and Near North Side Italian communities. These activities placed the Unione in direct competition with Capone's gang. As such, Capone engineered the election of one of his own followers, Antonio Lombardo, to the presidency of the Unione Siciliana. In an effort to overcome the negative publicity surrounding the Unione's participation in bootlegging, Lombardo changed the name of the organization to the Italian-American National Union and opened its membership to all Italians. Lombardo also asked Giovanni Schiavo of New York University to write about the experience of Chicago's Italian community. Schiavo's efforts resulted in the publication of the 1928 book *The Italians in Chicago*.[21]

After the fall of the Gennas, their bootlegging activities were taken over by the Aiello brothers. The Aiellos, a large and extensive family of nine brothers and numerous cousins, were the Near North Side's equivalent of the Terrible Gennas. Joey Aiello was the kingpin of the group. They owned a bakery at 431 West Division in the heart of Little Sicily, which gave them access to sugar, an important ingredient in making booze. The Aiellos, like the Gennas, were also major forces in the Unione Siciliana. Joey Aiello was unhappy about the ascension of Capone's man Lombardo to the throne of the Unione, believing it should be his instead because of his long years of service to the organization. Consequently, Aiello formed alliances with other North Side gangs, such as the O'Banion forces (now led by Bugs Moran), Billy Skidmore, and Jack Zuta, for the purpose of eliminating Lombardo and Capone.[22]

The Aiello and Moran forces made a number of attempts on the lives of Lombardo and Capone. The Aiellos promised fifty thousand dollars to anyone who would kill "The Big Fellow," as Capone was often referred to. (Federal wiretaps learned that Capone was also called "Snorkey" by his men.) On September 20, 1926, Moran, Weiss, and Drucci attacked Capone's headquarters at the Hawthorne Inn in Cicero. Gunmen in seven cars, positioned less than ten feet apart, fired more than one thousand bullets into the Hawthorne restaurant where Capone was eating. Strangely enough, no one was killed. Joey Aiello then hired Angelo La Mantio to shoot Capone and Lombardo as they were leaving Hinky Dink Kenna's cigar store at 311 South Clark, but the assassination attempt was interrupted by the police. In retaliation, the Aiello Bakery was attacked on May 29, 1927, when two hundred machine-gun bullets were fired from a curtained automobile into the store. Two men were struck by the gunfire, Tony Aiello and Charles Delio, a neighborhood resident.[23]

After three years in office, Antonio Lombardo was finally killed at 4:30 P.M. on the afternoon of September 6, 1928, at the corner of Dearborn and Madison Streets in the heart of downtown Chicago. He was replaced by another Capone appointee, Pasquilino Lolardo, who was murdered four months later. Lolardo was replaced by Joey Aiello, who finally attained the presidency of the Unione. The "War of Sicilian Succession," as the struggle for the control of the Unione Siciliana became known, had claimed two more lives. The objective of the war was gaining control of the home alky-cooking system originated by the Genna brothers, which had become a $10-million-a-year enterprise.[24]

Within a year a dozen more men were killed in Chicago's Near North Side Sicilian neighborhood, and seventy-five-thousand-dollars' worth of property had been demolished by bombs as the Aiello and Capone forces battled for control of the Unione. The situation was so desperate that people began to abandon the neighborhood until the violence ceased. Some sought temporary refuge in Wisconsin and Michigan. Others just moved away. Father Louis Giambastiani of the church of San Filippo Benizi, troubled by the killings, posted a sign on the front door of the local parish church that read: "Brothers! For the honor you owe to God, for the respect of your American Country and humanity; pray that this ferocious manslaughter, which disgraces the Italian name before the civilized world may come to an end."[25]

The war did come to an end on February 14, 1929, in the S.M.C. Cartage garage at 2122 North Clark Street when the remaining members of the Moran-Aiello alliance were murdered by forces loyal to Capone. Seven men were machine-gunned to death in what has become known as the Saint Valentine's Day Massacre. Although no one has ever been convicted of the murders, Vincenzo de Mora, alias "Machine Gun" Jack McGurn, and Joseph Lolordo, brother of Pasquilino Lolordo, whose murder Moran had engineered, were arrested. Also arrested were Capone gunmen Albert Anselmi and John Scalise. The car used in the murders was found in a garage at 1723 North Wood Street, around the corner from the Circus Café, headquarters of the Circus Café Gang, of which McGurn was a member. Capone is believed to have ordered the killings.[26]

By 1930 Al Capone, then only thirty-one years of age, had become the supreme overlord of vice in Chicago. The *Chicago Daily News* estimated that he controlled six thousand speakeasies and two thousand handbooks. The combined revenue from these activities plus prostitution and racketeering was estimated to be $6,260,000 a week. During the four-year "beer wars" (1922–1926), 315 gangsters had murdered one another, and Chicago police had killed another 160 gangland members in running gun battles. Colonel Robert Isham Randolph, president of the Chicago Chamber of Commerce, reported that the crime syndicate operated with impudence as Capone's men expanded into payroll robberies, jewelry holdups, labor unions, and the protection racket—all because of the money paid to law enforcement to protect the beer racket.[27]

The Saint Valentine's Day Massacre shocked the world. Something had to be done. Working with the *Chicago Daily Tribune*, municipal court judge

John Lyle developed a plan to charge Capone and his men with vagrancy—being an idle and dissolute person who neglected all lawful business and did not lawfully provide for themselves and for the support of their families. The plan was to arrest gangsters on vagrancy warrants and then ask them questions—such as "What is your source of income?"—to disprove the vagrancy allegation. If the alleged vagrant failed to answer, he would be fined two hundred dollars. If he paid the fine, he would have to explain where the money had come from. If he did not pay the fine, he would be sentenced to the Chicago House of Corrections to work out the fine. Judge Lyle obtained a list of the city's most notorious gangsters from the Chicago Crime Commission. The list contained twenty-eight names. Heading the list was Al Capone, "Public Enemy No. 1." The title caught the public's attention as books, radio shows, and moving pictures adopted the phrase, bringing additional attention to the gangster problem. Other names on the public enemies list included Frank Diamond, Frank McErlane, Frank Rio, Edward "Spike" O'Donnell, George "Red" Barker, and William "Three-Fingered Jack" White. The enforcement of the vagrancy statute also led to the development of a new word. When arrested by federal agents on charges of tax evasion, gangster Harry Guzik replied in relief that he thought the police were "vaging" him—that is, arresting him for vagrancy.[28]

The Saint Valentine's Day Massacre also shocked the underworld. Gang warfare and murder in Chicago were bringing national attention to the bootlegging problem throughout the country. Capone told Major L. B. Schoefield, the director of public safety in Philadelphia, that there had been an attempt to establish order in the underworld at a peace conference in Atlantic City attended by Capone's enemies Joe Aiello and Bugs Moran. Also attending was Johnny Torrio, now of Sheepshead Bay, New York. Under the terms of the pact, Torrio was to return to Chicago to take over the rackets, and Capone was to step down. Whether it was Capone's refusal to step down or a rising sentiment against Capone in Chicago, the peace pact failed. (Capone's fellow Chicago gangsters had accused him of spending too much time and money at his newly acquired home in Florida.) Fearing a threat on his life, Capone arranged to have himself arrested in Philadelphia and sentenced to one year in jail for carrying a firearm, believing he would be safer in prison than on the streets of Chicago.[29]

The Saint Valentine's Day Massacre not only marked the end of the O'Banion Gang but also established the supremacy of the Capone syndicate as the leading force in Chicago's underworld. One year later, on October 23, 1930, Joey Aiello was murdered. Cook County Coroner Herman Bundesen reported that Aiello had received wounds from fifty-seven shotgun slugs and machine gun bullets. Capone had regained control of the Unione Siciliana, appointing Agostino LoVerdo as president. The final conquest of the Unione, however, became a short-lived victory. The eventual end of Prohibition three years later forever marked the end of the importance of the Unione Siciliana to organized crime in Chicago.[30]

Crime ran wide open in Chicago. Police and judicial corruption were so widespread that the Better Government Association petitioned the United States Congress to intervene in the internal affairs of the city, arguing that its leaders were in league with gangsters and that the city was overrun with protected vice. The alliance between corrupt government and organized crime was made clear with Big Bill Thompson's return to city government. Promising that "he was as wet as the Atlantic Ocean," Thompson was returned to the mayor's office in 1927 with strong support from Chicago's criminal element. A number of Capone gangsters actually worked in Thompson's campaign headquarters. The Chicago Crime Commission reported that Capone donated $260,000 to Thompson's reelection fund. The money was used to purchase the right to run houses of prostitution, gambling dens, slot machines, and control the sale of outlawed beer and alcohol in all sections of Chicago south of Madison Street. The money was reportedly paid out to Thompson's workers from a bathtub in the Sherman Hotel that was filled with packages of five-dollar bills.[31]

With Thompson back in office, Capone returned to the Levee, setting up headquarters in the Metropole Hotel at 2300 South Michigan Avenue and in 1928 one block north at the Lexington Hotel. Speakeasies and vice again flourished in the First Ward, but they were not under the control of aldermen Bathhouse Coughlin and Hinky Dink Kenna. Vice remained strictly in the hands of the Capone organization. In fact, the aldermen were called into Capone's office and told that their future depended on their usefulness to the Syndicate. To this Coughlin was said to reply, "We're lucky to get as good a break as we did."[32]

Capone's gangsters roamed the corridors of Chicago's city hall seeking favors from friendly and not-so-friendly aldermen alike. Capone also set up offices for his gambling empire at Clark and Madison Streets, one block from the mayor's office. In charge of gambling operations were Jake Guzik and Jimmy Mondi. Guzik and Mondi summoned the owners of all Chicago gambling services to their office and instructed them that they would now have to pay 40 percent of their profits to the Capone syndicate in order to ensure protection from the police. The alliance between the Thompson administration and the Syndicate was an important milestone in the development of organized crime in Chicago. The Capone syndicate was now the official mediator between the underworld and Chicago's political structure. Independent gamblers could no longer seek out their own deals with local politicians. The alliance between gangsters and politicians was so powerful that a 1930 police raid found Capone henchmen Paul "The Waiter" Ricca, Ralph Pierce, Murray "The Camel" Humphreys, and Frank Rio meeting with Illinois state representatives Albert Prigano and Roland Libonati, and Saul Tannenbaum of the city attorney's office. Several firearms were also uncovered.[33]

Realizing that there was a total breakdown in municipal government, Chicago Crime Commission director Frank Loesch traveled with a group of prominent businessmen to Washington, D.C., in 1929 to meet with President Herbert Hoover to discuss crime conditions in Chicago. As a result of this meeting, the president ordered a full-scale attack on the Capone syndicate by the Prohibition Bureau and the Internal Revenue Service (IRS). Under the supervision of twenty-eight-year-old Elliot Ness, Prohibition agents battered down the doors of nineteen Capone distilleries and six breweries and seized or destroyed more than a million dollars' worth of whiskey, beer, delivery trucks, and other equipment. While the "Untouchables," as Ness's men became known, were busy dismantling Capone's bootlegging empire, agents of the IRS were also busy assembling tax cases against Capone and many of his leading hoodlums.[34]

Although it is commonly believed that it was tax evasion that finally sent Capone to prison, he was also charged with conspiracy to violate the Prohibition laws based upon the work of Ness and his men. The IRS charged that he had not paid taxes on the $1,038,654.84 he had earned between 1924 and 1929; Capone owed the federal government $215,080 in back taxes. The Prohibition conspiracy alleged that Capone's beer business had brought in gross receipts of $200 million in a ten-year period. The conspiracy involved sixty-eight of Capone's underlings and included five thousand overt acts of violating Prohibition laws. For example, the first overt act charged against Capone occurred in 1922 when as one of Torrio's runners he bought a used truck to convey illegal beer. Ness and his men were so successful in their efforts against Capone that Ness's life was threatened numerous times, and the Capone gang hired a private investigator to "get something on him."[35]

As the crime situation in Chicago worsened, a group of prominent businessmen joined in the effort against the Capone syndicate. Taking the law into their own hands, they established the Citizen's Committee for the Prevention and Punishment of Crime. The Secret Six, as they came to be known, were so named by the press because their chairman, Colonel Robert Isham Randolph, refused to name his five colleagues lest he endanger their lives. Working in cooperation with the Chicago Crime Commission and the Internal Revenue Service, the Secret Six donated one million dollars to fight organized crime. This money was used to hire private investigators who developed informants, tapped telephones, paid witnesses, and generally collected information on mob activity that was passed on to federal authorities. It was the Secret Six who spent ten thousand dollars sending star witness Fred Ries to South America until he was needed to testify against Capone in federal court on charges of income tax evasion.[36]

Recognizing that the illegal sale of alcohol had created a national crime problem, President Hoover established the National Commission on Law Observance and Enforcement. Headed by Attorney General George Wickersham, the commission was appointed to address the issue of Prohibition and the resulting increase in crime. The commission issued fourteen volumes dealing with crime in America, ranging from improvements in law enforcement to the causes of crime. Addressing Chicago, they found that crime was organized "to an amazing extent" and consisted of a series of lawless operations that were syndicated by rival gangsters and public officials. The commission also addressed Prohibition, recommending the retention of the Eighteenth Amendment and increased law enforcement efforts against the liquor trade. In spite of the commission's findings, President Hoover recommended the repeal of Prohibition, calling it a noble but failed experiment.[37]

When Prohibition ended in 1933, Al Capone was in jail for tax and bootlegging violations. The organization that he had helped to create now turned its attention to the control of gambling, prostitution, and other illegal activities. Because bootlegging had provided immense resources in terms of money and organization, an unprecedented consolidation and centralization of underworld power had occurred. Some members of the Capone syndicate entered into the legitimate liquor business after the end of Prohibition. Those who remained in organized crime continued in traditional vice activities, but now in the same highly organized fashion in which liquor was distributed. For example, the term *district man* was used for many years in Chicago to describe a person who was in charge of vice and payoffs in a particular area of the city.[38]

During the years that followed Prohibition, it became increasingly clear that the Capone syndicate dominated organized crime in Chicago. The Capone organization had emerged as the most vicious fighters in the war to control the distribution of illegal alcohol in Chicago. There is no evidence that Capone's men were members of the Sicilian Mafia, as is commonly believed. Capone himself was not Sicilian, but Neapolitan. In fact, most members of the Capone syndicate were not even Italian. A list of members of the Capone organization published in 1936 by the *Chicago Daily Tri-*

bune reported that the organization had 181 members during its heyday in the years between 1925 and 1931.[39] Of those 181 members, only 75 (41 percent) had Italian surnames. The *Tribune* organized the Capone syndicate into four departments: the Board of Directors, the Income Department, the Protection Department, and the Gunmen. Only the Protection Department was dominated by Italian members. The involvement of Capone, Torrio, Frank Nitti, the Gennas, and the Aiellos had fixed the image of the Mafia forever in the minds of Chicagoans, but as previous chapters have shown, organized crime was already firmly in place in Chicago when the first Sicilian immigrant set foot upon the shores of Lake Michigan.

There was, however, another ethnic group that played an important, but often unrecognized, part in the success of the crime syndicate: Chicago's Jewish community. Although Jews played an important part in the development of organized crime in New York City and were fundamental to the ethnic succession argument, there was no recognizable period of Jewish dominance in Chicago. Control of organized crime was transferred directly from the Irish to the Italians without an intervening period of Jewish control. Chicago, however, did have a number of Jewish gangsters.

The first Jews to arrive in Chicago lived along Lake Street behind or above stores in the central business district. By 1870 the center of the Jewish population was between Van Buren and Polk Streets from Clark Street to the Chicago River. When the Great Chicago Fire destroyed the downtown Jewish community in 1871, many moved to the area of Fourteenth and Halsted Streets, where a Jewish synagogue had recently been established. By 1889 ten thousand Jews lived in Chicago. The first Jews to settle in the West Side were Bohemian Jews who had moved into the area already populated by Bohemian immigrants who had settled in the Pilsen area. Construction of the elevated railroad embankment along Fifteenth Street split the community and separated the Jews from the rest of the Bohemian population.[40]

The center of the West Side Jewish community was the Maxwell Street Market. Maxwell Street, or "Jew Town" as it came to be known, was a hotbed of local politics and graft. There one could find "shyster" lawyers, political fixers, ward healers, and rival politicians who fought for control of the market. Vendors were forced to pay regular tribute to the "market master," who controlled selling space on the street. Those who did not make the necessary political contribution were banned from peddling in the area. Maxwell Street was also home to cigar stores and curtained gambling houses that were the haunts of the district's loafers and gangsters and of "sacramental" wine dealers during Prohibition. A 1911 newspaper exposé charged that Twentieth Ward alderman Emanuel "Manny" Abrahams controlled vice activity among the Orthodox Jews in the district.[41]

Like other immigrant areas, Maxwell Street produced its own group of young toughs, including Hershel Miller and Samuel "Nails" Morton. Miller and Morton were charged in the 1920 murders of two police officers resulting from a fight in the Beaux Arts black-and-tan club. Both, however, were acquitted, claiming self-defense. Morton, an accomplished hijacker, was also affiliated with the O'Banion gang. Morton was somewhat of a hero in the Jewish community, having protected local residents from the Jew-baiting Poling Gang, who had threatened their neighborhood. He also had received the Croix de Guerre from the French government during World War I while serving in the United States Army. Morton died when he was thrown from his horse during a riding accident in Chicago's Lincoln Park. He was with three of his friends, including Dion O'Banion, at the time of his death. After Morton's funeral, O'Banion gangster "Two-Gun" Louie Alterie stole the guilty horse from the Lincoln Riding Academy and shot it to death, marking it the only Chicago gangland hit to be directed at a horse.[42]

Like other ethnic groups, second-generation Chicago Jews left the central city area for more desirable neighborhoods. By 1930 the West Side Jewish community had moved to Chicago's Lawndale area. Centered at Kedzie and Twelfth Street, the neighborhood became one of the largest concentrations of Orthodox Jews in the world. Of the sixty synagogues in the area, all but one was Orthodox. At its height, 110,000 Jewish people lived in the neighborhood. The Jews of Lawndale were strongly Democratic and helped to elect Henry Horner, Illinois' first Jewish governor. Lawndale's voting power also made Twenty-fourth Ward alderman Jacob Arvey a powerhouse in Chicago politics. Arvey was no stranger to the workings of the machine in Chicago. The Twenty-fourth Ward had its share of gambling. Junk dealer Moe Rosenberg and Ben "Zookie the Bookie" Zuckerman ran a number of gambling houses in the ward and were lieutenants in Arvey's ward organization.[43]

The most important Jewish gangster in Chicago history was Jake "Greasy Thumb" Guzik. (The name Greasy Thumb stemmed from the days when, as a waiter, his clumsy thumb constantly slipped into the bowls of soup he was carrying.) Guzik was, without question, one of the most important members of the Capone syndicate. He had earned Capone's friendship after tipping him off to an assassination attempt. Later, Guzik was the hapless victim of a drunken slapping from a freelance beer runner, burglar, and three-time killer named Joe Howard. Unable to defend himself, Guzik reported the offense to Capone. Capone caught up with Howard in a South Wabash Avenue saloon, where, after a brief exchange of words, Capone shot Howard six times with his revolver. Initially a small-time Chicago pimp, Guzik became the trusted treasurer of the Capone mob.[44]

When Capone went to prison, Frank "The Enforcer" Nitti took control of the Syndicate. With Nitti at its head, the Capone syndicate branched out into new forms of crime, such as "call operations," "B-girls," and business and labor racketeering. Nitti had been born in Italy and was brought to New York by his parents when he was three years old. After serving as a member of the Five Points Gang, he came to Chicago and worked for Capone. His understanding of business and accounting procedures set him apart from other gangsters. He is credited with directing the Capone syndicate's successful takeover of gambling in Chicago after the fall of Prohibition and the organization's movement into racketeering. Although Nitti was the recognized head of the Syndicate, Jake Guzik, Murray Humphreys, and Edward Vogel (the slot machine king) were also recognized as the "bosses" of the organization.[45]

It was racketeering that provided the Capone syndicate with its major source of revenue following the demise of Prohibition. Capone gangster Murray Humphreys told the secretary-treasurer of the milk wagon driver's union in 1933, "Prohibition is going out and soon there won't be an 18th Amendment. We've got a big organization and must take care of our boys." Racketeering also provided an alternate source of revenue during the economic depression that followed the crash of the stock market in 1929. Money was tight and people no longer could afford to spend what little they had on gambling and prostitution. The city of Chicago itself was broke. Its debts totaled $280 million with 40,123 public employees going unpaid.[46]

Racketeering can be defined as a scheme for making a dishonest livelihood through illegal or criminal practices that often involve the extortion of money by threat or violence. The word *racket* can be traced to the gangs of New York.[47] During the early part of the nineteenth century, it was a common practice for political and social clubs to sponsor benefit dinners on their own behalf. These were such loud affairs that they were known as "rackets" because of all the noise that was made. Grasping the opportunity for easy money, gang members would announce a benefit dinner and, with threats of violence and property damage, encourage local businessmen to buy tickets.

The racketeer might be the boss of a supposedly legitimate business association, or he might be a union leader. As early as the late nineteenth century, small shopkeepers and peddlers paid money to neighborhood gangs to protect them from violence and property damage perpetrated by the gang itself. Later, racketeers organized small businessmen into business and trade associations in order to regulate competition and guard against price undercutting in a particular market or area. Any merchant who didn't join the association and pay his dues was bombed, assaulted, or otherwise intimidated. For example, members paid the Midwest Garage Owners Association one dollar a month for every car that they handled. Those who were not members of the association often became the target of attacks as tires were slashed on cars parked at their garages.[48]

In 1927 the Employers Association of Greater Chicago issued a list of twenty-three businesses that were manipulated by racketeers. These included laundries and dry cleaners, parking garages, garbage collectors, and fish and poultry stores. Many Chicago unions were also under the control of local racketeers. For example, Mike Carrozzo's power had grown from control of Colosimo's street sweepers to the sole boss of more than twenty-five locals of the International Hod Carriers, Building, and Common Laborers Union representing more than twenty thousand workers, all under the control of the Syndicate. In 1928 the Office of the Cook County State's Attorney reported that ninety-one Chicago unions and trade associations were dominated by organized crime. These included the Municipal Clerks' Union, the Union of Commission Wagon Drivers, the Newspaper Wagon Drivers' Union, and the Filling Station Owners' Union.[49]

Another area of commerce dominated by the Syndicate involved coin-operated devices such as pinball machines and jukeboxes. In 1946 the *Chicago Sun* estimated that there were more than five thousand pinball machines being operated illegally in the city of Chicago and that 75 percent of the coin music industry was dominated by the Capone mob. In 1940 members of the Illinois Phonographic Owners Association, a group of jukebox distributors, complained to the Chicago Crime Commission that the hoodlum element was muscling in on their business. Four Syndicate jukebox distributors were promising owners that if they did business with the Syndicate, no one would "bother" their taverns. The four firms included those owned by "Sugar" Joe Peskin, Edward Vogel, "Tough" Tony Capezio, and a black group headed by policy baron Dan Gaines.[50]

Gangsters did not always "infiltrate" trade associations and unions as is popularly believed; some were invited in. When dry cleaner Morris Becker began having trouble with rivals and employees seeking to unionize, he voluntarily formed a partnership with Capone stating, "I don't need the police to help anymore. I have the best protection in the world now." The end result was a campaign of terror by Capone gangsters seeking to force all cleaners and dyers in Chicago to join the Cleaners and Dyers Institute, a trade association that sought to regulate prices and competition. Those who did not join were subjected to a wave of acid spraying, bombing, and slugging. Probably the largest and most extortionate racket ever imposed on Chicago commerce was the Truck and Transportation Exchange (TNT). TNT levied tribute on employees and unions alike, setting the amount that could be charged for truck deliveries. Both owners and drivers paid dues to set the delivery rates.[51]

The Capone syndicate's racketeering interests even reached as far as Hollywood, California. George Browne and Willie Bioff, of the International Alliance of Theatrical Stage Employees, were convicted in 1941 of extorting $550,000 from Warner Brothers, Paramount, Twentieth Century-Fox, and Loew's studios in exchange for not calling strikes and otherwise keeping labor peace within the film industry. The two men wielded absolute power over 125,000 moving picture operators, studio workers, and stagehands. Prosecutors described Browne and Bioff as members of the Al Capone gang. During the early days of Prohibition, Browne was a stagehand and eventually the business agent of the union's Chicago local. It is believed that Browne met Frank Nitti in 1931, while Browne was a Chicago saloon keeper, and eventually gained Nitti's support in his ascension to president of the international union a few years later.[52]

The Capone syndicate's move to take over gambling focused on control of the Continental Press, a racetrack wire service. Owned by James Ragen, Continental provided race results to much of the country; the Chicago outlet was Midwest News. Control of the wire service meant control of the bookmakers who relied on the wire service for horse race results. The Syndicate informed Ragen that they wanted to buy controlling interest in the service because they controlled more than one-half of the six hundred handbooks in Chicago. When Ragen refused, Syndicate gangsters Murray Humphreys and Jake Guzik demanded 40 percent of Midwest's earnings. Ragen's steadfast refusal resulted in his poisoning death in 1946. Control of Chicago's handbooks was also politically important. The Chicago Crime Commission estimated that by 1949, handbook operators in Chicago could deliver a minimum of two hundred thousand votes and unlimited financial support toward the election of favored candidates.[53]

Backlash against Thompson's permissive view of vice had helped to elect Anton Cermak to the mayor's office in 1931. After his mayoral defeat, Thompson retired to obscurity except for a feeble attempt to reenter politics at the state level in 1936. When he died in 1944, his bank safety deposit boxes were found to contain nearly $1.5 million in cash and another $20,000 in negotiable securities and liberty bonds.[54] Citizens believed that the defeat of Thompson and the election of Cermak marked the beginning of Chicago's political redemption. True, an attempt was made to change the relationship between the gangsters and the politicians, but organized crime continued. Although the Capone syndicate was tied to the Republican Party under Mayor Thompson, it is important to remember that corruption in Chicago has long been associated with the Democratic Party. Corrupt Democratic ward healers such as John Powers, Hot Stove Jimmy Quinn, Bathhouse Coughlin, and Hinky Dink Kenna had been around for years.

The Democratic takeover of political power and underworld revenue in the city of Chicago following the defeat of Thompson can be traced to the activities of Roger Sullivan, George Brennan, and John O'Malley. "Sullivan's Democrats," as they were called, consisted of saloon keepers, gamblers, brothel keepers, and other criminals who sought protection from political reformers. The emerging Democratic organization knew that to remain in power they would have to work in secret and avoid controversy. Graft would continue, but undercover, and there would be a pretense of good government. They had all learned from the mistakes of Thompson, who had appropriated everything in sight and, though popular, lost the sentiment of the public.[55]

Born in Bohemia, Cermak immigrated to the United States as a child. At age sixteen he came to Chicago, worked in various jobs, and became involved in politics in the Pilsen district, which was populated chiefly by Czechs and other Eastern Europeans. By the age of thirty, he was elected to the Illinois legislature and later served four terms on the Chicago City Council. In 1922 he was elected president of the Cook County Board of Commissioners.[56]

Cermak was also the leader of the United Societies, an organization of saloon keepers, brewers, and distillers who opposed the regulation of taverns and saloons by the city of Chicago.[57] The group was a formidable political force that exploited the liberal liquor philosophy of Chicago's foreign-born element. The members of the United Societies were steadfastly against Chicago's Sunday closing ordinance and had sponsored an ordinance allowing the sale of liquor in public dance halls frequented by teenagers. During the aldermanic campaign of 1915, the United Societies also endorsed many of the old "gray wolves" of the city council, such as Powers, Coughlin, and Kenna.

Cermak was not involved with the Capone mob. In fact, Cermak personally directed the organization of a vice and gambling unit within the police department in an effort to increase police efforts. Not only did Mayor Cermak heighten vice and gambling enforcement, but also it is alleged that members of his personal police detail had intentionally shot Frank Nitti in an effort to weaken the mob's hold on the Chicago underworld. On December 19, 1932, two Chicago police officers, Harry Lang and Harry Miller, visited Nitti in his downtown office. Nitti was shot by the detectives after they alleged that he had resisted arrest. This story was first accepted, but it later came out that Miller actually fired the first shot. He had allegedly been offered fifteen thousand dollars to kill Nitti.[58]

Although Cermak was anti-mob, he was not anti-vice. Recognizing the financial importance of gambling to the political structure in Chicago, he moved to rationalize the city's gambling enterprises under his own control. Cermak attempted to reorganize gambling under the supervision of his own political followers, including gamblers Ted Newberry and Martin Guilfoyle.

After Cermak was shot and killed in 1933 while speaking with president-elect Franklin Delano Roosevelt in Miami, it was alleged that his death was the result of his activities against the Capone syndicate.[59] Regardless of Cermak's anti-mob activities, his murderer, Giuseppe Zangara, maintained until the time of his death in the electric chair that Roosevelt was his intended target.

Alderman Frank Corr was chosen as Cermak's temporary successor. He was soon succeeded by former funeral director and sanitary district engineer Edward J. Kelly, who served as mayor of Chicago from 1933 to 1947. Kelly was no stranger to controversy. He had been indicted by a Cook County grand jury in May 1930 on charges of graft and corruption stemming from his position as chief engineer of the Metropolitan Sanitary District of Chicago; however, the case never went to trial. After Kelly became mayor, the federal government began looking into his tax returns. Strangely, between 1919 and 1929, Kelly reported an income of $724,368, although his government salary totaled only $151,000 for the same period of time. Even more perplexing was his close relationship with Chicago politician Frank Harmon, the man who held the mortgage on Al Capone's Miami Beach estate.[60]

Kelly was the choice of Cook County Democratic Party chairman Pat Nash. "P. A.," as Nash was called by his friends, made a fortune building sewers in Chicago, including $14 million in work from Kelly's sanitary district. Although Nash boasted that he would never be connected with "anything crooked," his right-hand man in his racially changing Twenty-eighth Ward bailiwick was Negro policy king Big Jim Martin.[61]

Kelly was an advocate of the "liberal-town policy," a more refined version of the "wide-open town" policy advocated by Big Bill Thompson. While official pronouncements informed the public that the Capone syndicate did not exist, the streets of Chicago were lined with handbooks, and policy gambling flourished in Chicago's South Side. The Kelly-Nash combination had turned to the Syndicate for revenue to fund their political organization. Tribute paid to the Democratic Party by the vice lords was a vital source of political funding. The supervision of gambling revenue was entrusted to each ward committeeman. A portion of the money collected went to Democratic offices downtown while the rest stayed in the ward to defray campaign expenses.[62]

The Kelly-Nash machine had a more ruthless and efficient alliance with the underworld than any previous Chicago administration, with a reported seventy-five hundred protected gambling establishments operating openly. Financial records obtained by the *Chicago Daily Tribune* in 1943 showed that the Syndicate was paying $300,000 a year to politicians, police, fixers, and public officials in Cook County and its country towns. The records also showed that Syndicate profits from slot machines and gambling houses in Cook County outside of Chicago were approximately $2.7 million a year. The *Tribune* obtained the records after gangster Jake Guzik left them in the oven of his apartment when he moved out of a fashionable North Side hotel.[63]

Although frequently overlooked, Kelly's contribution to organized crime in Chicago rivaled that of Big Bill Thompson. A 1946 investigation of the police department by the Chicago Crime Commission found that the police department was ruled by Kelly's city hall machine. Gambling was controlled in each police district by the "captain's men," plainclothes officers who worked directly for the district captain. Their job was to collect tribute from gamblers, bawdy houses, and cheating nightclubs and taverns. Other officers were not allowed to interfere. Any officer who was brash enough to set out against these activities was quickly disciplined and transferred to some undesirable assignment. Even if some cases did make it to court, they were often "fixed" by Kelly's precinct captains who were employed as court clerks. Judge Edward Casey, a Republican, even alleged that the city's newly established "rackets court" was created by the Kelly-Nash machine to ensure that no bookmaker could be convicted of a crime.[64]

After fourteen years as mayor, Edward Kelly was asked to step down in 1946. Kelly's administration had been tied to organized crime, which, along with the deterioration of the public schools and his efforts to bring blacks into the Democratic Party, had alienated many voters. The public had such a poor view of the Democratic Party that before the 1947 election the charge was made that the Democratic machine had brought pressure on police to suppress the facts in the Ragen murder case. The reasons advanced were that the city administration did not want the graft payments and gambling war discussed in the election campaign. When Kelly left office, *Tribune* reporter Clayton Kirkpatrick wrote: "It is agreed that Prohibition thoroughly corrupted the police department. The corrupting influence was prolonged by tolerance of horse race gambling during the 14 years that the late Edward J. Kelly was mayor."[65]

To take Kelly's place, Democratic leaders, including Jake Arvey, chose Martin Kennelly, whose integrity and respectability were unquestioned. Kennelly was a self-made man. He had built Allied Van Lines and chaired the American Red Cross in Chicago during World War II. Under Mayor Kennelly flagrant gambling disappeared. Bookmaking continued on a "sneak" basis, but visible commercial gambling establishments were closed down. Although Kennelly was generally viewed as an honest man, he was viewed as the "reform" mayor who did not "perform." Robert Hunter, the 1951 Republican candidate for mayor of Chicago, charged that Kennelly's municipal administration was the worst ever inflicted on a free people and that the Syndicate still had considerable influence in Chicago.[66]

Frank Nitti took his own life on March 19, 1943, after successfully leading the Capone syndicate for ten years. Reportedly in poor health and under indictment in New York for extorting substantial sums of money from Hollywood movie executives and their union employees, Nitti shot himself in the head near his home in North Riverside, a Chicago suburb. His suicide was the first instance of a big-time Chicago gangster taking his own life. Under Nitti's direction the Capone syndicate was revived after Prohibition and expanded to control gambling, prostitution, and other kindred rackets. He also took the organization into union racketeering and dominated fifteen unions totaling a membership of twenty-five thousand employees.[67]

Nitti was succeeded as the head of the Syndicate by Paul Ricca (Paul DeLucia), who remained in the position for one year until he entered the penitentiary on extortion charges. Ricca's position was subsequently filled by Anthony Accardo, an old Capone gunman who had risen under Nitti. Accardo had been suspected of killing *Chicago Tribune* reporter Jake Lingle and being the chauffeur in the Saint Valentine's Day Massacre. Accardo remained the boss until 1952 when Ricca returned from prison. Together they ruled the Syndicate until 1958, reaping profits from gambling and muscling in on labor unions.[68]

Elliot Ness (back, far right) and the Untouchables. Courtesy of John Binder, private collection.

Police raiding an illegal liquor still. Courtesy of John Binder, private collection.

Chicago mayor William Dever (right) and Al Jolson. Courtesy of John Binder, private collection.

Police destroying illegal liquor during Prohibition. Courtesy of John Binder, private collection.

James H. Wilkerson, the judge who tried Al Capone. Courtesy of John Binder, private collection.

Policy gambling slips. Courtesy of John Binder, private collection.

Policy King Teddy Roe fought Syndicate takeover of policy gambling. Courtesy of John Binder, private collection.

Chicago mayor Martin Kennelly. Courtesy of John Binder, private collection.

Police Captain Joseph Morris led the Scotland Yard organized crime squad. Courtesy of the Chicago Police Department.

Police raid of an illegal racetrack betting parlor. Courtesy of John Binder, private collection.

Cook County sheriff Richard Ogilvie (center) and Arthur Bilek (right), chief of sheriff's police. Courtesy of John Binder, private collection.

Police destroying illegal slot machines. Courtesy of Charles Molnar, private collection.

William H. Thompson campaign parade. Courtesy of John Binder, private collection.

Chicago alderman Benjamin Lewis. Courtesy of John Binder, private collection.

Chicago Police Intelligence Division commander William Duffy. Courtesy of the Chicago Police Department.

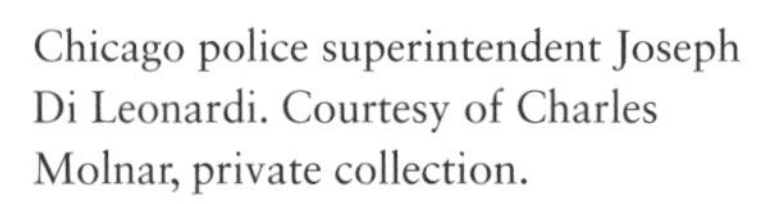

Chicago police superintendent Joseph Di Leonardi. Courtesy of Charles Molnar, private collection.

5

THE FORTY-TWO GANG

This chapter reviews the history of the Forty-two Gang and its significance for the continued development of organized crime in Chicago. The Forty-two Gang was a group of teenage boys and young men who committed an endless series of crimes in Chicago's Near West Side during the years between 1925 and 1934. Although they concentrated on auto theft, the Forty-two Gang engaged in nearly every other form of crime, from coin-box looting and smash-and-grab burglary to armed robbery and murder. During Prohibition the gang also furnished cars for their elders in the alcohol and bootleg rackets. They even robbed Mrs. William H. Thompson, the wife of the Chicago mayor. Promising members of the Forty-two Gang graduated into the various adult gangs in Chicago, including those led by Bugs Moran, Joseph "Red" Bolton, and Al Capone.[1]

The story of the Forty-two Gang is an important one. Other than Frederic Thrasher's 1927 classic, *The Gang: A Study of 1,313 Gangs in Chicago,* and Herbert Asbury's 1940 volume, *The Gem of the Prairie,* researchers have written little about the early history of gangs in Chicago. One of the reasons for this lack of information is the fact that gangs existed before the advent of social science. We have had gangs throughout the history of Chicago, but they did not become the focus of academic investigation until the 1920s and the establishment of the Chicago School of sociology.[2]

One of the fundamental problems in researching gangs is that the word *gang* has a number of different meanings. The outlaws of the Old West, the bank robbers of the Depression, and the bootleggers of Prohibition have all been referred to as gangs. Until the work of Frederic Thrasher, gangs were typically viewed as criminal groups: gangs in Chicago, such as the Quincy Street Gang, the Henry Street Gang, and the Gloriana Gang, engaged in robbery, burglary, and all manner of other crimes. However, it was Thrasher's work and its sociological focus that changed this definition, forever linking the word *gangs* to successive generations of troubled immigrant youth. Thrasher focused primarily on adolescent youth in order to understand both the conditions and the stages of gang development. He was also concerned with the effects of the city on the immigrant community and the process by which young gang members were socialized into adult crime.[3]

Thrasher argued that adult gangs were formed in two ways: some criminal gangs were the direct continuation of teenage groups, which had drifted into crime;[4] other adult gangs represented a coalescence of various elements in the gang community. Thrasher described these elements as criminal "residue," sorted and sifted from the gangs of adolescent youth. Studying the Forty-two Gang provides a unique opportunity to not only view the stages of development of a 1920s Chicago gang but to also examine the process by which young men were recruited into adult crime. Boys as young as thirteen joined the Forty-two Gang and remained in the gang into their early twenties, committing various criminal acts.

The data for this chapter comes from a number of different sources, the most important of which are the unpublished Landesco papers found in the manuscript archives at the University of Chicago, and newspaper accounts of the day. John Landesco is best known for his study of organized crime in Chicago. In 1924, as a graduate student at the University of Chicago, he received a grant from the university's Local Community Research Committee to study organized crime. The results of Landesco's study were published as part 3 of the Illinois Crime Survey in 1929 and appropriately titled "Organized Crime in Chicago."[5] Although the report was not widely circulated, it received considerable attention when it was reprinted as a stand-alone volume in 1968. In fact, Landesco's book is widely acclaimed to be the most important book ever written on the subject.

Landesco also developed an interest in boys' gangs, and after completing his research on organized crime, he began a study of the Near West Side Forty-two Gang. Although he intended to publish the results of his study in book form, the book was never completed. His investigation of the Forty-two Gang was interrupted by his appointment to the Illinois Parole Board. The preliminary, typewritten draft of the manuscript, titled "The Forty-two Gang: A Study of a Neighborhood Criminal Group," consists of twelve chapters of various lengths and is part of the John Landesco Collection at the University of Chicago Library.[6]

Although he never completed the book, Landesco published chapter 11, "The Failure of Institutions of Reform and Control," in an article titled "Crime and the Failure of Institutions in Chicago's Immigrant Areas" in the

Journal of Criminal Law and Criminology in 1932. Landesco also published chapter 3, "The Origin and Formation of the Gang," and chapter 4, "Its Criminal Activities," in an article titled "The Life History of a Member of the Forty-two Gang," which appeared in *Criminal Law and Criminology* the following year. Of the remaining chapters, two are worthy of note. Chapter 6, "Formation, Consolidation, and Dissolution," describes the formation of the gang, the recruitment of new members, and the final breakup of the gang. Chapter 7, "The Diffusion of a Criminal Culture," concerns the delinquent exploits of young boys in the area of the Forty-two Gang and explores the relationship between childhood delinquency and gang participation. All of this work was completed with the aid of Landesco's research assistant Corrado De Sylvester, an Italian and resident of Chicago's Near West Side.[7]

Landesco's work traces the history of the Forty-two Gang from a neighborhood play group to an adult criminal gang. He also traces the influence of the original members of the gang on future generations of delinquent youth. Most of the original members of the Forty-two Gang were killed or imprisoned by the time of Landesco's study, but the tradition of the gang lived on. The "legend and mythology" of the Forty-two Gang affected future cohorts of young delinquents and crime syndicate members.

The Forty-two Gang was largely made up of Italian youth from Chicago's Near West Side, most of whom resided in the Maxwell Street police district. Maxwell Street contained a number of different communities, the most prominent of which were the Jewish ghetto, the largely Irish Valley district, and the Italian Taylor Street neighborhood. Although early newspaper accounts attributed the Forty-two Gang to the Valley district, most were from the neighboring Taylor Street community.[8]

The genesis of the gang involved two groups. The first group included Rocco Marcantonio, Pete "Mibs" Gallichio, and Louis Pargoni. They had been together since 1924 when, as seventh graders at Rees Elementary School, they began "bumming" (skipping) class. The boys began their criminal careers by stealing silk shirts from backyard clotheslines and selling them to friends in their neighborhood. They remained in the shirt stealing business for the next two years and then began "robbing pennies" from peanut machines along Roosevelt Road. They soon graduated to stealing bicycles in the Chicago suburb of Oak Park, which they sold from the basement of a neighborhood delicatessen that they had turned into a clubhouse. They then moved on to stealing tires from automobiles.[9]

The boys eventually began to associate with an older group—Joseph "Babe Ruth" Calaro, "Sharkey" Icola, Sam Giancana (Gagiano), and a teen known only as Salvi—who introduced them to hijacking "butter and egg" trucks. Before long, twenty more boys were brought into their group. They were recruited by the "older fellows," who offered them apprenticeships in crime and protection from the police. Many of the new recruits were young boys, who formed small "mobs" of three and four followers around each of the older boys. The groups varied in size depending on the criminal activity being pursued. The boys did not yet have a central hangout but were mutually acquainted from school, neighborhood play, the local police station, jail, and reform school.[10]

In 1925 the boys established their first headquarters at Bonfiglio's poolroom at Elburn and Loomis Streets. Two months later they moved to Mary's Restaurant located at the corner of Taylor and Bishop. Soon thirty more boys joined the group. By Landesco's account this brought the number of members to fifty-eight. Although no one knows how many boys and young men joined the Forty-two Gang, the Chicago Police Department reported in 1932 that the gang had 500 members. I have identified 192 of them from newspaper accounts and from published and non-published sources. They included 160 Italians, 7 Jews, 2 Greeks, 5 Irishmen, and 1 Pole.[11]

There are a number of different explanations for the Forty-two Gang name. Landesco reports that the name is derived from the legend of "Ali Baba and the Forty Thieves." The gang originally had forty plus two members, hence the name Forty-two Gang. Patsy Pargoni reportedly came up with the name after the boys began to frequent Mary's Restaurant. Chicago Chief of Detectives William Shoemaker told the *Chicago Daily Tribune* that the name Forty-two Gang was a derivation of the original name of the gang, the Forty Thieves, which by corruption of language became the Forty "Teefs" and later the Forty-twos.[12]

The difference between the various accounts of how many members were in the gang can easily be attributed to the time at which each census was taken. When the name Forty-two Gang was decided, they most likely had 42 members. Although the police department's count is probably high, it is certainly possible that the gang eventually had 190 members. Landesco's descriptions of the gang suggests it was a fluid group, almost an umbrella organization for Near West Side delinquents. Young criminals came and went during the nine-year history of the gang. Some were killed, some were sent to reform school, some matriculated into adult crime, and some just matured out of crime.

Bonfiglio's poolroom and Mary's Restaurant were central to the growth of the gang. So were the older, more experienced criminals who frequented those two places. Once the gang had a hangout, a central location, it began to attract other delinquents from around the neighborhood. Delinquents were attracted by the cars, clothes, guns, and girlfriends of the older gang members. Groups of young boys whose crimes consisted of stealing roller skates and coaster wagons were now exposed to young men who taught them how to steal tires and automobiles. The grammar-school youth who stole toys from department stores for excitement were now taught how to steal resalable items for profit. In spite of the importance of Bonfiglio's poolroom and Mary's Restaurant for the growth of the gang, they soon became known to the police and subject to police surveillance and exploitation (shakedowns). As a result, the gang began to move about the neighborhood, alternately frequenting the corner of Taylor and Laflin, a local barbershop, a neighborhood florist, and a local car wash.[13]

The leaders of the gang were referred to as "smart heads," smart because they knew the way of the streets. Although the Forty-twos never had an official leader, the smart heads assumed a leadership role because of their experience and longevity in the gang, often taking advantage of the newer boys. For example, Joseph Calaro was known to have recruited younger boys to steal cars. Calaro would drive around with an aspiring gang member until he saw a car that he wanted to steal. He would then direct the new boy to steal the car. Calaro would tell the new recruit that anyone could steal a car, but the real skill was to follow along in another car and "cut off" the police or victim if the theft was discovered. In reality, the youthful offender was at risk of being shot by the police or the intended victim while Calaro was safely following behind. In fact, Calaro lost two of his protégés to police gunfire during an Oak Park robbery. Calaro was not alone in his exploitation of aspiring members. Other smart heads played the same game of exploitation, shamefully referring to the aspiring members as "suckers."[14]

Hopeful gang members continued to work with the smart heads in spite of their exploitation, because the smart heads had established relationships with the police and neighborhood "fences" (receivers of stolen property).[15] Once the new recruits became familiar with the police and were able to deal directly with a fence themselves, they broke away from their gang mentors. There was, however, a downside to this progression in their criminal careers. Once the gang members became known to the police, they became subject to regular shakedowns and were regularly stopped by police officers who wanted to share in their illegal profits.

The crimes of the Forty-two Gang included murder, robbery, burglary, auto theft, kidnapping, and various other misdemeanor and felony crimes. Those who were arrested varied in age from thirteen to thirty-three, although the median age of those identified in Landesco's records and newspaper accounts was twenty-one. By 1927 almost every car stolen in the Near West

Side of Chicago was recovered, stripped of its necessary parts, in old barns and garages in the neighborhood of the Forty-two Gang. Few, however, were stolen from their own neighborhood. As their proficiency grew, the Forty-twos began to steal autos for bootleggers to be used in the transportation of illegal liquor. The gang used children as young as six years old to break into automobiles and thirteen- to sixteen-year-olds to drive them away, believing the police would not shoot at children.[16]

An important challenge faced by the Chicago police when dealing with the Forty-two Gang was their driving. Police were reluctant to chase gang members for fear of harming innocent bystanders. Chases often ended up in fiery crashes and gun battles with the pursuing officers. So determined were the members of the Forty-two Gang to evade the police that they would hold practice driving sessions on Sunday mornings. One of their drills was to "sweep" an auto from the street into a narrow alley at fifty miles an hour. Whipping corners was especially dangerous to neighborhood bystanders. Many of the young drivers were so small that they could not see above the seat of the car.[17]

Although auto theft appears to have been the main crime committed by the members of the Forty-two Gang, armed robberies were common. By 1930 they were suspected in more than a dozen robberies. They robbed the Everett Coal Company and the Goldenrod Ice Company. They robbed hat shops, bank messengers, department stores, dance halls, mail carriers, liquor stills, and handbook operations, killing at least one innocent bystander. Robbing a liquor still or a handbook was a dangerous business, because it directly challenged adult organized crime. Forty-two Gang member Michael DeStefano even robbed a fellow prisoner while being held in the lockup of the Warren Avenue police station.[18]

Probably the most daring raid carried out by the Forty-two Gang was the alleged robbery of the C & O Cabaret in the North Clark Street rialto. The C & O was owned by John Connors, the brother of William "Botchie" Connors, the political boss of the Near North Side of Chicago. Robbing the C & O demonstrated an utter disregard for the established political structure. The resulting gun battle left five people wounded. Information developed by the Secret Six revealed that Sam "Teets" Battaglia and several other members of the Forty-two Gang had shot up the C & O Cabaret at the request of the remnants of the Aiello gang. It seems that the C & O had dropped the Aiellos and switched their liquor purchases to the Capone mob after the death of Joe Aiello.[19]

Even the police were not safe. Two of the five people shot in the C & O battle were police officers. There was no love between the police and the members of the gang. Some officers were despised because they could be paid off; others were hated by the gang because of the rough treatment the gang members received in police custody. Landesco argued that this hatred of the police contributed to the violent nature of the gang. The gangster who had paid the police, bought himself out of jail, and had beaten cases in court developed an abusive attitude toward the law, one that often resulted in bitterness in court and violence out on the street. To the gang member, there was no justice, only the power of the "pull"—the ability to fix a case in court. As a result, gang members were filled with confidence and daring, believing they would not be held accountable for their crimes.[20]

Their hatred of the police was so great that during their nine-year reign of terror, members of the Forty-two Gang killed at least four police officers. In 1929 Forty-two gangster Willie Doody killed Berwyn police chief Charles Levy, who saw Doody driving a stolen auto and attempted to apprehend him. Unknown to Chief Levy, Doody was wanted by the authorities for the murder of postal inspector Evan Jackson, whom he had shot in a gun battle with federal authorities a few weeks earlier. Eighteen months after the Levy murder, members of the Forty-two Gang killed police officer John Vondruska, of the Fillmore Street station, when he tried to prevent the robbery of a Yellow Cab Company garage in the Far West Side. Finally in 1933, Forty-two Gang member Tony Rocco killed policeman Maurice Marcusson when he tried to prevent the robbery of a dress shop in downtown Chicago.[21]

The gang also turned to kidnapping and rape. On one occasion two members of the gang kidnapped a seventeen-year-old girl and drove her to a nearby garage, where seven men attacked her. On another occasion three members of the Forty-two Gang kidnapped a twenty-year-old woman in the Near West Side, but she managed to escape before she was harmed. In yet another case, three members of the Forty-two Gang attempted to abduct two women sitting on the front steps of their home, but were driven off by the fiancé of one of the girls. So many gang rapes were attributed to the Forty-two Gang that Thomas Courtney, the Cook County state's attorney, sought to amend the Illinois criminal code to make gang rape punishable by the death penalty.[22]

Landesco attributed these rapes to the breakdown of old world traditions. According to Landesco, eight Italian girls were raped in 1930, all within six blocks of the headquarters of the Forty-two Gang.[23] Only ten years earlier, a young man who harmed an Italian girl would have been killed by her father. American jurisprudence, however, outlawed the vendetta and prevented Italian fathers from taking justice into their own hands. Local women told Landesco that Americanization had contributed to the raping of Italian girls, who were now going out on dates, attending drinking parties, and coming home late at night.

The Forty-two Gang was also involved in bootlegging. Working for the Red Bolton Gang, they branched out as peddlers on Bolton's less important routes. When not looking for new customers, they also hijacked liquor stills. In fact, one of the Forty-twos' most active thieves, seventeen-year-old Frank Petitto, was found murdered on Joliet Road, south of Lyons, Illinois. Police reported that Petitto "had been taken for a ride." They suspected that he had been preying on still owners and alky runners "hoisting" stills and robbing whoever was present, taking hundreds of gallons of bootleg booze. Two months after the death of Petitto, Peter Nicastro, one of the early members of the Forty-two Gang, was also murdered. Police believed that Nicastro was also killed for hijacking liquor stills. Further investigation revealed that Petitto and Nicastro had been murdered by fellow Forty-two Gang members for hijacking stills belonging to the Bolton Gang. Hijacking Bolton stills constituted a betrayal of the gang because of the working relationship between the Bolton bootleggers and the Forty-twos.[24]

No crime seemed to be out of the question for the Forty-two Gang. Working with Forty-two Gang members Joseph Muscato and Albert Woodrick, Dominick DePalma told his cousin, Attillo Scalditti, that two men had been hired to kill him.[25] DePalma then told Scalditti that he knew the men and could dissuade them if Scalditti paid twenty-five hundred dollars. Scalditti told DePalma to negotiate the deal and then called the police. When Muscato and Woodrick arrived to pick up the extortion money, police attempted to make the arrest, but Muscato fled and was shot by the police. He died a short time later at the county jail hospital. Newspapers incorrectly reported the incident as Black Hand extortion. The Black Hand was not a criminal organization, but a method of crime, common in the Italian community, involving the use of a blackmailing letter. No letter was involved in the Scalditti extortion, nor was the Forty-two Gang a Black Hand gang.

The Forty-two Gang also tried its hand at bank robbery. Louis "The Louse" Clementi and nine other members of the Forty-two Gang robbed Chicago's Main State Bank, escaping with $16,300. They also robbed the South Holland Trust and Savings Bank on two separate occasions. During the first holdup, Peter De Young, a replacement bank guard, was killed by the robbers. One year later Forty-two Gang members tried to rob the bank a second time. This time their efforts were averted by the alert action of the local police. Noticing a suspicious car parked near the bank, the local police chief notified bank security personnel. When three Forty-two Gang members entered the bank brandishing shotguns, the on-duty bank guard,

Jacob De Young (father of the previously slain bank guard), opened fire, killing two of the robbers and wounding the third.[26]

One of the most famous crimes committed by the members of the Forty-two Gang was the home invasion robbery of Mr. and Mrs. William H. Mitchell in Lake Forest, Illinois. The robbery occurred on the night of November 21, 1931, while the Mitchells and seven guests were playing backgammon. Five masked youths entered the Mitchell home waving pistols and robbed the Mitchell party, escaping with money and jewelry valued at $150,000. William Matheson, the Mitchell chauffeur, however, reached a telephone in the confusion and called the police. The robbers then fled, but not before exchanging gunfire with Lake Forest officers. The following day, an overcoat with the stolen jewelry in the pockets was found on the Mitchell estate. Frank Tufano, a member of the Forty-two Gang, was implicated in the robbery after an automobile with license plates issued to his mother was found near the Mitchell property. Servants in the Mitchell home then identified a picture of Tufano as one of the robbers. Tufano was arrested with three other Forty-two Gang members, and all were identified as the men who committed the Mitchell holdup. The four defendants—Frank Tufano, Joseph Perello, Paul Ross, and Nick Maentanis—were all convicted of the robbery and sentenced to one year to life in the Illinois State Penitentiary.[27]

In response to the growing number of crimes committed by the Forty-two Gang, Judge Francis Borrelli of the Des Plaines Street court launched a two-pronged attack on the activities of the gang.[28] The first stage of the attack was Borrelli's personal expedition into the Near West Side of Chicago, the stronghold of the gang. For one month, the judge, dressed in shabby clothes, mingled with the young hoodlums, frequented their haunts, and through personal observation satisfied his need to smash the gang. The second prong of the attack was carried out by the Chicago Police Department. Ten squads of heavily armed detectives were sent into the territory of the Forty-two Gang with orders to arrest gang members on sight.

Within days 134 suspected gang members had been charged with disorderly conduct and brought before Judge Borrelli's court, most of them boys between the ages of seventeen and twenty-one. Addressing the defendants, Borrelli told them that they were a disgrace to the Italian name. Unfortunately, most of those arrested were not actually gang members, and after intense police questioning and standing in multiple police lineups, 115 of those arrested were discharged. Twelve others were fined from one hundred to two hundred dollars. A second wave of arrests was carried out one year later. Acting on information supplied by Judge Borrelli, police arrested 36 suspected Forty-two Gang members. This time the police got lucky. They seized eight shotguns, two pistols, three bulletproof vests, and a bushel basket filled with ammunition. Three robberies were also solved.[29]

Even when the police were successful in bringing charges against Forty-two Gang members, it seemed that the criminal justice system functioned in the gang's favor. If they could not bribe the arresting officer, they often found a friendly judge to writ them out of police custody in order to avoid standing in a police lineup at the detective bureau.[30] Lineups were dangerous. Even if gang members were not identified by their current victim, they might be identified by a victim from a prior crime. When gang members were charged with an offense, friendly judges were often available to lower their bond, and if they went to trial, witnesses could be intimidated or bought off. In one case Forty-two Gang members actually kidnapped a prosecuting witness from the Chicago Criminal Court Building to prevent him from testifying. Finally, if all else failed and they went to prison, there was always the chance of obtaining an early parole.

Another reason that authorities were having problems controlling the Forty-two Gang was their inability to send the younger members to prison. Boys under seventeen could only be punished by sending them to the Saint Charles School for Boys. Saint Charles was created to handle boys who committed minor delinquent offenses and was not equipped to manage the dangerous hoodlums of the Forty-two Gang. In addition, Saint Charles had gone through a reform period in which corporal punishment and military decorum had been replaced by psychological counseling, which led some to believe that the school was no longer capable of handling more troubled youths, such as those of the Forty-two Gang. A sentence to Saint Charles provided so little deterrence to the Forty-two Gang that on at least two separate occasions, gang members simply drove up to the school and rescued their fellow gang members from custody. Even those members sent to adult prisons were a problem for authorities. In fact, the Pontiac Reformatory refused to accept Rocco Capra, a Forty-two Gang member, because they did not want a "Chicago gunman" in their prison.[31]

Even if a Forty-two Gang member was sent to prison, there was no guarantee that he would remain there. Many were paroled before serving the full length of their sentence. Take the example of Ralph Greco. In 1922 he was sentenced to serve twenty years at the Pontiac Reformatory for burglary but was paroled just three years later. After a few months on the street, he violated his parole and was returned to Pontiac. In 1928 he was again paroled and remained at liberty until 1929, when he was arrested with other members of the Forty-two Gang and sent back to prison. A third parole was granted in 1932. Shortly thereafter he was arrested again and returned to prison. Another Forty-two Gang member, Solly Goldsmith, had been sentenced for burglary and subsequently paroled twice before receiving a life sentence as a habitual criminal. In still another case, Nick Maentanis, one of the Mitchell home invaders, was paroled after serving only four years of a one-year-to-life sentence. The remaining Mitchell bandits were paroled into the United States Army in 1943 during World War II after serving only eleven years of their sentence.[32]

There is substantial evidence to support allegations of corruption in the Illinois parole system. A 1928 report on parole abuses in Illinois, written by such notables as Andrew Bruce of Northwestern University, Dean Albert Harno of the University of Illinois, and Ernest W. Burgess of the University of Chicago, attributed abuses in the parole system to politics.[33] The report found that state legislators often represented prisoners at parole hearings. Although they were attorneys, inmates did not retain state representatives and senators because of their legal acumen, but because of their political influence.

Landesco blamed the formation of the Forty-two Gang on social conditions in the Near West Side of Chicago. Neighborhoods like Taylor Street were abandoned by those families who were able to adapt to modern society, leaving behind a community composed of those whose burdens were far too great for their own solutions. In contrast to orderly society, gangs in these neighborhoods were as close as the street corner. There the older gangsters lured younger boys into crime. The stolen cars, the clothing, the shows, the cabarets, and the excitement all offered a way out of slum life.[34]

As a university professor, Landesco was a member of the emerging Chicago School of sociology, which sought to understand the relationship between crime and the organization of the urban environment. Like Clifford Shaw and Henry McKay, Landesco challenged the notion that crime was the result of the organic makeup of the offender or his ethnic background. He identified the conditions in the Near West Side of Chicago that contributed to the formation of the Forty-two Gang as the failure of political, educational, and religious institutions; unemployment; and the lack of what he called recreational and character-forming institutions.[35]

Nineteenth Ward alderman John Powers controlled the Taylor Street area for forty years, elected to office when the neighborhood was largely Irish. Powers controlled votes through patronage jobs, favors, and other courtesies. When his constituents were arrested, he furnished them with bond money and "fixed" cases in court. Aside from the police, Powers was the only direct contact the people of the Near West Side had with American government. Powers was known as the "Prince of Boodlers" because of his ability to push corrupt measures through the Chicago City Council. He was so corrupt that he was caught attempting to fix a Black Hand kidnapping case involving a six-year-old boy. Together the gangsters and politicians ruled the civic life of the community and provided the only examples of success for young boys to emulate. Corrupt politicians also taught aspiring Forty-two Gang members that justice could be bought and that they had nothing to fear from the police, even those officers who were honest, because the police were under political control.[36]

There were also vast differences in the quality of the schools in the Near West Side. The inability of immigrant parents to speak English often prevented them from working with the schools to educate their children. As a result, the school authorities with whom immigrant parents came into contact were often principals and truant officers. Further, the schools in the neighborhood were old and poorly equipped and not desirable places for teachers to work. Because politics played a large role in the assignment of teachers, the best teachers were often assigned to better areas, leaving the unwilling and discouraged behind. Even the best of students had enormous difficulties to overcome when they left school and sought a job. Poor dress, grooming, speech, and broken English worked against them.[37]

Religious institutions also suffered from conditions in the Near West Side. Although churches, synagogues, and parochial schools originally flourished, the exodus of the legitimately successful increased the financial burden of the poor residents, who became resentful of the Church's increasing demand for support. Additionally, Americanization led to conflict between immigrant parents and immigrant children about church attendance and religious beliefs.[38]

Unemployment among fathers also contributed to delinquency in the area. Failure to find employment imposed not only a financial hardship on the family but also ineffective parental control. The father who could not provide for his family found it difficult to control the boy who found economic independence through participation in the gang. While there was strong initial opposition from the parents, the financial inadequacy of the father's earnings and periodic unemployment often led to an acceptance of a child's illegal activity. Some families were even forced to live on the illegal earnings of their children in order to survive.[39]

Finally, Landesco argued that Taylor Street and the Near West Side were devoid of recreational and character-forming institutions. Boy Scout troops, settlement houses, and parks were almost entirely absent from these areas, whereas orderly communities had these facilities as well as functioning religious, educational, vocational, and recreational institutions, all contributing to the formation of the character of the child. If these conditions had been equally present in the inner city, then it could be argued that delinquency was the result of cultural practices and transplanted old world traditions, but they were not.[40]

In contrast to the social disorganization of slum life, Landesco reported that the gang provided an attainable life plan and a way out of the opportunity-deprived inner city. The gang not only furnished partners for truancy; it provided friends, sources of spending money, and economic independence. The gang also provided examples of manly courage. A gang boy watched his friends endure beatings by the police, was carried from the gunfire of his enemies by his gang friends, and rescued his pals in turn. The Forty-twos had a steadfast rule that members must carry their wounded partners to safety. The gang also provided access to the adult gangster and liquor boss, the one element in the community feared by local politicians who had sought to repress the Italian community.[41]

Landesco's description of the Near West Side is one that is familiar to all gang researchers. Recent studies by James D. Vigil, William J. Wilson, and Sudhir A. Venkatesh have documented the effects of social disorganization on gang formation. What is not familiar is the rampant corruption of government that existed in Landesco's time. Once successful Italians left Taylor Street, the only models for success that young people had left were the gangsters and the politicians. Today, inner-city youth have successful drug dealers as role models, but wholesale alliances between gangs and politicians are rare. During the time of the Forty-two Gang numerous alliances between politicians and gangsters existed. Take the example of Illinois state representative John Bolton, former Forty-two Gang member and brother of bootleg boss Red Bolton. He was killed in July 1936 because of his involvement in the illegal handbook racket. There was also Joseph "Diamond Joe" Esposito, Nineteenth Ward (Taylor Street) Republican ward committeeman, restaurateur, and local bootlegging boss.[42]

By 1927 many of the original members of the Forty-two Gang were dead, in prison, or had given up a life of crime. Joseph Calaro, one of the original smart heads, was killed by the police as he fled from a "stripped" auto. Louie Pargoni had also been killed by the police, but in a separate incident. Salvi was killed in an automobile crash. Sam Giancana was in prison for rape, and Rocco Marcantonio had left a life of crime after serving time at the Saint Charles reformatory. Sharkey Icola also left a life of crime and went to work for the city of Chicago. Pete Gallichio outgrew the gang and became a "big shot" gangster. Although the original members had fallen away, their exploits had a direct impact on the next generation of children in the Taylor Street community. While the original gang was in dissolution, having lost many of its members to death or imprisonment, the younger boys were still eager to emulate their actual or imagined exploits. The traditions of the Forty-two Gang had become the delinquent culture of the neighborhood, and it was through this delinquency culture that young boys graduated to become adult criminals.[43]

This new generation of little ruffians, hardened by the exciting life they witnessed in the Taylor Street area, became hardened delinquents. Gunfire between the police and the Forty-twos was a daily affair; fast cars were constantly being chased by the police; and the guns, whiskey, and flashing of rolls of money all led the boys to a life of crime. In his unpublished manuscript, "The Diffusion of a Criminal Culture," Landesco provides a rich description of the lives of these young people. His observations include case studies of aspiring Forty-two Gang members, daily accounts of the lives of neighborhood boys, and his general observations of the play life of children in the neighborhood of the Forty-two Gang. Landesco believed that the data should speak for itself. As such, he provided a "thick description" of the lives of these boys in their own words, one that takes the reader into the setting being described so that they can understand the phenomena studied and draw their own interpretations. Three of these accounts are summarized in the following paragraph. They concern the lives of a clique of three boys—Mike, Tom, and Jo—whose behavior was typical of other boys in the neighborhood.[44]

Thirteen-year-old Mike was considered the "brains" of the group. Mike's stated ambition in life was to become a gangster like Al Capone. Mike started his criminal career "robbing" (shoplifting) at the Wieboldt's department store. Initially his thefts included socks and cap guns. He then progressed to stealing milk, pencils, and books at school. Although he didn't like school, he liked to read gangster books. When not at school, Mike spent his free time hanging around with the older members of the Forty-two Gang. Tom, the "muscle man," was fourteen years of age. His delinquent career began by stealing baseballs and baseball bats from the children at a local Greek school. He also stole paper, books, and pencils from the school and burglarized a local candy store. Tom hung around Mary's Restaurant and helped out with stripping autos. Like Mike, he read books about gangsters and favored newspaper accounts of robberies and murders. His ambition was to be a bootlegger. Jo, the last of the three boys, was known as the "ambassador" and began his delinquent career at twelve when he "robbed" a bicycle. He also stole toy guns from the Wieboldt's department store and pilfered bananas and watermelons from local peddlers. He then progressed to stealing automobile parts from parked cars. At school he stole cakes, candy, and milk. Jo said that he didn't like school and that his teachers never bothered him, because they knew he was a member of the Forty-two Gang. Like the other boys, Jo read gangster books and newspaper accounts of murder and robbing stores.[45]

These boys all took pride in living near the Forty-two Gang and were delighted when the members of the gang spoke to them or praised their driving skills. They spoke with pride of Babe Ruth Calaro, a deceased smart head, and wanted nothing more than to become a "real" Forty-two. The influence of the gang was so great that young children, boys and girls, would "whip" corners with their bicycles and coaster wagons, emulating the reckless driving of the gang.[46]

The new generation of Forty-twos formed little "mobs" on almost every block in the Taylor Street area.[47] Most were led by the older gang members and were in constant communication with one another. All considered themselves Forty-twos and "followed a single tradition, a mutual confidence, and a single code." They were also considered Forty-twos by the police, who did not differentiate between the various groups. This diffusion of the Forty-two Gang to various locations in the Near West Side is similar to the groupings within today's gangs. In Chicago, for example, the Vice Lords street gang has "sets" throughout the West Side of the city. Most do not even know each other, but they all "ride" under the same name, reputation, and code of conduct set by the original gang members.

In spite of their ability to attract new members, the Forty-two Gang abruptly ended in 1934. The end of the Forty-twos brought an end to large criminal gangs in Chicago. Gangs became groups of adolescent, street-corner youths who occasionally engaged in delinquent activity. Sure, there were small bands of robbers and burglars, but they never approached the size and dedication to crime that the Forty-two Gang, and its predecessors, had. One may ask about the "super" gangs of today. Groups in Chicago like the Latin Kings, Vice Lords, and Gangster Disciples are large criminal organizations, but their focus is on drugs. They do not principally engage in robbery, burglary, and auto theft like the Forty-two Gang once did. The reason for this change in the nature of gangs in Chicago may have been the ascendancy of the Chicago Outfit, the traditional organized crime group in Chicago.

When the Capone syndicate expanded its bootlegging activities into the area of the Forty-two Gang, many gang members were recruited as "militia men" and even given the opportunity to run liquor stills. This was called "being put on the payroll or given a spot or a job," much like the gang members of today who are given a "spot" to sell drugs. It is noteworthy that this word continues to have the same significance nearly eighty years later. What is even more noteworthy is Landesco's claim that the Capone syndicate, with the cooperation of the local police, helped to clean up the Near West Side, bringing unattached hoodlums, like the members of the Forty-two Gang, under Syndicate control. This position is supported by the work of Gerald Suttles, who studied the Taylor Street area some forty years later. Suttles argued that the presence of the crime syndicate in the Taylor Street community provided an additional dimension of social control that few were willing to challenge. The Forty-two Gang continued to commit other crimes, but they became more selective, and once they were involved with the Capone mob, they also benefited from the huge amounts of graft paid by the bootleggers to police and politicians.[48]

A number of forces other than organized crime also contributed to the end of the criminal gang in Chicago. Many Irish gangs were rationalized into the established political structure. Street-corner youth who may have turned to crime gained access to city jobs through neighborhood political clubs sponsored by local politicians. All they had to do in return was turn out the vote. In Chicago's Italian neighborhoods, the Chicago Area Project had a significant impact on delinquency. Begun in the 1930s by sociologist Clifford Shaw to address juvenile delinquency and prevent crime, the program was well received by the Italian community, and literally thousands of teenage boys, and girls, participated in its programs, preventing their participation in crime.

Another factor that contributed to the end of the Forty-two Gang was the improved police response to the gang's criminal activities. In spite of widespread political corruption, the police were effective. One hundred and fifty members of the Forty-two Gang were sent to prison by city and suburban police forces for crimes ranging from petty larceny to murder. In addition, the Taylor Street neighborhood that was home to the Forty-two Gang began to disappear. The encroachment of industry and the eventual building of the Dan Ryan Expressway claimed most of the original neighborhood. Taylor Street today begins at Morgan Street; in the days of the Forty-two Gang, the neighborhood ended there. The ecological conditions that had contributed to the development of the gang are gone.

Almost everything we know about early twentieth-century gangs comes from two sources: Thrasher, and Shaw and McKay. Examining the Forty-two Gang provides another look at gangs during this important time in the development of sociological thought. In particular, the unpublished Landesco manuscripts provide insight into four important theoretical areas. The first concerns the gang itself. Although the Forty-two Gang was largely made up of teenage offenders, it was a *criminal gang*. It was not a *youth gang* in the Shaw and McKay sense of the term. Landesco's work provides valuable insight into the formation of a criminal gang, an area that has often been overlooked in gang literature.

Landesco's second important insight involves the diffusion of gang culture. Once the reputation of the Forty-two Gang became established in the Near West Side, it became the magnet that drew young delinquents to gang participation independent of the involvement of the original gang leaders. Landesco's findings support the work of Shaw and McKay, who argued that "delinquency subcultures" developed in socially disorganized communities and that these delinquency subcultures became the dominant pattern of criminal life in the area. Additionally, Landesco's findings support Thrasher's argument that some criminal gangs were the direct continuation of adolescent groups that had carried over into adult crime.

Landesco's work also provides a fresh insight into the evolution of organized crime in Chicago. So many senior members of the Forty-two Gang were recruited into the Capone mob that they became the foundation of the Taylor Street Crew, one of the five "street crews" (branches) of the Chicago Outfit. The Forty-twos were reportedly recruited by Capone strongman Jack McGurn, who grew up at Polk and Morgan in the Taylor Street neighborhood. One member of the Forty-two Gang, Sam Giancana rose to head the Chicago Outfit during the 1950s.[49]

Lastly, Landesco's work demonstrates that the chief causes of crime are not found in the physical and mental makeup of the criminal or in his transplanted culture, but in the community where the person resides. It wasn't a transplanted Mafia culture that allowed young people to enter organized crime but, rather, the social conditions in which they were raised.[50]

6

THE OUTFIT

The 1950s brought new leadership to the Capone syndicate. Things were changing. The old-timers who had known Al Capone were dead, in prison, or living in lavish suburban homes, and a new group of younger men was taking their place. These new gangsters weren't born in Sicily, nor did they grow up running beer during Prohibition. They were former delinquents who had terrorized the streets of Chicago's river wards. Among them were many members of the Forty-two Gang. The entrance of the Forty-two Gang had marked a turning point in organized crime in Chicago. Until this time the Capone syndicate was controlled by Levee gangsters. With the advent of the Forty-two Gang, however, control of organized crime moved to the West Side of Chicago. Former Forty-two Gang members such as Sam "Teets" Battaglia, Marshal "Joe Russo" Caifano, William "Potatoes" Daddano, "Mad Sam" DeStefano, Charles "Chuckie" English, and Albert "Obie" Frabotta attained prominence during the 1950s. In 1958 Sam "Mooney" Giancana, another Forty-two Gang member, rose through the ranks to head organized crime in Chicago.[1]

The 1950s also brought the accelerated use of the term *Outfit*. Capone biographer Robert Schoenberg traces the use of the term to the days of Johnny Torrio. It was a less lurid name than the term *Syndicate* used by crime reporters and novelists. A former gangster told this author that the word Outfit was a casual name used by gang members when they were talking among themselves and about their group. They would say, "I joined the Outfit two years ago." It was supposed to be a secret—"the Outfit." Nobody was supposed to know what it meant except the guys involved, but it eventually grew out of hand and became the name of the group.[2]

The Outfit also differed from the Capone syndicate in another significant way: the ethnicity of its members. Most of Capone's gangsters were not

Italian; most of the members of the Outfit are. By the 1950s 78 percent of the members of the Outfit had Italian surnames, and that trend continues today. As late as 2003, 77 percent of the members of the Chicago Outfit had Italian names. The decision to limit membership to those of Italian descent is attributed to Paul Ricca, who allegedly decreed during his reign as the Outfit's leader that only Italians would be permitted to hold top positions.[3]

The Takeover of Policy Gambling

One of the factors that helped bring members of the Forty-two Gang to power in the Chicago Outfit was the takeover of policy gambling. As the successor to the Capone syndicate, the Outfit worked tirelessly after Prohibition to control all vice activities in Chicago. By 1950 the one remaining racket they did not control was policy gambling. Despite the economic and political importance of policy to Chicago's African American community, blacks would lose control of the policy racket. Although Mayor Kelly was on good terms with Chicago blacks, the Kelly-Nash political machine that ran Chicago had relinquished control of all gambling to the Syndicate. The reason for the complicity of the Chicago Democratic Party was the estimated $12 million collected annually from illegal gambling and vice activities. This association between the Kelly-Nash machine and organized crime set the stage for the Outfit's attack on policy.[4]

After Al Capone succeeded Big Jim Colosimo as the vice lord of Chicago's Near South Side, he declared his intention of moving into the Second Ward and taking over all the illegal rackets operating there. Capone henchmen made plans to swoop down on policy, dice, and off-track betting. The "Spigoosh," as Chicago blacks called the Italian crime syndicate, first moved against a policy wheel operated by a man named Roberletto in the Entertainers Building on Thirty-fifth Street near Indiana Avenue. Sam Ettleson, a power in the Illinois state senate from the second congressional district, and Senator Adolph Marks, of the first district, brought pressure on Capone to give up the idea. As a result, Capone warned his men that the entire South Side black area and the policy racket were to be left to African Americans in exchange for their staying out of the beer racket. The deal made by Capone with the black underworld lasted until after World War II, when the Outfit began to take over policy gambling.[5]

Was Capone's agreement with South Side blacks simply good business, or were there other reasons for the concurrence? Capone biographer Laurence Bergreen argues that Capone was sympathetic to blacks because they, like

Italians, were part of an outcast ethnic group. In fact, as late as 1910, blacks were less segregated from native whites than were Italian immigrants. In addition, immigrant blacks and Italians often lived together in the slums of American cities. Ernest Burgess reports that cities like Chicago often had wards that comprised more than 10 percent of both the Italian and black populations of the city. This does not mean that Italians never discriminated against blacks; indeed, in 1929 Harvey Zorbaugh recorded conflicts between blacks and Italians in the Near North Side of Chicago. What it does mean is that Italians and Italian gangsters probably had a greater familiarity with African Americans than any other ethnic group had.[6]

In the spring of 1939, federal agents arrested Sam Giancana and fourteen others for operating an illegal liquor still on a farm near Garden Prairie, Illinois. Giancana, past member of the Forty-two Gang, was subsequently sentenced to four years in the federal penitentiary at Terre Haute, Indiana. There, Giancana met Big Ed Jones, who was serving time for income tax evasion. Jones reportedly told Giancana about the vast sums of money he had made in the policy racket. After being released from prison in 1942, Giancana began making plans for the Outfit's takeover of the policy racket. The opening salvo against black policy operators was the kidnapping of Jones upon his release from Terre Haute prison.[7]

The kidnapping took place on May 11, 1946, in the presence of Jones's wife, Lydia. Lydia's screams attracted the attention of a passing patrol car manned by two police officers, who immediately took up the chase. The abductors, seeing the police, broke out the rear window of their auto and fired a volley of bullets at the pursuing squad car, wounding one of the police officers Michael Derrane. Having made good their escape, the kidnappers eventually released Jones upon collecting a $100,000 ransom payment. Shortly thereafter, Ed Jones and his brother George moved to Mexico and left the policy racket to Theodore "Teddy" Roe, their partner in the Maine-Idaho-Ohio wheel.[8]

Outraged by the shooting of the officer, Police Commissioner William Prendergast directed the Chicago Police Department to stamp out the policy racket. Jones also received the wholesale condemnation of his fellows in the numbers racket, who charged that he had destroyed the game after having made millions of dollars from it. Some fellow policy operators charged that Jones had made an "unholy" alliance with West Side gangsters whom he had met while serving time in the federal penitentiary. On several occasions Jones was criticized for placing too much trust in his "white friends" who had enjoyed visits to his home in Chicago and his villa in Mexico City.

Policy operators were not sorry to see the Jones brothers exit the racket. It seems they had a reputation of being tightwads and had contributed little to local charities or the black community.[9]

Ed Jones had violated the unwritten law of the policy fraternity by associating with members of the Outfit. His association with Chicago mobsters resulted in his kidnapping and drew the attention of the police, who had been happy to cooperate with the policy barons while it was a local racket unconnected to the Capone mob. Contrary to popular writings, Jones may not have been simply an innocent victim of underworld extortion. According to the *Chicago Defender*, Jones was seen meeting with West Side mobsters on a number of occasions and was reportedly seeking to invest one hundred thousand dollars in the jukebox racket. It appears that Jones contracted with the gangsters to obtain two thousand jukeboxes to be placed in South Side taverns and restaurants. The result of Jones's association with the Chicago mob was an assault on the policy racket by both the police and the Outfit.[10]

Ed Jones's successor, Teddy Roe, ran his policy operations from the Boston Club in Chicago's South Side. Described as an elaborate gambling den, the Boston Club was equipped with policy wheels, dice games, and other gaming devices. The Chicago Outfit lost no time in moving against Roe. On September 7, 1946, four syndicate gangsters attempted to kidnap Roe as he left the Boston Club. A confidential informant told the Chicago Crime Commission that four shots had been fired at Roe as he fled the gangsters. In addition, the informant predicted the end of black control of the policy racket in Chicago. Chicago was the only city left in the nation where blacks continued to control the game.[11]

Three days after the unsuccessful kidnapping attempt of Roe, Robert Wilcox was murdered in a printing shop under the Boston Club. Wilcox was a partner with Roe in the club and held a monopoly on the manufacturing of policy wheels. The *Chicago Sun Times* reported that Wilcox received seven hundred dollars for each policy wheel that he sold, which also included a small printing press. The *Sun Times* also reported that Wilcox was murdered because he had refused to sell policy equipment to mobster Paul Labriola. The *Chicago Defender*, however, had a different story. The *Defender* reported that Wilcox was killed by the black policy syndicate to prevent him from selling policy equipment to the Chicago Outfit.[12]

Even the Benvenuti brothers were not safe from Syndicate extortion. Both Al Capone and Julius Benvenuti had died. The Erie-Buffalo wheel was now under the control of Benvenuti's two brothers, Leo and Caesar. In 1949 two Syndicate gangsters, Sam Pardy and Tom Manno, became partners in the wheel and placed the Benvenutis on a fixed salary. "Consulting" money was also paid to Anthony Accardo and Jake Guzik. With their policy wheel now under the control of the mob, the Benevenutis left for an extended visit to Europe.[13]

Policy employed many people in Chicago's South Side and contributed to the area's economy, despite being illegal. The important thing was that the money stayed in the community, but Ed Jones's association with the Outfit had changed all that. The added pressure from the police forced many policy station operators, checkers, pickup men, cashiers, and the like out of work, depriving the black community of needed income. The assault on policy by Chicago gangsters also stirred police into action to wipe out the game before the Outfit could take it over by force.[14] The police believed the attack on Jones was the initial move in the Outfit's attempt to muscle in with "gun and bomb" to take over the racket. They feared that the South Side would be utilized only for "pillage and plunder," with the bulk of the money leaving the black community to benefit white gangsters.

Responding to the attempted takeover of the policy racket by the Chicago Outfit, Congressman William Dawson summed up the black community's sentiment toward policy gambling when he stated, "If anyone is going to make money out of the frailties of my people . . . it's going to be my people." In fact, Dawson fought to protect black numbers racketeers against invasion from the mob. Once when local police captains, working with Italian gangsters, were harassing black policy wheel owners, Dawson went to the mayor of Chicago and had the offending police officers transferred out of his bailiwick. So important was policy to the black community that reform-minded Chicago mayor Martin Kennelly lost his reelection bid in 1955 partly because of his efforts against policy operations in black wards. As a result of his crackdown on policy gambling, Kennelly lost the support of black politicians. Democratic politicians in the South Side expressed concern that the crackdown on policy would have disastrous results on their political machines at the precinct level. Most of the policy runners had developed into outstanding precinct workers. They were exceptionally helpful in getting out the vote, because they had developed direct connections with voters, visiting them once or twice each day to collect, pay off, and distribute policy results.[15]

The records of the Chicago Crime Commission indicate that Congressman Dawson may have had a greater involvement in the policy racket than protecting the interests of the black community. In fact, numerous letters from concerned citizens and memos from confidential informants indicate that Dawson was the conduit for protection money paid to city officials. So convinced was the public that Dawson was involved in policy that on

March 29, 1947, a local black newspaper, the *Chicago World*, publicly accused Congressman Dawson of participating in the numbers racket. Dawson retaliated by filing a one-hundred-thousand-dollar lawsuit against the *World*. His alleged gambling activities were the subject of a Cook County grand jury inquiry in 1955, although no indictment ever resulted from the inquiry.[16]

In an interview granted to the Chicago Crime Commission, Dawson admitted taking money from gambling operators, but only for "political purposes." Like Dan Jackson before him, Dawson led one of the most powerful political organizations in the city. The black South Side vote was tightly organized and could be directed at election time. In fact, Dawson's political organization was probably the most powerful in Chicago. The Chicago Crime Commission reports that one of the reasons Dawson's political organization was so powerful was because policy operators were required to hire political workers to act as policy writers.[17]

The Chicago Outfit's effort to take over policy gambling was not confined to the South Side of Chicago. A large African American community also existed in the city's West Side. First settled at the turn of the century, more than six thousand blacks lived along Lake Street by 1920. This area continued to grow until the 1970s when most of the West Side of Chicago became entirely black. Big Jim Martin ran policy in the West Side from his tavern in the 1900 block of West Lake Street. On October 1, 1940, the Outfit planted a bomb at Martin's bar and made a demand for twenty thousand dollars. Martin ignored the demand, however, because he believed his position as the political leader of the West Side black community would protect him.[18]

The Outfit eventually made Martin the same offer they had made the Jones brothers. When Martin refused to switch allegiance to the Outfit, he was shot on November 15, 1950. The assailant was future mob boss John P. "Jackie" Cerone. Left for dead, Martin recovered and, following the example of the Jones brothers, left Chicago. It appears that the political protection Martin once held was gone. George Kells, the ward's alderman, had resigned, citing the ill health of his wife. Her problems stemmed from the threatening telephone calls she had received from Syndicate gangsters suggesting that it was ill advised for her husband to seek reelection.[19]

Teddy Roe was the one man left who held firm against the mob. The *Defender* reported that Roe knew he was marked for death but swore he would never let the Chicago Outfit take over the policy racket.[20] Roe became a hero in the black community. He was all that stood between the racket and the Outfit. Roe was also a Robin Hood figure to many people. He was the unofficial referee and Supreme Court of the policy game. As reported in the *Chicago Defender*:

> One of his [Roe's] favorite stories was about the elderly woman who bet $2 against another wheel and won but was not paid. She came to him and complained and he sought out the owner to lay down the law. There was a scene complete with name calling, but the woman got her money. This was Roe's sense of fair play. It was the kind of fair play learned when family men had to provide today's meal and next month's rent without a job or the opportunity to get one.

The first time Roe met Sam Giancana, a fight broke out between the two men. The next time the two met, Roe and his men killed gangster "Fat" Lenny Caifano and badly wounded Vince Ioli, another Giancana gangster, in a gun battle in Chicago's South Side. The Outfit retaliated a few months later, killing Roe on August 4, 1952. Chicago's black community was filled with indignation at Roe's murder. Third Ward alderman Archibald Carey blamed city hall for the death of Roe and for their failure to stop the Outfit's assault on policy gambling. Chicago police eventually ordered the arrest of Lenny Patrick, David Yaras, and William Block, three West Side gangsters, in connection with the Roe murder. It was clear that the days of the black policy barons in Chicago were over.[21]

Less than two weeks after the killing of Roe, mobsters Tony Accardo, Jake Guzik, and Pat Manno were indicted by the U.S. attorney for failure to pay income taxes on the proceeds of policy gambling. The indictments revived speculation that Roe had been executed for showing the federal government how to catch policy operators who were faking their income tax returns. In fact, Roe did testify at the Kefauver hearings about policy operations in the South Side of Chicago and named prominent wheel operators, including Chicago mobsters Pat Manno and Pete Tremont.[22]

Policy gambling was important to politicians and the Outfit alike because of the large amount of money it produced. The extraordinary profitability of policy was demonstrated in 1964 by an incident that occurred in the South Side of Chicago. While on a routine inhalator call, an ambulance squad noticed a large stack of coin wrappers and a bag of money on a table in the home of Lawrence Wakefield and notified the police.[23] The next day, detectives secured a warrant and searched the Wakefield home. They recovered $809,058, two policy wheels, eleven policy presses, and seven firearms. When asked why the Outfit had not muscled in on the Wakefield operation, Captain Edward Egan of the Kensington Police District reported that he had heard the crime syndicate had thought about taking over the Wakefield wheel but decided not to bother, because it was thought to be too small to be concerned about.

The Outfit's takeover of policy did not sit well with the black community. In fact, the *Crusader* newspaper became the African American community's voice against the Outfit's attempt to control the racket. The *Crusader* argued that mob-controlled policy was crooked and called upon black policy operators to stand firm against the mob, criticizing them for not fighting back. The *Crusader* also listed the names of the black policy operators who were cooperating with the gangsters. The newspaper predicted the end of policy, reporting that blacks were shunning the game as they became increasingly aware that their wagers were ending up in the coffers of the mob, who returned nothing to the community. The newspaper even asked players to boycott the mob-controlled Windy City wheel.[24]

Although the Outfit used violence in their takeover of policy gambling, they also sought to control it politically. Take the example of Dr. Edward A. Welters, an African American Illinois state representative, who announced that he was running for state senate from the predominantly black first senatorial district. Congressman William Dawson reportedly offered Dr. Welters fifteen thousand dollars to withdraw from the race.[25] Welters refused, but the nomination still went to someone else. Fred Roti received the nomination and was ultimately elected to the senate seat. Roti was sponsored by Peter Fosco, Democratic committeeman of the First Ward and member of the bipartisan "West Side Bloc" of elected officials tied to the Chicago mob.

By 1953 traditional organized crime's takeover of policy was complete. The Chicago Outfit, the successor to the Capone syndicate, had displaced African American gangsters and controlled policy gambling in the South and West Sides of Chicago. Policy had become the Outfit's biggest single money maker. The Outfit's takeover of policy gambling in Chicago did not mean the end of African American participation in the racket. Blacks were indispensable. They were the ones who gambled, and they were the ones who collected the bets. What the Outfit did was share in the profits. The Chicago mob, run by Tony Accardo, kept blacks as employees but took a percentage of the policy profits. Chicago's black policy gangsters became underlings in the Chicago Outfit.[26]

After Prohibition, Capone-era gangsters Murray Humphreys and Sam "Golf Bag" Hunt established a vast gambling empire in Chicago's South Side.[27] Located in mostly white communities, the Chicago Outfit oversaw a network of wire rooms where bets on horse races and sporting events could be called in and smaller walk-in bookmaking operations where off-track gambling took place. In addition, the Outfit oversaw a number of casino gambling operations, including the Beach Club in Hyde Park and a craps game at the famous Club De Lisa jazz emporium on South State Street.

As Chicago's black belt expanded, Ralph Pierce, the successor to Murray Humphreys and Sam Hunt, organized a circle of black lieutenants who supervised gambling in African American areas. Pierce was reportedly the Outfit's overlord of the Fifth, Sixth, and Seventh Wards, which included Hyde Park, Woodlawn, Grand Crossing, and other South Side communities. Pierce's black lieutenants included Osborn Fraser, John Womack, and James Robinson.[28]

African American involvement in traditional organized crime activity in Chicago was not limited to policy gambling. The *Chicago Sun Times* reported in 1965 that African Americans in Chicago were key figures not only in the Cosa Nostra policy racket but also in drug trafficking. The *Sun Times* went on to list four blacks who were active in drug activity tied to traditional organized crime. They were ex-boxer James "Kid Rivera" Williams, Carl Irving, Cornelius Haynes, and Jesse Hoskins.[29]

Other evidence of the link between Chicago blacks and traditional organized crime can be found in the records of the Permanent Subcommittee on Investigations of the Committee on Government Operations of the United States Senate, more commonly referred to as the McClellan Committee. The McClellan Committee reported in 1964 that "Mafia" groups controlled the bulk of the interstate distribution of heroin smuggled into the United States. We know from modern research that what the committee was referring to as the "Mafia" was really the American La Cosa Nostra (LCN). According to the findings of the committee, the LCN was responsible for channeling vast quantities of heroin from New York to other major cities on America's eastern seaboard and to Chicago. From Chicago, narcotics were subsequently distributed to the leading cities of the Midwest and the southwestern United States. In Chicago the committee went on to state that Italian drug organizations distributed heroin to Italian violators of lesser importance and to major Negro violators.[30]

The *Chicago Defender* reported in 1952 that early black drug peddlers in Chicago were ex-bootleggers who had turned to narcotics after the end of Prohibition. The reason for this was twofold: it was no longer possible to make money in bathtub gin, and black bootleggers already had the essential contacts with the Capone mob. Although Chicago's African American community produced a number of prominent drug traffickers in the 1930s, 1940s, and 1950s, it was always an accepted fact that the "big wheels" in the drug trade in the black community were Italian gangsters. Blacks obtained their drugs from the Chicago mob and in turn passed them on to the peddlers and pushers who sold heroin at the street level.[31]

According to the McClellan Committee's report, many of Chicago's most important African American drug distributors received their heroin from organized crime figure Joe Bruno. They included Rupert Kelly, Archie Robinson, Marvin Moses, Auckland Holmes, Moses Hightower, and Harry "King of the Dope Peddlers" Schennault. Bruno had an interest in two drugstores in the heart of Chicago's South Side African American community. The McClellan Committee reported that Bruno, who was considered the major source of supply for heroin in the Chicago area, used the drugstores to obtain quantities of quinine and milk sugar, which were needed for diluting heroin. Grace Pine, a black woman, managed Bruno's interests in the drugstores when he began serving an eight-year prison sentence in 1958.[32]

Bruno was not the only Italian source for African American violators. Two other members of the Chicago underworld—Michael De Marco and Americo DePietto—were charged with distributing heroin to Nolan Mack, Opal "Pat" Cole, and Johnny Green, all African Americans. Prior to his involvement with De Marco and DePietto, Mack had been receiving heroin from Medio Mancione and Joseph Iacullo, two other Chicago Italian American drug wholesalers. The McClellan Committee reported that Iacullo was an associate of Tony Accardo, longtime boss of the Chicago Outfit.[33]

Rocco Infelise, who later became the boss of the Outfit's Taylor Street Crew in the 1980s, was arrested in 1972 for distributing heroin to Thomas "Big Stein" McGarry and Ernest Brown, both African Americans. In referring to the Infelise investigation, the Chicago press stated that the Federal Bureau of Narcotics "uncovered evidence linking a number of white organized crime figures to their black counterparts in a racket to smuggle drugs into this country and sell them."[34] These indictments clearly established the link between the Chicago Outfit and black narcotics sellers in Chicago. Mafia groups in Sicily sold narcotics to the American LCN, which in turn sold drugs to black distributors in Chicago and other areas of the country.

The arrest of Bruno, Infelise, DePietto, and other Italian American violators led to a moratorium on drug trafficking by the Chicago Outfit, whose members feared that those who were arrested would cooperate with authorities in investigating other mob-related activities. In fact, Tony Accardo is alleged to have told Rocco Iacullo, brother of Joseph, to move out of his neighborhood because Accardo did not want to be tied to Iacullo's participation in drug trafficking. Accardo's reluctance to be associated with Iacullo was probably the result of his fear of being arrested on narcotics conspiracy charges. So severe was the Outfit's eventual ban against drug trafficking that Anthony Dichiarinte was murdered because he ignored the edict to get out of the drug business. Dichiarinte's murder was seen as a warning to the members of the Chicago Outfit to steer clear of narcotics trafficking.[35]

The position that Italian American drug dealers in Chicago were in fact part of the Outfit has been the subject of some disagreement. Many believe that the Outfit never sold drugs. However, Outfit participation in drug trafficking is supported by the fact that Outfit drug traffickers participated in other mob-related activities. For example, the McClellan Committee reported that Joseph Iacullo participated in the murder of Anthony Ragucci, another Chicago hoodlum. Carlo Urbinati, listed as a member of one of the three major narcotic groups existing in Chicago's West Side black community during the 1950s, was also involved in the policy racket with his brother-in-law Charles English, a "made guy" in the Chicago Outfit.[36]

The 1950s also brought extensive change to Chicago's South Side black community. Working- and middle-class blacks, attracted by the lure of the suburbs, began to move out of Chicago's South Side. In addition, Chicago's economy was undergoing a massive restructuring, which saw a tremendous decline in the number of blue-collar jobs. Chicago lost 326,000 manufacturing jobs between 1967 and 1987. The disappearance of work had tremendous consequences for life in the inner city. The departure of the middle class was followed by the exit of the commercial institutions they once supported. With no jobs available, young men made rational decisions to "hustle on the streets," resulting in an increase in crime.[37]

As the crime rate soared and street gang activity increased, it became increasingly more difficult for white gangsters to operate in black areas. This point was brought home when one of mobster Ralph Pierce's top lieutenants suffered a merciless beating at the hands of street gang members who had ordered him out of their turf.[38] Mobster Angelo Volpe, who had obtained control over the Windy City policy wheel, also found himself the victim of intimidation by black gang members and was forced to hire his own group of black gang youths to protect him on the day-to-day rounds of his policy operation.

The decline of traditional organized crime activity in the black community was under way. Changing political and social realities made it increasingly difficult for the Outfit to operate in inner-city areas. Government action against policy operators and the decline of Chicago's celebrated Black Metropolis all contributed to the decline of policy gambling. The creation of the Illinois Lottery in 1980 further hastened the decline. Policy, however, did not disappear entirely. Chicago police and federal authorities were taking enforcement action against policy operations as late as 1989 when representatives of the U.S. Attorney's Office seized ten policy stations in a civil forfeiture action. The properties seized were part of the Reuben-Linda lottery, so named for the couple who ran the policy wheel.

Chicago police estimated that the Reuben-Linda lottery had been in existence for six years, from 1983 to 1989, and had taken in an estimated three million dollars a year in revenue.[39] The interesting thing about the Reuben-Linda lottery was that its writers took bets, ranging from twenty-five cents to fifty dollars, on the results of the daily Illinois Lottery. This allowed the bettors to see the numbers drawn on television each night, which ensured the integrity of the game. In spite of persistent rumors, no evidence was ever uncovered of Outfit involvement in the Reuben-Linda operation. The Outfit had lost its control of Chicago's South Side while black organized crime continued.

The Outfit Comes of Age

In May 1950 U.S. Senator Estes Kefauver began a series of investigative hearings into organized crime. The "Kefauver hearings," as they were called, were unique in that they were the first congressional hearings to be televised. Some believe that Kefauver began the hearings to position himself to run for president, which he did in 1952 when he sought the Democratic Party's nomination. Although the hearings were initially looked upon with favor by the Truman White House, the murder of two gangsters in Kansas City's First Ward political clubhouse cooled the ardor of the president, who feared that the hearings would cast light on the connection between the Democratic Party and corruption in his home state.[40]

In Chicago, Kefauver subpoenaed a number of gangsters, including Paul Ricca, Murray Humphreys, Jake Guzik, and brothers Rocco and Charles Fischetti. Testimony was also taken from Virgil W. Peterson, the operating director of the Chicago Crime Commission. Peterson's forty-two-page statement provided a history of organized crime in Chicago and became the basis of the Kefauver Committee's final report. The report traced the beginning of organized crime to the 1920s and the Torrio-Capone gang. Despite the national attention directed at organized crime, the *Chicago Tribune* argued that the amazing thing about the Kefauver Committee was that they didn't learn anything that wasn't already public knowledge.[41]

The Kefauver hearings, however, did cause a renewed effort by the Internal Revenue Service to target hoodlums and led to the establishment of the Organized Crime and Racketeering Section within the U.S. Attorney's Office. It is interesting to note that the list of 126 Chicago gangsters under scrutiny by the IRS revealed that only 48 (30 percent) of them had Italian surnames. This was despite the fact that the hearings concluded, "There [is] a nationwide crime syndicate known as the Mafia whose tentacles are found in many large cities," and, "The Mafia is the cement that helps to bind the Costello-Adonis-Lansky Syndicate of New York and the Accardo-

Guzik-Fischetti Syndicate of Chicago as well as smaller criminal gangs and individual criminals throughout the country."[42]

The Kefauver hearings also resulted in a renewed effort by the Chicago police. The "Scotland Yard" unit that had been set up by Mayor Cermak in 1931 to investigate important murders and major crimes was expanded to include the investigation of organized crime. Charles Gross, a Republican ward committeeman, had been shot to death, and Chicago hoodlums had begun a bombing campaign against the Teamsters Union. Headed by Lieutenant Joseph Morris, Chicago's Scotland Yard would now concentrate its efforts on the Outfit's attempts at labor racketeering, gambling, and extortion.[43]

Labor racketeering was nothing new in Chicago. Gangsters had extorted labor unions since the days of Prohibition. The 1950s, however, brought new efforts to gain control of the Teamsters Union. Controlling Chicago's teamsters would give tremendous power to the Outfit. Striking truck drivers could strangle the city with labor unrest and stop deliveries of food and other materials. On September 16, 1950, three Syndicate gangsters accosted William Lee, president of Teamsters Local 734, stating, "We want in." Lee was also the reigning president of the Chicago Federation of Labor. Lee's assault was followed by a campaign of violence in which two union officials were murdered, one shot, and ten homes and offices bombed.[44]

Scotland Yard's efforts against organized crime began in 1952. Its activities were so successful that by 1953 it was rumored that Tony Accardo was moving to California to avoid the surveillance of the Scotland Yard detail. Morris had ordered his men to arrest Accardo anytime he was seen inside the city of Chicago. So aggressive were Scotland Yard officers that Sergeant William Duffy, disguised as an ice cream peddler, pushed his ice cream wagon into a Fourth of July party at Accardo's River Forest mansion and sold ice cream to the gangsters' children while eavesdropping on their parents' conversations.[45]

In spite of its success, the Scotland Yard organized crime unit was disbanded in 1956 after only four years of operation. Virgil Peterson of the Chicago Crime Commission charged that the unit had been knifed by its political enemies, but police commissioner Timothy O'Connor said the unit was broken up as part of a detective division decentralization plan. Not only was the unit broken up but also its extensive files had vanished. More than six file cabinets, listing more than 10,000 criminals, 600 hoodlums, and 150 businesses taken over by gangsters, had disappeared. The real reason for dissolving Scotland Yard may have been the election of Richard J. Daley to the mayor's office. The Cook County Democratic Party had dropped its support of reform-minded mayor Martin Kennelly. During the campaign,

Lieutenant Joe Morris had been investigating a bookmaker, Michael Farr, who had powerful connections to the Cook County Democratic Central Committee, and word got to Daley that the Scotland Yard detail was working against him. Farr was known as the private bookie of the top brass of the Democratic machine. In spite of Morris's denials, the unit was disbanded when Daley came into office. Morris had also testified in the 1954 federal prosecution of nine men charged with vote fraud in the First Ward, the center of the Outfit's political power. After the trial, U.S. Attorney Robert Tieken wrote Chicago police commissioner Timothy J. O'Connor to say that after asking six police officers to testify, including one police captain, only Lieutenant Joseph Morris was willing to appear in the vote fraud case. The *Chicago Daily Tribune* condemned the whole episode, arguing that it underscored the relationship between local law enforcement and the worst elements of the criminal community.[46]

While the Kefauver hearings provided little new information about Chicago's gangsters, they did highlight the connection between the underworld and Democratic politicians. Testimony was obtained that certain members of the Illinois legislature associated freely with gangsters and voted against legislation designed to curb gangster activity as well as legislation sponsored by the Chicago Crime Commission. Known as the West Side Bloc, the group was a bipartisan coalition of elected officials tied to the Chicago Outfit who supported every corrupt politician since William Hale Thompson. Originally referred to as the "Capone Bloc," the West Side Bloc included a coterie of corrupt Chicago aldermen, Illinois state legislators, and U.S. congressmen who attempted to thwart every worthwhile piece of anticrime legislation brought to vote in the general assembly in Springfield, Illinois, and in Washington, D.C. It included Chicago's First, Twenty-seventh, and Twenty-eighth Wards and the legislative districts that encompassed these areas.[47]

The West Side Bloc's ability to defeat anticrime legislation was demonstrated in 1967 when the Chicago Crime Commission tried to pass a series of anticrime bills in the Illinois General Assembly. Recognizing that the enforcement of existing laws was not enough to defeat organized crime, the commission proposed nine new laws to provide police and prosecutors with modern, legal weapons to defeat the criminal element. The proposed laws included, among others, a ban on pinball gambling, a bill to license bartenders, and gun control legislation. All but one of the proposals failed. All were opposed by the members of the West Side Bloc. The records of the Chicago Crime Commission listed thirty-four Illinois legislators as members or affiliates of the West Side Bloc in the years between 1951 and 1967. While no more than a handful of these elected officials were actually members of the bloc, the remaining legislators voted to support West Side Bloc initiatives because of "log rolling" or the "swap system" of exchanging votes. West Side Bloc members would support any legislation in return for support of their initiatives. Because the bloc was interested in only a dozen of the two thousand plus bills introduced each year, they were willing to support other legislators whose initiatives the bloc had no interest in, thus guaranteeing support for their positions.[48]

The name West Side Bloc came from the fact that most of its members were from the West Side of Chicago and voted as a bloc. Their point of origin was the inner-city wards along the Chicago River, where the crime syndicate had a strong voice in politics, gambling, and vice. These wards often contained skid row areas—South State Street, West Madison Street, and North Clark Street—each lined with cheap saloons, flophouses, and burlesque shows. Each was a descendant of an older tenderloin district developed under the protection of a political boss. The reason for the enduring affinity between politicians and skid row derelicts was that politicians needed their votes on Election Day.[49]

There was also a Republican component to the West Side Bloc; however, it was under the control of the Democratic Party. This was made possible by the Illinois system of cumulative voting for the state House of Representatives. By agreement, the majority party nominated candidates for two of the three legislative seats at stake in each election and gave the third to the minority party. As a result of this arrangement, Republican organizations in the river wards continued to exist through the tolerance of the Democratic Party as long as they cooperated behind the scenes with the Democrats.[50]

The 1952 murder of acting Republican ward committeeman Charles Gross of the Thirty-first Ward, a vigorous opponent of attempts by gangland elements to dominate Northwest Side politics, was one of a number of attempts by the West Side Bloc to expand its control beyond Chicago's river wards. The Outfit earlier had forced George Kells out of office in the Twenty-eighth Ward and Sidney Schiller in the Twenty-seventh, and it was not the first time the Outfit had used murder to dominate ward politics. Authorities suspected that the Outfit had also killed Twenty-seventh Ward Republican committeeman William Granata. Granata had earlier challenged James Adduci, a member of the West Side Bloc, in the race for the Second District seat in the Illinois House of Representatives.[51]

Responding to the Gross murder, Cook County Republicans announced that they would purge their party of all eight ward committeemen accused of membership in the West Side Bloc and strip them of the more than three hundred municipal and county jobs they controlled. Stripping the ward committeemen of their patronage jobs would effectively strip them of their ability to deliver the vote. Each job holder was potentially worth nine votes from his family and friends. Additionally, they served as precinct workers at election time, hustling to bring in the vote. Cook County Republicans called on the Democratic Party to follow their lead and discharge those party officials who were members of the West Side Bloc. After the Democrats failed to do so, Republican sheriff John Babb described the Republican effort as "political genocide," because it would strip the Republican Party of its political workers.[52]

Eight days after the Gross murder, a special session of the city council was called to consider crime and corruption in Chicago. The aldermen called for the replacement of police commissioner Timothy J. O'Connor and the creation of a nine-member City Council Emergency Committee on Crime. The "Big Nine," as they were called, began a yearlong investigation into the link between crime and politics in Chicago. Only volume 6 of their 863-page final report was made public. The first five volumes contained names and instances of police and government corruption. The committee was warned not to release these volumes for fear of litigation. Named the "Kohn Report," after the committee's chief investigator, Aaron Kohn, the report concluded that the "criminal syndicate" in Chicago consisted of political officials who maliciously withheld law enforcement power in exchange for money and support from hoodlums, vice operators, professional gamblers, and other community enemies in return for help in furthering their political ambitions.[53]

Chicago's civic leaders were also moved to action by the Gross murder. Within a week, four hundred citizens, including many business leaders, met at the La Salle Hotel to map out a campaign to reform the city and eliminate any link between politics and crime. The group was called the Citizens of Greater Chicago and was led by a committee of nineteen members. The "Big Nineteen," as they came to be known, denounced the West Side Bloc and demanded that a special prosecutor be named to investigate crime and corruption in Chicago. They also endorsed the City Council Emergency Committee on Crime. Within six months, the cry to avenge the death of Charles Gross was all but forgotten as the Big Nineteen became embroiled in a controversy over a city-imposed head tax for suburban workers.[54]

The Gross murder also became an election issue. Fifth Ward Republican alderman Robert Merriam, a member of the city council's Big Nine committee, faced Richard J. Daley in the 1955 mayoral election. Merriam charged that the crime syndicate in Chicago had operated with the political protection of the Democratic Party, the only party that had been in control of city government for the previous twenty-four years, and that if he was elected mayor, he would build a police department that would "break the back" of the crime syndicate. Daley responded that organized crime was a "Republican" problem and that he would end organized crime in Chicago if elected. Merriam, a social reformer, was the "fusion" candidate for mayor. So tired were the people of Chicago of vice, crime, and the Outfit that more than sixteen thousand Republican, Democrat, and independent voters filled Chicago Stadium on March 30, 1955, in support of Merriam and his anti-hoodlum policy.[55]

Despite Daley's promise that the crime syndicate would be driven out of the city if he was elected to the mayor's office, the common expectation was that gambling would run wide open if Richard J. Daley became mayor of Chicago. To the surprise of many, the amount of organized gambling was still down thirteen months after Daley came into office. However, Daley was instrumental in ending the work of the city council's Big Nine committee, and its chief investigator Aaron Kohn was placed under surveillance by the police department's "Red Squad." The failure to "reopen" the town did not sit well with Chicago's underworld, which had helped Daley gain the mayor's office. His victory in the 1955 Democratic primary came largely from the wards controlled by the Outfit's West Side Bloc.[56]

The Gross murder had also led to the discovery that a number of mob figures were on the city and county payrolls. For example, gangster Samuel DeStefano worked as a foreman at a city garbage dump. West Side Bloc member James Adduci was receiving regular county payroll checks under the name James Addison while working as a state representative. Loop gambling boss Louis Briatta, the brother-in-law of First Ward alderman John D'Arco, had a no-show job as a paving foreman. Jerry Cataldo, the president of the journeymen barbers union, had a phantom job as a sewer laborer. He also lived in Elmwood Park, a suburb of Chicago. (Chicago city workers are not permitted to live beyond the city limits). Others who were found with city jobs included bookmaker Nick Cashia and suspected hit man Sam Mesi, who won his city job by delivering votes in the Twenty-sixth Ward. There were also a number of convicted felons on the city payroll, such as Anthony De Rosa, who collected gambling debts for Louis Briatta. Even Tony Accardo's daughter had a job under the sponsorship of a West Side Bloc ward committeeman. When questioned about criminals on the city payroll, Mayor Daley responded that it was the city's policy to rehabilitate men with criminal records by giving them government jobs.[57]

In November 1959 an inmate in the Cook County Jail sent word to state's attorney Benjamin Adamowski that he had information to trade for a reduction in charges. The inmate, Richard Morrison, told state's attorney investigators that he had been involved in a burglary ring with eight Chicago police officers assigned to the Summerdale Police District. The scandal rocked the police department and forced the retirement of Police Commissioner O'Connor. Seeking to reestablish the integrity of the department, Mayor Daley appointed a committee to find a nationally recognized expert to lead the Chicago police. After weeks of searching, the committee chose its own chairman, Orlando W. Wilson, to lead the department. Known as "O. W.," Wilson, a former police officer and college professor, was a student of police organization and management. His book *Police Administration* was viewed as the bible by progressive police managers across the nation. Recognizing that Chicago had an organized crime problem, Wilson appointed now captain Joseph Morris to lead the newly formed Bureau of Inspectional Services to fight police corruption, vice, and organized crime in Chicago. Morris, in turn, appointed his former protégé William Duffy to command the bureau's newly created Intelligence Division and lead the fight against organized crime.[58]

Morris and Duffy lost no time in reorganizing Chicago's efforts against the underworld. Housed in a secret location at Chicago's Navy Pier, the Intelligence Division attacked gambling, narcotics, pornography, and policy gambling. Intelligence Division detectives even cracked a major juice loan operation. Duffy also assisted the McClellan Committee in its investigation of organized crime in Chicago. Following the lead of the federal government, Wilson attempted to have a wiretap law passed in Illinois; however, the West Side Bloc killed the bill. When Wilson left the department, Duffy was demoted by Wilson's successor, James B. Conlisk, for "failing to bend to political pressure." Captain Joseph Morris had already retired. This was the second time that Duffy had been demoted for his efforts against organized crime.[59]

Despite the attention given to Gross's murder, he was not the last political figure to be killed by the Chicago Outfit. After World War II, Chicago's Lawndale community changed from almost 100 percent Jewish to 90 percent black. Jewish political leaders, however, tried to retain control of the ward. The ward had always produced tremendous Democratic majorities at the polls and had been the setting for several major gambling operations. In 1958 Benjamin Lewis, a Negro, was elected alderman. Although he had been brought into politics by the regular Twenty-fourth Ward Democratic organization, Lewis attempted to ease out the white precinct captains and had been talking about keeping a larger share of the ward's gambling money. It was also suspected that he supported the Comet-Neptune-Atlas policy wheel's attempt to remain independent of Outfit control. On February 28, 1963, Lewis was found in his West Side ward office handcuffed to a chair and shot three times in the head.[60]

When asked why people did not organize against the West Side Bloc, Near West Side activist Florence Scala told the *Chicago Daily News* that the bloc's hold was so powerful that people in her community were afraid to vote against it. Murder was a reality to the residents of the First Ward, having lived with it all their lives and seeing people killed on their streets. When asked why they didn't act, Taylor Street residents told Gerald Suttles that there was no use in organizing against the Outfit when they couldn't get city hall to help. As proof, they recalled the failed efforts of the Italian White Hand Society to fight Black Hand extortion. Suttles was working in the Taylor Street community doing research for his 1972 book, *The Social Construction of Communities.* Similar evidence was provided by a local community leader who related that people on Taylor Street were afraid to vote against the Outfit for fear of violence. Residents believed that there was no police protection and that the police could not be trusted. They also believed that the city knew how they voted and that if they voted against the Chicago machine, city property inspectors would show up at their houses the next day and find thousands of dollars in code violations. It was okay to be a social reformer as long as you did not go against the interests of the Outfit and the politicians.[61]

In 1954 Richard B. Ogilvie, a member of the Young Republican Club of Cook County, joined the U.S. Attorney's Office in Chicago. A World War II tank commander, Ogilvie was especially alarmed by revelations of growing gangland power in Chicago. In 1958 he was appointed to the attorney general's task force on organized crime. Ogilvie was assigned to the Chicago office, one of four set up by the government in response to the 1957 underworld conclave in which sixty-seven gangsters were found meeting in Appalachian New York. For the next two years, he directed a special grand jury investigating the Chicago Outfit. Ogilvie's work, however, seemed to be blocked at every turn. Although promised a staff of lawyers and investigators, he was given one assistant—Bill Carey. Even the FBI in Chicago had strict orders from J. Edgar Hoover to limit their cooperation. Hoover had publicly stated that he did not believe in the existence of organized crime. Despite these obstacles, Ogilvie and Carey were able to convict Tony Accardo on charges of income tax evasion, but the case was later overturned by an appellate court.[62]

Upon leaving the U.S. Attorney's Office, Ogilvie again became active in Republican politics. Addressing the Cook County Republican Veteran's League in 1961, Ogilvie charged that the federal government was failing in its responsibility to stop Syndicate crime. He also charged that FBI director Hoover had not kept up with the times. Ogilvie argued that Hoover, and other policy makers, viewed the fight against organized crime as a local law enforcement problem but that local agencies were hopelessly inadequate to cope with this menace. While the federal government may not have had the jurisdiction to fight organized crime, the FBI did begin the "Top Hoodlum Program" in 1953 to collect information on America's gangsters. Proving to be the one political leader who stood firm against the mob, Ogilvie ran for Cook County sheriff in 1962, arguing that organized crime was the biggest business in Chicago and that law enforcement had done nothing to suppress Syndicate leaders.[63]

Ogilvie was right about the organized crime problem in Chicago. Local law enforcement was helpless largely because of the political power of the mob. The Outfit sold narcotics, muscled labor unions, and forced saloon keepers and restaurant owners to install their jukeboxes and pinball machines. They also ran handbooks, dice games, gambling casinos, and brothels. The *Chicago Daily Tribune* estimated that the Outfit controlled one thousand places in Chicago and suburban Cook County where a person could gamble in one form or another—all made possible by a powerful alliance between elected officials and crooked politicians. The Outfit was so powerful that virtually every organized illegal activity came under its control. When members of the Outfit heard of an independent gambling operation or a tavern where strippers and bar girls solicited drinks, they demanded a percentage of the profit to ensure police protection and peace with the Outfit.[64]

Ogilvie's run for sheriff so troubled the Outfit that word came down from mob leader Sam Giancana that Ogilvie's candidacy had to be stopped. The Outfit had a substantial investment in suburban Cook County that would be threatened by an unfriendly sheriff. In south suburban Calumet City, for example, gambling and strip clubs ran all night. According to the Chicago Crime Commission, wide-open gambling also flourished in the suburbs of Forest Park, Melrose Park, and Lyons.[65]

Mounting public disapproval of crime conditions led to a Republican victory in the sheriff's race. Ogilvie defeated the Democratic candidate, Roswell Spencer, chief investigator for the Cook County state's attorney. Once in office, Ogilvie declared war on the Chicago Outfit. One of his first official acts was to appoint Arthur Bilek chief of the sheriff's police. Bilek was the director of training for the Chicago Police Department and had earlier gained a squeaky-clean reputation while assigned to organized crime investigations under Republican state's attorney Benjamin Adamowski.[66]

Within a month of taking office, Ogilvie's police, working with the Chicago Police Department, arrested 250 people in gambling raids throughout Chicago and suburban Cook County. Ogilvie's police even raided mob-infested Cicero, Illinois, clamping down on gambling and vice activity in the suburb. Cicero was especially famous for its striptease shows. Clubs like the Dream Bar featured women who stripped down to their G-strings, coaxed on by the applause of the excited clientele. The sheriff's police department established sixteen-hour-a-day uniformed patrols in Cicero to ensure that vice activity did not reopen. Ogilvie also presented Cicero police chief Erwin Konovsky with a ten-point plan to clamp down on criminal activity and threatened to ask the state's attorney to charge Konovsky with malfeasance if he did not implement the plan. So aggressive were Ogilvie's efforts that his men arrested future mob boss Joey "Doves" Auippa for the attempted bribery of police officer Donald Shaw stemming from a Cicero gambling case.[67]

Ogilvie also clamped down on vice activity in the unincorporated areas of Cook County, where vice often ran openly. Unincorporated areas are those that are not governed by any village or municipality. Administratively, their control falls under the Cook County Board of Commissioners, and they are under the law enforcement jurisdiction of the Cook County sheriff. The vast size of the county, weak township government, and lax enforcement by the sheriff made these areas prime locations for crime syndicate activities. Gambling houses such as Vic's Tavern and the Ballard Inn in Main Township, the Sunrise Inn in Leyden Township, the Forest Lounge in Niles Township, and the Wagon Wheel and Norwood House in Norwood Park Township flourished in the unincorporated areas. Vice activity in these areas became particularly important before a Chicago mayoral election, because the Outfit provided financial support without which the ward and precinct organizations could not function.[68]

Ogilvie's success and popularity as sheriff propelled him to the presidency of the Cook County Board of Commissioners in 1966 and two years later to the office of governor of the state of Illinois. Within a year of taking the governor's office, Ogilvie created the Illinois Bureau of Investigation to fight organized crime and drug trafficking in the state. The IBI, as it came to be known, was intended to be state's version of the Federal Bureau of Investigation. Despite the need for heightened enforcement against the crime syndicate in Chicago, liberal reformers and Chicago mayor Richard J. Daley fought the creation of the IBI, fearing a "super police" state. Richard Ogilvie was ultimately a one-term governor, losing to Democrat Daniel Walker in 1972. Ogilvie's loss was blamed on his support for a state income tax. Like Ogilvie, Walker was also a one-term governor, losing to former U.S. Attorney James R. Thompson in 1976. Thompson, who was generally viewed as a reformer, disbanded the IBI, forever ending the state's efforts against organized crime.[69]

In 1967 the Chicago Crime Commission issued a report titled "Spotlight on Organized Crime." In it the commission reported that the revenue received by organized crime from gambling and other illicit activities was being used to infiltrate almost every sector of legitimate business, from liquor sales to coin-operated vending machines. Once established in a legitimate business, the Outfit sought to create a monopoly through extortion and the threat of violence. Many of these businesses revolved around tavern operations. Corner taverns often doubled as bookmaking operations where local residents could bet on their favorite horse race. Taverns also needed towels, jukeboxes, pinball machines, and other amusement devices, all of which could be provided by legitimate businesses affiliated with the mob. In their report, the crime commission listed ten businesses that were owned outright by Outfit members. An additional thirty-one businesses employed a member of the Outfit, were owned by a relative of a member of the Outfit, or were owned by "associates" of members of the Outfit. In 1969 the crime commission added an additional thirty businesses to the list, for a total of seventy-three legitimate businesses in the Chicago area that had some relationship to organized crime.[70]

One industry targeted by the Outfit was the jukebox business. In 1970 Illinois attorney general William Scott filed an antitrust suit against the Outfit's domination of the jukebox racket. Of the 7,745 licensed jukeboxes in Chicago, all but 83 were under a monopoly controlled by the Chicago Outfit. Prime targets of the suit included the Commercial Phonograph Survey and the Recorded Music Service Association, two trade groups that allegedly conspired to restrain trade through the regulation of the jukebox industry. Under the monopoly setup, no tavern owner or businessman was allowed to own his own jukebox or to lease one from a distributor that was not a member of the group. Another target was the Outfit-controlled Lomar Distributing, which had a monopoly on supplying the phonograph records used in the jukebox machines. Although the state prevailed in the litigation, the two convicted protective associations paid their fines by collecting a "special assessment" from the jukebox operators: the very victims of the jukebox racket![71]

Also at the state level, the Illinois Law Enforcement Commission, led by Ogilvie's former police chief Arthur Bilek, awarded a grant to the Illinois Institute of Technology and the Chicago Crime Commission to study organized crime in Illinois. The commission was created by the Illinois General Assembly to serve as the state's official criminal justice planning agency. Their final report, *A Study of Organized Crime in Illinois*, was published in 1971. The study concluded that

- Large-scale organized crime, both Outfit and not, existed in all major Illinois communities.
- Organized crime persisted because it catered to the public's desire for illicit goods and services.
- Organized crime persisted because a sufficient number of influential politicians and criminal justice officials had been corrupted.
- A continuing conspiracy existed between racketeers, politicians, businessmen, and labor and government officials to extract unearned dollars from both willing victims and unknowing customers.
- The people of Illinois were ambivalent in their attitudes about organized crime.
- A large majority of the population wanted and used the services offered by organized crime.
- Organized crime had caused a state of fear and continuing anxiety in the minds of the citizens in many parts of the state.[72]

Data was gathered for the study through a review of court records; interviews of federal, state, and municipal officials; and a household survey conducted in four hundred separate locations throughout the state. The household survey found that 20 percent of all Illinois residents—an astonishing 2,016,231 people—had firsthand contact with organized crime, whether through gambling, narcotics, or some other form of illegal activity. Seventy-five percent of the same surveyed population believed that organized crime was securing important favors from local politicians, and 62 percent believed that organized crime was securing protection from police personnel. Finally, 86 percent of the survey population wished that something could be done to stamp out organized crime in Illinois.[73]

The Federal Government Begins to Act

The Kefauver and McClellan hearings exposed the American public to the threat of organized crime in a way that had not been done before. Organized crime was now part of the national agenda. Between January 1967 and April 1971 the Justice Department's Organized Crime and Racketeering Section, established in 1954, created eighteen federal "strike forces" to fight organized crime in major cities across the country staffed with assistant U.S. attorneys and representatives from federal law enforcement agencies.[74]

In 1965 Lyndon Johnson formed the President's Commission on Law Enforcement and the Administration of Justice. As part of this effort, Johnson directed the Department of Justice, the secretary of the treasury, and the heads of the other federal law enforcement agencies to submit legislative proposals to Congress that would strengthen and expand their enforcement efforts against organized crime. As a result, Congress passed a series of laws aimed at eradicating organized crime in America. The Omnibus Crime Control and Safe Streets Act of 1968 authorized wiretapping and electronic surveillance to collect evidence in criminal investigations. The Organized Crime Control Act of 1970 authorized the creation of special grand juries to investigate crime, the issuing of grants of immunity to witnesses, and created the witness protection program. Title IX of the act created a racketeering statute. The Racketeer Influenced and Corrupt Organizations (RICO) Act is a group of federal laws passed by the United States Congress to deal with organized crime. RICO is specifically directed at individuals or organizations involved in systematic, long-term illegal activities. It increases criminal penalties and allows civil claims to be pursued by the injured parties. A person can be charged with racketeering under the RICO statutes if within a ten-year time period he or she, as part of a criminal enterprise, commits two crimes from a list of predicate offenses.[75]

Despite these growing federal efforts against organized crime, a new effort was made by the Outfit to expand its activities. Led by Taylor Street gangster Joseph "Joe Nagal" Ferriola, a group of young Turks referred to by the FBI as the "Black Leather Jacket Bunch" began a renewed effort in the 1970s to bring all independent bookmakers, off-track messenger services, and pornography shops under the Outfit's control. This was usually accomplished through a demand for "street tax," payments made to the Outfit for the right to conduct illegal activities such as gambling. Those locations that did not pay were targeted for violence, and their proprietors were often beaten and even killed. The imposition of street tax on illegal activity not only increased revenue but also provided a way for a shrinking Outfit to control criminal activity. Part of the reason for a smaller Outfit was reluctance on the part of the mob hierarchy to share profits and recruit new members. Instead, the Outfit "franchised" the right to conduct criminal activity such as bookmaking. Rather than collect the bets themselves, they taxed independent bookmakers for the right to gamble and provided such services as the collection of overdue gambling losses.[76]

Those reluctant to pay were often the victims of violent retribution. When pornographic movie distributor Rene Nawodylo refused to split 50 percent of his profits with the Outfit, his warehouse in Chicago was bombed. Bookmaker Hal Smith was found dead in the trunk of his car after he refused to pay street tax and began talking to federal authorities. The renewed push by the Outfit to control criminal activities in Chicago led to as many as twenty-eight gangland executions. Gangsters killed not only reluctant victims but also each other in an attempt to seize a greater share of the illegal profits, or to prevent members who were on their way to prison from cooperating with government authorities.[77]

Much of the violence was carried out by Joe Ferriola's nephew, Harry Aleman. He was the "hammer" of the Chicago mob. One of the killings he was charged with was the 1972 murder of Teamsters Union steward William Logan.[78] Even though Aleman had been identified by an eyewitness, he was acquitted in a bench trial before Cook County judge Frank Wilson. It later came out that Wilson received a ten-thousand-dollar bribe from attorney Robert Cooley to throw the case. Aleman was later retried and convicted of killing Logan. The case made history in that it was the first time a defendant had been tried again after an acquittal. The court determined that Aleman had not been put in jeopardy during the first trial. He was sentenced to one hundred years in prison.

When Jane Byrne became Chicago's mayor in 1979, she forced James E. O'Grady, the superintendent of police, to resign. O'Grady had openly supported incumbent mayor Michael Bilandic in the mayoral primary. In O'Grady's place, Byrne appointed former homicide commander Joseph Di Leonardi as acting superintendent of police. Di Leonardi immediately appointed William Duffy to lead the Bureau of Inspectional Services and the department's Intelligence Division. Duffy's appointment signaled a crackdown on organized crime. Almost immediately, police stepped up gambling enforcement in the First Ward. Di Leonardi also moved to clean up the scandal-ridden police motor maintenance division. The U.S. attorney in Chicago was investigating reports of double billing for supplies by First Ward political appointees working at the police motor pool.[79]

Before long Di Leonardi was called to city hall by mayoral aides William Griffin and Michael Brady, who informed him that John D'Arco, the First Ward Democratic committeeman, wanted Duffy demoted. Di Leonardi refused and withdrew his application to become Chicago's permanent police superintendent. Government informant and mob insider Robert Cooley wrote in his book *When Corruption Was King* that First Ward alderman Fred Roti had explained to him that Jane Byrne had been told that either she must get rid of Di Leonardi or municipal unions would shut down the city during upcoming contract negotiations. Such was the power of the Chicago Outfit, of which Roti was a "made member." Soon Di Leonardi, Duffy, and James Zurowski, who had run the police garage for Di Leonardi, were demoted to meaningless jobs and banished from police headquarters. It was the third time Duffy had been demoted for his stand against organized crime. What was even worse, this time the department tried to justify the demotion by labeling Duffy a stumblebum and a fraud, questioning his reputation as a crime fighter. Then police superintendent Richard Brzeczek, who had been appointed by Byrne to succeed Di Leonardi, went so far as to claim that the charges made by Di Leonardi, Duffy, and Zurowski were baseless and that the three men were "shooting their mouths off because they were demoted." Byrne's concern for D'Arco's wishes may have stemmed from the fact that D'Arco had arranged a reconciliation between Byrne and her two political enemies, aldermen Edward Vrdolyak and Edward Burke.[80]

Although Byrne had succumbed to pressure from D'Arco and the First Ward, the police department actually stepped up its enforcement efforts against the Outfit. Veteran gambling investigator Donald Herion was placed in charge of a special squad to attack syndicated gambling, and Captain Julian Gallet was placed in command of the Intelligence Division. Gallet had a vision of police and federal agents working together to build cases against organized crime. Under his command, Chicago police continually raided the Outfit's dice and barbooth (a Middle Eastern dice game) games and worked with the FBI on the "Operation Chisel" chop shop investigation. Intelligence officers were also instrumental in arresting members of the FALN (Fuerzas Armadas de Liberación Nacional), a Puerto Rican terrorist group, who had planted explosives in downtown Chicago.[81]

The election of Ronald Reagan in 1981 brought new pressure on the mob. Reagan appointed a national commission to study organized crime. Headed by former New York judge Irving R. Kaufman, hearings were held throughout the country to develop new remedies to cripple America's crime syndicates. Reagan had firsthand experience with organized crime when as a member of the Screen Actors Guild he watched as the Chicago Outfit tried to muscle in on the motion picture industry. The commission recommended that an aggressive effort be launched to root out organized crime, concluding that previous efforts had been disorganized and largely ineffective. The commission also recommended that steps be taken to rid labor unions of mob influence through the extended use of electronic surveillance, aggressive enforcement of federal anti-racketeering laws, and the decertification of unions that were found to be mob-controlled.[82]

It wasn't long before the Outfit's luck began to change. In 1986 mob boss Joseph Auippa and three other Chicago gangsters were convicted in a Kansas City trial of skimming profits from the Stardust casino in Las Vegas. Skimming is the practice of removing money from a casino counting room before income taxes are determined. Gambling has been legal in Las Vegas since 1931. In 1946 the Chicago Outfit invested money to build the Flamingo Hotel, one of the earliest on the Las Vegas strip. Through their influence with the Teamsters Central States' Pension Fund, the Outfit arranged financing for San Diego businessman Allen Glick to purchase the Stardust Hotel and Casino in 1974. Over the next ten years, Auippa and company skimmed two million dollars in profits from the casino. Chicago gangster Anthony Spilotro, Chicago's man in Vegas, not only watched over their investment in the Stardust Hotel, but he also collected gambling debts and ran a juice loan operation.[83]

In 1990 the federal government brought a RICO prosecution against members of the Chicago Outfit. There had been prosecutions of Chicago gangsters before, but never a RICO case. After years of prosecuting individual gangsters, the government announced a three-pronged racketeering attack against organized crime in Chicago. The first case, known within the government as the "Commission" investigation, was expected to bring indictments against the bosses of Chicago's five street crews. The second, an attack on the mob's political influence in Chicago, was directed at First Ward alderman Fred Roti and First Ward Democratic committeeman John D'Arco. The third was a racketeering prosecution of the Joseph Ferriola Street Crew.[84]

The first case to be announced was the indictment of mob chieftain Rocco Infelise and nineteen other members of the Ferriola Street Crew. Infelise commanded the crew after Ferriola's death. The indictment charged the crew with using murder, intimidation, and payoffs to protect their illegal operations. A key factor in obtaining the indictments was the cooperation of William Jahoda, a member of the Ferriola Street Crew, who had turned to the government for protection, fearing he was on the outs with fellow mobsters. After a week of deliberation, the jury returned a combination of convictions, acquittals, and indecisions. Although all of those prosecuted were not convicted, the case was the beginning of a series of federal prosecutions that would help to bring the Chicago Outfit to its knees.[85]

Six months after the Ferriola indictment, veteran gangster Lenny Patrick and four others were indicted by the U.S. Attorney's Office for extorting substantial sums of money from the owners of various restaurants, car dealerships, and illegal gambling operations. Although this case was not among the three announced earlier, it was a significant step against organized crime. The victims were apparently chosen because they had some familiarity with the Chicago Outfit. All total, the defendants collected $376,000 from their victims, which included the restaurants Billy and Company, Hole in the Wall, Myron and Phil's, and Father and Son Pizza as well as King Nissan and the Motor Werks of Barrington. The group also sought to collect an illegal gambling debt from contractor Alex Tapper and to impose street tax on two illegal gambling businesses. They were also charged with trying to set fire to the Lake Theater in order to settle "union problems." In a surprising turn of events, Patrick agreed to cooperate with the government and testified against his boss, Gus Alex, making him the highest-ranking mobster ever to become a government witness.[86]

The attack on the mob's political influence was dubbed "Operation Gambat," a code name for "gambling attorney," referring to FBI informant Robert Cooley.[87] First Ward alderman Fred Roti, First Ward Democratic Party secretary Pat Marcy, Illinois state senator John D'Arco Jr., and former Cook County chancery judge David Shields were all indicted by the federal government for what was described by the *Chicago Daily Tribune* as a "Corruption Feast." The importance of the investigation was that it finally broke the connection between organized crime and politics in Chicago. Roti was charged with accepting money to "fix" a Chinatown murder trial, and Marcy was charged with bribing Judge Frank Wilson in the murder trial of Syndicate killer Harry Aleman. Senator D'Arco Jr. was charged with accepting money to introduce a bill in the Illinois General Assembly to expand the kinds of insurance sold by travel agents.

While not the "Commission" case mentioned earlier, the Justice Department announced another racketeering prosecution in 1992 when eleven members of the Outfit's Carlisi Street Crew were indicted. The indictment charged that Samuel "Wings" Carlisi and his codefendants ran an extensive sports bookmaking operation and had engaged in loan sharking, extortion, attempted arson, and income tax evasion in furtherance of their criminal enterprise. The crew also financed Lenny Patrick's juice loan operation. They operated in west suburban Cook County and DuPage County, Illinois. All but one, Joseph Braccio, were convicted in federal court.[88]

In 1997 the Chicago Crime Commission reported that despite this impressive string of prosecutions, the federal government had not yet killed off the mob. Down but not out, the Outfit reorganized into three street crews, rather than five, and renounced the indiscriminate use of violence. The mob now had fewer members and made less money. RICO had made street crew bosses just as guilty of mob murders as the guys who pulled the trigger. The mob had also found a new source of revenue: video poker machines. Video poker was a perfect source of revenue for the Outfit. The machines were growing in popularity and were legal, but they could be used in an illegal fashion—they could be used to gamble.[89]

Even after the convictions of Roti and D'Arco, the influence of the Outfit was still felt in Chicago's city hall. Rather than purchase its own trucks, the city of Chicago often leased them through the "Hired Truck Program." A 2004 exposé by the *Chicago Sun Times* found that one out of every ten trucking firms in the city's program was owned by alleged mobsters, Outfit associates, and family members. Trucking companies wanting to work in the program had to go through city employee Nick "The Stick" Coco, a reputed mob loan shark. The trucking companies doing business with the city were owned by such Outfit luminaries as loan shark Jimmy Inendino, bookmaker Gregory Paloian, and Fred Roti's nephew Fred Barbara, who earlier had tried to collect a twenty-thousand-dollar juice loan from an undercover FBI agent. City government had become one of the Outfit's most lucrative rackets.[90]

On April 25, 2005, the Justice Department announced that it had indicted the Chicago Outfit as a "criminal enterprise." Dubbed "Operation Family Secrets," fourteen gangsters were arrested on charges stemming from murder to bookmaking and tax fraud. Described by U.S. Attorney Patrick Fitzgerald, as a "hit on the mob," the case was a milestone event in the battle against organized crime. What made this case particularly important was that it charged the defendants with committing seventeen murders in furtherance of crime syndicate activities. The murders occurred between 1970 and 1986 and read like a history of organized crime in Chicago. One man, Frank Calabrese, was charged with participating in thirteen of the alleged killings. He was so feared that his own brother and son testified against him in the Family Secrets trial. Calabrese, Joseph "Joey the Clown" Lombardo, and James "Little Jimmy" Marcello were found guilty of participating in ten murders. Three others were convicted on racketeering charges. The jury remained deadlocked, however, on the remaining eight cases.[91]

In spite of the far-reaching effect of the Family Secret's prosecution, west suburban rackets boss, Michael "The Large Guy" Sarno, was indicted in May 2009 by the federal government and accused of leading an illegal gambling ring and playing a key role in the 2003 pipe bombing of a competitor's video poker business.[92] Six others, including Outlaw motorcycle gang members Anthony and Samuel Volpendesto and Mark Polchan, were also charged with racketeering conspiracy. The ring was alleged to have committed jewelry heists, auto theft, arson, and witness intimidation. Sarno allegedly oversaw nine robberies and thefts that yielded more than $1.8 million. The six-week trial proved that Sarno had carved out an alliance between the Chicago Outfit and the Outlaws motorcycle gang.

Today the Outfit is a mere shadow of its former self, but it still exists. As long as society seeks to regulate vice, there will be a role for the Outfit to play. While the Illinois Lottery and riverboat gambling have cut into the Outfit's take, they have not eliminated it. People still bet with bookies and people still make juice loans.

7

THE OUTFIT AS A COMPLEX ORGANIZATION

Since the 1950s, sociologists have debated the structure of organized crime in American society. Two basic positions have emerged. The first portrays a nationwide association of Italian American criminals bound together by a rigid code of conduct within a rational, bureaucratic structure with an elaborate division of labor and detailed general rules of conduct. The second presents a system of Italian American criminal units tied together by a patrimonial network of social relationships within a structure that is not rational, but traditional.

This debate places organized crime somewhere on a continuum between a rationally defined formal organization and a naturally organized criminal group. As a rational organization, American organized crime, or the Cosa Nostra, would be organized in the pursuit of relatively specific goals and would exhibit a formal social structure. In contrast, the natural systems perspective maintains that members of the Cosa Nostra are not necessarily guided by their organization's goals but that they share a common interest in the survival of the system and engage in collective activities informally structured to secure this end. They are, fundamentally, social groups attempting to adapt and survive in their particular circumstances. As such, these organizations can be seen as ends in themselves.

The view that organized crime follows a bureaucratic structure can be traced to the work of the 1967 President's Task Force on Organized Crime.[1] The task force detailed the internal structure of each crime family and argued that the Cosa Nostra closely resembled a formal organization. They described organized crime as a complex system, like a business or government bureaucracy, with a specialized division of labor rationally designed to achieve specific goals. The report presented a picture of a hierarchical organization with orders coming from the top and passing through various levels to the workers, who operate under official rules of conduct that are based upon the code of the Sicilian Mafia.

In contrast to the findings of the President's Task Force is a view that conceives of the Cosa Nostra as a band of ethnic criminal gangs whose structure can best be understood in terms of culture and kinship and patron-client relationships. Italian American crime families are not formal organizations like governments or business corporations, rationally structured in order to maximize profits and carry out tasks efficiently. Rather, they are traditional social systems, organized by action and by cultural values that have nothing to do with modern bureaucratic virtues. Francis Ianni and Elizabeth Reuss-Ianni argue that Italian American organized crime can be better explained by examining kinship networks. Membership is based simply on blood, marriage, godparenthood, and fictive kinship.[2]

The bureaucratic view of organized crime has also been criticized by Joseph Albini, who writes that the Cosa Nostra consists of a number of criminal syndicates in a loose system of power relationships, in contrast to a rigidly organized secret society. He characterizes the bureaucratic model as the "evolutional" approach, which assumes that Italian American organized crime represents the evolution of the Sicilian Mafia. On the other hand, Albini offers the "developmental" approach, which argues that organized crime emerged from social conditions and factors within American society itself.[3]

Howard Abadinsky also takes exception to the bureaucratic model of organized crime. Although he found that rules and other signs of formal organization do exist, he contends that patron-client networks are better able to describe the structure of organized crime than bureaucratic analogies. For example, he states that the soldiers of an organized crime family act as patrons to nonmember clients, both legitimate and criminal. The soldier, in turn, is a client of a higher-ranking member, a lieutenant. These lieutenants form the group that surrounds the boss. The bosses form a loose network based upon kinship, friendship, mutual interest, and tradition.[4]

There have been attempts to integrate rational and natural systems theory into what has been described as the open systems perspective. One such attempt, the contingency model, might help to explain the true organizational nature of the Cosa Nostra. Contingency theory argues that the form an organization takes is determined by its environment. The more homogeneous and stable the environment, the more appropriate will be a formalized and hierarchical form; the more diverse and changing, the more appropriate a less formalized organic form. This is the contingency argument: there is no one best way to organize. Organizations have fluid structures that adapt to changes in their environment.[5]

The contingency argument is supported by the work of Annelise Anderson.[6] Anderson's research revealed that organized crime has a hierarchical structure similar to that described by Donald Cressey, though not as complex. She found that Cosa Nostra groups did have positions for boss, underboss, and so on, but they also included various "associates" who were not true members. These associates carried out many activities necessary for the success of the organization. They ran both illegitimate gambling activities and legitimate business fronts for the criminal organization.

This chapter attempts to resolve the ongoing debate surrounding the structure of traditional organized crime through an examination of the Outfit, Chicago's traditional organized crime group. The Syndicate/Outfit has been in existence since the early 1930s, a period of some eighty years. Although its activities have been severely curtailed, it continues to exist today and continues to be organized in much the same way as it has since the 1950s.

The formal structure of the Outfit in Chicago is well defined. Newspaper and law enforcement accounts of its activities suggest that positions exist for bosses, members, and associates, who are said to be "connected." Additionally, the data gathered for this analysis suggests that at the height of its influence the Chicago Outfit also had an organized public made up of gamblers, thieves, and wannabes (people who want to be associated with the Outfit), who provided a ready source of participants for organized criminal activities as well as recruits for the Outfit itself.

This chapter is divided into two sections. In the first section, I describe the formal structure of the Chicago Outfit and its criminal activities. In addition, I argue that people who are connected to organized crime are, in fact, part of the organizational structure. In the second section, I describe the people with whom the Outfit is regularly in contact and suggest that they, too, are an integral part of the organization.

The Criminal Organization

A review of the history of the Chicago Outfit indicates that it has been described in a number of different ways. For example, in 1967 the Chicago Crime Commission divided the "Chicago Syndicate" into six geographically based subdivisions: the Chicago Loop, the Near North Side, the Far North and Northwest suburbs, the Far West and West suburbs, the South Side, and the South and Southwest suburbs. In 1970 the *Chicago Today* newspaper divided the Chicago "Crime Syndicate" into four segments: Cicero, Melrose Park, the North Side, and the South Side. The creation of the Cicero group in the 1970s can be explained by the fact that then syndicate boss Joey Auippa maintained an office in Cicero, Illinois. In 1983 the *Chicago Tribune* divided the "Chicago Mob" into South Suburban and Indiana, Lake County, Milwaukee, Las Vegas, and South, West, and North Side groups. In 1985 the *Chicago Sun-Times* divided the Outfit into three segments: the West Group, the South Group, and the North Group. A similar division (North, South, and West Sides) was made by the Chicago Crime Commission in 1997.[7]

Law enforcement, however, divided the Outfit differently. In 1981 the Chicago Police Department divided the "Chicago Crime Syndicate" into five sections named for each of the group's leaders: Vincent Solano, Joseph Lombardo, Joseph Ferriola, Angelo La Pietra, and Al Pilotto. A similar list was published by the Chicago Crime Commission and the Illinois attorney general in 1983. These groups were further defined in 1987 when the Chicago police assigned geographic names to them: Chicago Heights, Taylor Street, Twenty-sixth Street, Grand Avenue, Rush Street, and the North Side.[8] Somewhere along the line these groups became known as the "street crews" of the Chicago Outfit. Street crews are organizational groupings in which the Outfit's activities are carried out.

The Chicago Crime Commission reported in 1990 that there were six street crews, but characterized them as Twenty-sixth Street, the West Side, Elmwood Park, the North Side, Grand Avenue, and Lake County. They also stated that there were sixty-six members of the Outfit, but that more than three hundred additional people derived significant portions of their income from mob activities. The members of the West Side, Elmwood Park, and Lake County Street Crews as indicated by the Crime Commission by and large corresponded to the members of the Taylor Street Crew as indicated by the Chicago Police Department. The need for this further diversification of the Taylor Street Crew can be explained by two factors: the resettlement of many Taylor Street residents in the suburb of Elmwood Park and the Taylor Street Crew's eventual takeover of gambling in the Lake County, Illinois area.[9]

The Twenty-sixth Street Crew is also referred to as the "Chinatown Crew" because of its proximity to Chicago's Chinese community. The Rush Street Crew was added to the 1987 Chicago Police Department chart because of the division of the North Side Crew. The Rush Street and North Side Crews had traditionally been one but were divided into two separate crews during the 1980s. The North Side Crew, made up of mobsters from other sections of Chicago, was brought into the area to handle organized crime activities north of Fullerton Avenue and into the northern suburbs. The Rush Street Crew was made up of the remnants of the original North Side Crew, who continued to control what little organized crime activities remained in the Rush Street area. One explanation for the division of the North Side Crew was the unavailability of new recruits in the Near North Side neighborhood. This community has been completely changed because of social and economic development and is no longer viewed as an organized crime community. The old neighborhood in which North Side organized crime activity was previously centered no longer exists.

The 1990 racketeering prosecution of Rocco Infelise and a group of Chicago Outfit members gives an inside look at street crew activities. In all, twenty members of the Chicago Outfit were indicted and charged with forty-two counts of racketeering. According to the indictment, there existed in Chicago a criminal organization sometimes referred to as the "Joseph Ferriola Street Crew." This street crew was part of a larger criminal organization commonly referred to as the Chicago Outfit or the Chicago Mob. The Ferriola Street Crew is another name for the Taylor Street Crew. Joseph Ferriola was the boss of the Taylor Street Crew during much of the time of this investigation. The indictment states that the Ferriola Crew existed primarily for the purpose of providing income to its members in several ways, including the operation of various illegal gambling businesses such as sports bookmaking, parlay cards, and casino games; the collection of interest, known as "juice," on usurious loans made by the enterprise; the collecting of protection money, known as "street tax," from various illegitimate as well as questionably legitimate businesses; and the use of the proceeds from those activities in the enterprise and in other business ventures.[10]

In order to accomplish the purposes of their criminal conspiracy, members of the Ferriola Street Crew were charged in the indictment with the murder of a number of people who either posed a threat to the street crew or who failed to pay street tax for operating various illegal enterprises. Members of the crew were also charged with engaging in an illegal gambling business and extortionate credit practices stemming from that business. In addition, some crew members were charged with failing to file federal income taxes.

The indictment also states that it was the purpose of the Ferriola Street Crew to recruit and retain members and to maintain loyalty, discipline, and control over the members of the illegal enterprise. In order to carry out these activities, the street crew maintained the following structure: a leader or boss, assistants to the boss, supervisors of the various income-producing activities, and agents and employees who were compensated out of the earnings of the enterprise.

The role of the boss of each street crew was further defined in the 1992 RICO indictment of Sam Carlisi and eleven other members of the Outfit in

Chicago. This indictment states that the boss of the crew was ultimately responsible to the head of the Outfit and was required to ensure that the leadership of the Outfit received a share of the proceeds from the crew's activities.

As described in the previous chapter, fourteen members of the Chicago Outfit were indicted in 2005 by the U.S. Justice Department for participating in a forty-year-long RICO conspiracy after a lengthy FBI-led investigation code-named Operation Family Secrets. The indictment set forth a detailed overview of the Outfit's structure, chain of command, and criminal activities. According to the Justice Department, the Outfit's criminal activities were carried out by subgroups called street crews that were known by their geographic names and included the Elmwood Park Street Crew, the Rush Street/North Side Street Crew, the South Side/Twenty-sixth Street/Chinatown Street Crew, the Grand Avenue Street Crew, the Melrose Park Street Crew, and the Chicago Heights Street Crew. Each of the street crews was led by a leader known as a street boss or capo.[11]

The purpose of the street crews was criminal activity. Their substantive crimes included murder in furtherance of Outfit business, collection of street tax to allow illegal businesses to operate, usurious juice loans, and illegal gambling.[12] They also committed other crimes to facilitate the operation of the criminal enterprise, including obstruction of justice, witness intimidation, and income tax evasion. Illegal violence was also used to instill discipline within the organization and to punish members whose conduct was adverse to the continuation of the Outfit's interests.

Each street crew, for the most part, acted independently of the other crews, and each boss was solely responsible for the activities of his crew. However, they worked together as needed. The head of the Outfit, the boss, settled disputes between the crews and handled relations with those outside the organization, such as corrupt public officials and organized crime groups in other cities. However, he was more of an arbitrator than a director of a large corporation. The street crews deferred to his authority in order to avoid violence and the news media attention that is associated with it. The meetings in which disputes were settled were referred to as "sit-downs."[13]

The Chicago Crime Commission reported in 1990 that a capo, or captain, was in charge of each of the street crews and that each crew was composed of "made guys," who were sometimes referred to as "soldiers," and associates who were said to be "connected." In charge of all the crews was a boss and a second in command, an "underboss." There were also advisors, who were usually older successful members who served as elder statesman.[14]

This position is supported by the Family Secrets investigation, which reported that each crew was led by a crew leader or "street boss," also known as a capo. These crew bosses reported to an underboss, or *sotto capo*, who was second in command of the Outfit. The Outfit also utilized a "consigliere," who provided advice to the boss. There is some disagreement, however, about the various terms used to describe positions within the Outfit. Informants report that members of the Chicago Outfit never use the terms *soldier, capo* or *consigliere*. These terms originated in New York with Joe Valachi. Valachi, a self-admitted member of the New York Genovese crime family, supplied the terms when he testified before the Senate Permanent Subcommittee on Investigations (McClellan Committee) in 1963 regarding the existence and structure of organized crime in America.[15]

There is a definite distinction between being a made guy and being a worker within the Chicago Outfit. To be a made guy, one has to be a boss or a person of special status within the organization, and not just a member. The head of the Outfit and his advisors are made guys. The heads of the street crews and their "lieutenants," persons with a definite area of responsibility, are also said to be made guys. Being a made guy grants certain rights and privileges that other members do not have. Made guys manage the operations, give orders, and profit more than everybody else. Becoming the boss of a crew is a good indication that the member has been "made." Associating with made guys and assuming responsibility within the organization is also an indication of who is likely to be a made guy.[16]

To be a made guy one also has to be Italian, and not just any kind of Italian, but southern Italian, Neapolitan, or Sicilian. Some non-Italians carry great stature within the Outfit because of their advanced age or accomplishments within the organization, but they are not made guys. Take Jewish gangster Lenny Patrick, for example. Patrick grew up in the West Side of Chicago and went to the penitentiary for armed robbery. After he came out, he went to work for the Outfit booking horses and eventually controlled gambling in the Jewish community. Although he was a boss and killer in his own right, he could never be a made guy, because he was not Italian.[17]

The requirement that made guys must be Italian did not exist in the Capone syndicate, whose leaders were largely non-Italian. This new requirement has helped to ensure that members of the Outfit share the same values and has helped to prevent infiltration of the organization.[18] Many of the early southern Italian and Sicilian immigrants who were attracted to organized crime subscribed to the code of *omerta* (manliness) and had lived under a Mafia-dominated social order before coming to the United States, both of which facilitated their participation in organized crime. Today, the requirement of being Italian accomplishes a similar goal. Although the average recruit today has never been exposed to the Mafia, many were raised in neighborhood areas where organized crime was part of the social structure, thus ensuring that potential recruits have been exposed to values that are conducive to life in the rackets.

It is commonly believed that to become a made guy one must have killed someone in furtherance of crime syndicate business. This may not always be true. Evidence suggests that one can get credit for killing someone simply by assisting in a murder as opposed to carrying out the killing itself. For example, government informant William Jahoda told federal investigators that Salvatore "Sollie" DeLaurentis had not killed anyone himself, but that the Outfit had given him credit for being present and helping to "set up" bookmaker Hal Smith. Just being there and knowing about it counted.[19]

Becoming a made guy may also involve a ceremony in which the inductee swears allegiance to the Outfit. This ceremony is normally attended by the prospect's street crew boss and other ranking members of the Outfit. Once he is made, the inductee is accorded greater status and respect in the organization. Jahoda told federal law enforcement officials that the Infelise Street Crew made people the "old way." Infelise told him he had been expecting to be made and said, "We do it the way they used to do it with the paper and the fire"—that is, burning a holy card in his hand. During a consensually recorded conversation between gangster Nicholas Calabrese and an undisclosed government informant, Calabrese stated that he became a made member of the Outfit in a ceremony, presided over by the bosses, involving the letting of blood and the burning of a holy picture.[20]

Reporting to the made guys are the members of the various street crews. In Chicago they are commonly referred to as "Outfit guys." There is a distinction between being a made guy and being a crew member. There is also some disagreement regarding whether crew members are in fact made guys. The Chicago Crime Commission, for example, states that each crew consists of soldiers who are made guys, but that is not consistent with the data gathered for this book. For example, in a statement given to the FBI, Gerald Scarpelli stated that he was not a member of the Outfit, although he readily admitted being part of one of the street crews, collecting juice money, and participating in a number of sanctioned murders. Scarpelli apparently attributed membership to being a made guy.[21]

Scarpelli is a good example of an Outfit guy. He was originally from the Taylor Street neighborhood.[22] At age seven he moved to the Chicago Avenue area in the city's West Side. Scarpelli told the FBI that he was a member of the street crew run by Ernest Rocco Infelise and reported that his principal duties involved the collection of street taxes. He also said he was personally responsible for fifteen individual accounts, mostly bookmakers and a few whorehouses run by panderer Vito Caliendo.

Another one of Scarpelli's duties involved the identification of new illegal activities to be taxed.[23] He would develop his own leads and then go back and tell his street crew boss that he found a guy who was doing something illegal. The boss then checked with the other crew bosses to see if the potential shakedown victim was already paying another member of the Outfit. If not, the boss would give the okay for Scarpelli to shake him down. The victim would have to pay street tax or enter into a 50 percent partnership with the Outfit. Street tax was usually fifteen hundred to two thousand dollars a month. Scarpelli gave his boss whatever he collected. The boss would then give a portion of the money back to Scarpelli.

Scarpelli received a salary of two thousand dollars per month for collecting street tax for the Outfit. In addition, he committed various acts of violence as part of his duties. He admitted to participating in three murders and two beatings. Scarpelli was never paid money for his participation in these crimes, because they were just part of his responsibilities as a member of the Outfit. To supplement his measly income, he also committed burglaries and had taken part in three Brinks armored car robberies. When Scarpelli wanted to commit a robbery, he would have to get permission in advance and then go back to his boss and give him a percentage of the take.[24]

At the time of his arrest in 1988, Scarpelli was receiving only twenty-four thousand dollars a year in salary from the Chicago Outfit—not very much money! He was even told at one point by his crew boss that he should not participate in any "scores" (thefts) because of government heat. One may ask why he would continue to involve himself in organized crime activities and take the chance of going to prison for such small sums of money. The data gathered for this volume suggests that he did so because being an Outfit guy gave him status and provided a sense of importance.[25]

The fact that Scarpelli did not make a lot of money from his organized crime activities highlights the idea that the status provided by membership is often more important than the financial benefits it provides. The status of membership seems to take on even greater importance at the lower end of the organized crime hierarchy. Much of the money taken in by the Outfit moves up the organizational chain, leaving relatively little to be shared by those at the lowest levels. It seems, therefore, that people are not in the Outfit solely for the money. They are also in it for the prestige that is associated with membership.

Despite the prestige that accompanies membership, not everyone involved in the Outfit wants to move up the ladder. According to one Chicago bookie, not everyone wants to become a "wise guy"—another name used to describe organized crime members, both soldiers and made guys. Many are happy just booking (taking bets). Although bookmaking is not an important position, it is one in which a lot of money can be made. Even some Outfit guys themselves are reluctant to become made guys and take positions of authority, because they will be targeted for prosecution. Nevertheless, if you are ambitious, an important way to move up the ladder is to bring in money for your crew and the Outfit in general.[26]

Besides made guys and workers, the Chicago Outfit also includes associates who are said to be "connected." There is a definite distinction between membership and being connected. Made guys and Outfit guys are members; connected guys are not. Being connected means you do business with the Outfit. For example, Chuck Giancana, the brother of crime syndicate leader Sam Giancana, was employed by the Outfit as both a bookmaker and the manager of a hotel owned by the crime syndicate. Chuck Giancana was connected. The fact that connected people are part of the criminal organization but not seen as members of the Outfit was highlighted by a Christmas party hosted by the Chicago Heights Crew at the Alcazar Club in Chicago Heights during the 1990s. Albert "Caesar" Tocco, the head of the crew, separated wire room clerks (connected employees) into a different party room from the made guys and Outfit guys.[27]

People doing business with the Outfit are generally connected only to the person they are working with. People who are associates, like those who are bookmakers, are connected only to the guy they are answering to. Family members and professional people who work for the Outfit are also said to be connected. Jackie Cerone made his son a lawyer in charge of a union. Was he in the Outfit or not? He was a legitimate lawyer, but he was taking care of Outfit business, so he was still connected. Only people who are beneficial to the Outfit become connected.[28]

Being connected has its benefits; it gives one contacts in the mob and grants him the ability to get a favor done if he has a problem. But if someone receives a favor from the Outfit, he might be asked to commit a crime at a later time to return the favor. Being connected also enables one to go to the Outfit with business propositions, both legal and illegal; it doesn't make you a member, but it allows you to go to them with a score or a profitable venture. If you are connected, you are worthy of being listened to. Being connected also gives a person status. A person who is connected with the Outfit is said to carry some "weight." If he gets into trouble, he can go to them to ask for help in straightening things out.[29]

During the 1960s the Chicago Police Department maintained a list of 3,015 people who they believed were connected to organized crime in Chicago. In 1992 there were still 1,500 people listed as "associates" of the Chicago Outfit. They worked in labor unions, for the city of Chicago, and even in the police department. There were so many people that even the Outfit guys did not know who all of them were.[30]

An example of the role played by associates within the Chicago Outfit was made public in 2001 when the inspector general of the Laborers' International Union of North America filed a complaint for trusteeship alleging that managing members of the union had received over four hundred thousand dollars in improper pension, health, and welfare payments. The scheme was carried out to allow ineligible persons to receive financial benefits based upon false or misleading statements of work. These managing officials were all associates of the Chicago Outfit; most even received their positions of authority within the union with Outfit sponsorship.[31]

The Organized Public

Most organizations operate in an environment where they are not related to the public they are in contact with. In some organizations, however, the public is actually part of the organization. This situation routinely occurs in hospitals, prisons, and mental institutions; none of which would exist without patients and inmates. It also occurs in organizations that provide a service, such as schools, whose public is their students.

What makes organized crime in Chicago unique among criminal endeavors is that the public with whom the Outfit is in contact is also part of the organization. This public may be as diverse as an individual gambler or thief or a person who simply wants to be associated with organized crime. Although, gamblers, juice loan victims, and thieves all use services provided by the Outfit, they are also part of organized crime. Although they are not made guys or Outfit guys, they are critical to the survival of the organization.

Historically, gambling and professional theft have been particularly important for the continuation of the Outfit in Chicago; both have provided social structures that support this criminal group. Gambling and professional theft provide distinct sets of activities that not only produce income but also identify the public that the Outfit is in contact with. Support for organized crime is also provided by a segment of the public who seek to be associated with members of the Outfit. These wannabes, people who want to be connected to the Outfit, provide willing candidates for recruitment.

The Chicago Outfit makes most of its money through illegal gambling. There is some casino gambling and a few card games, but these events are largely a thing of the past. Today illegal gambling generally involves sporting events and poker machines. The control of illegal gambling has traditionally taken two forms: Outfit gambling and street-taxed gambling.

Outfit gambling is operated directly by street crew members who have people working for them in wire rooms (places where bets on horse races and sporting events are called in over the telephone) or at dice and card games. There are also a number of independent gambling operators, usually bookies, who pay street tax to the Outfit.

The importance of gambling for the Chicago Outfit goes beyond the revenue it produces. Gambling also provides a setting where a number of important organized crime activities are carried out. Gambling provides access to juice loans, a means of identifying gambling operations that are not paying street tax, and a mechanism for identifying potential burglary victims. Gambling also provides a mechanism for introducing people to organized crime and a setting for organized crime recruitment.

In reference to juice loans, let's assume you gamble. You lose your money at a card or dice game and you borrow from a loan shark. The loan shark has permission from the Outfit to lend money at the game and has paid a fee or tax to whoever gave permission for the game.[32] Regarding street tax, gambling also provides a means for the Outfit to identify potential victims. Most gamblers know other gamblers and hear about different card and dice games throughout the Chicago area. If a gambler finds out that a new game is not "sanctioned" by the Outfit and he owes juice money, he could go to his juice man and tell him about the game for a break on his juice. The Outfit will reduce the amount owed if the information checks out. They will also send someone to the game and tell the operator that they need the okay from the Outfit to remain open. If the game keeper doesn't cooperate, the Outfit may even call the police.[33]

A game keeper who doesn't cooperate could be taken care of in other ways, including violence. Violence may also be committed against those who fail to pay their gambling and juice loan debts. If a gambler falls behind, the loan shark will talk to him and try to get him to pay up. The Outfit doesn't like to kill people for a small amount of money, because it draws too much attention from the police. But if a guy gets too far behind and everyone knows about the situation, they might kill him as a lesson to others. According to one Chicago bookie, only "deadbeats" fail to pay their just debts. These debts, though illegal, are seen as just because no one is forced to gamble or borrow money from the Outfit. Outfit enforcer Frank Schweis stated in a secretly recorded conversation that people "who did not follow the rules" deserved to get killed.[34]

Gambling also provides a mechanism for identifying potential burglary and theft victims. If a bookmaker goes to a house to collect on a bet and sees objects of value, he is going to tell someone connected to the Outfit about it and receive a cut from the proceeds of the resulting burglary. Dice and card games are also great sources of information about organized crime activities. Everyone talks at the game. "Who is playing?" "Who is dealing?" "Who is on the hook for juice?" "Who is stealing?" "Who is hijacking trucks?" "Who has stolen merchandise for sale?"[35]

Lastly, gambling provides a setting for organized crime recruitment. This is accomplished in two different ways. First, bookies and game operators can become members of a street crew if they are productive. Gambling is the most labor-intensive part of the Outfit. They need people to work at dice and card games and in wire rooms as phone clerks. They also need collectors and payout people to settle gambling wagers. Although these are not difficult jobs, they provide a way for the Outfit to see how well a person works and if he can be trusted. Second, card and dice games provide a setting where information is exchanged about a person's criminal activity and reliability. If a person is believed to be reliable, he can be asked to participate in some form of criminal activity.[36]

Professional theft is another activity that has supported organized crime in Chicago. It provides a source of both revenue and potential recruits for the Outfit. Revenue is derived from street tax as well as from the proceeds of the crime. Some Outfit members are thieves like Gerald Scarpelli. There are also other thieves who are connected with the Outfit. Street tax is paid by burglars and thieves for the right to steal in the Chicago area. Not all thieves pay street tax, only those who are associated with the Outfit. If you are a connected guy and you are a burglar, you have to pay. Thieves who are residents of street crew neighborhoods also pay street tax. For example, if you are a thief from a street crew neighborhood and you go out and pull a good score, and the Outfit guys from your neighborhood find out, they will want a share.[37]

Street tax is not paid by blacks, Latinos, or inner-city street gang members who engage in professional theft. It is only paid by thieves who come from street crew neighborhoods, because they are part of the organized public of the Outfit. They understand how the racket subculture works. Professional theft also provides a ready source of recruits for organized crime. Thieves who aspire to membership in the Outfit traditionally have hung around social clubs and card rooms in street crew neighborhoods where young delinquents are trained by older gangsters. They learn how to steal cars, follow jewelry salesmen, and circumvent burglar alarms. The Outfit uses burglary and theft to make money and to test the trustworthiness of aspiring hoods.[38]

The life of Frank Cullotta provides a good example of the relationship between professional theft and organized crime. In a series of articles excerpted from federal court documents, the *Las Vegas Sun* newspaper reported that Cullotta was born in the Grand Avenue neighborhood and eventually moved to the Northwest Side of Chicago. When Frank was about twelve years of age, he met Tony Spilotro, who was also from the Grand Avenue area but had moved into the Northwest Side. The two quickly became friends and began stealing together. By the time Cullotta was fifteen, he was committing armed robberies of taverns and gas stations. By eighteen he had graduated to robbing bank messengers, which netted him a new car and a substantial amount of money. He was also committing home invasion robberies and burglaries. In 1960 he went to jail for one year for the burglary of an appliance store. After he was released from jail in 1961, Cullotta returned to stealing.[39]

During the time that Cullotta was in jail, Tony Spilotro became involved in the Outfit's loan shark business. Spilotro was working for Chicago mobster Sam DeStefano, a notoriously violent man who had killed his own brother for using drugs. Dubbed the "Marquis de Sade" of the Chicago Outfit, DeStefano was soon found murdered himself. The prime suspect was Tony Spilotro. At age twenty-seven, Spilotro had become the youngest loan shark and hit man in the Chicago Outfit.[40]

Eventually Cullotta was offered a position in the Outfit and went to work with Spilotro in Las Vegas. Cullotta worked for Spilotro leading a contingent of burglars known as the "Hole in the Wall Gang," so named because they would enter the homes or establishments of their intended targets through holes that they cut in the walls in order to avoid burglar alarms around the doors and windows. Cullotta was arrested twice in 1981. While in jail, he realized that Tony Spilotro had failed to care for his family. This was a signal to Cullotta that something was wrong. When he eventually learned that Spilotro had decided to have him killed, Cullotta decided to cooperate with the federal government and testify against Spilotro and others in exchange for protection for himself and his family.[41]

Access to organized crime through professional theft is not limited to those who are from racket neighborhoods. Take the case of Nick Gio. In an interview given to the Bureau of Alcohol Tobacco and Firearms at the time of his arrest, Gio stated that he had grown up in the suburb of Niles with John Daddano, son of organized crime figure William Daddano.[42] When Gio was sixteen years of age, he began committing burglaries with John Daddano at the direction of John's father. William Daddano had contacts in the insurance industry who provided potential burglary targets. By reviewing insurance riders, these contacts were able to determine the locations of expensive items of jewelry. Armed with this information, Gio and John Daddano committed approximately three hundred burglaries. For providing the information and a fence to dispose of the jewelry, William Daddano received between 30 and 40 percent of the net profits.

When Gio was arrested for burglary in 1983, he went to jail without telling the police about his accomplice John Daddano.[43] Because he did not talk, he was highly regarded by the Daddano family. When he was released from jail, Gio received a new Corvette from William Daddano for not squealing on his son John. After being released from jail, Gio also went to work in a money-counting room at Fox Amusement and was paid three hundred dollars a week to assist in counting money and making sure that the subterfuge owner, Mike Lizzio, was not stealing from the Outfit. In 1985 Gio began collecting juice, gambling debts, and street tax for William Daddano. He made twenty-five hundred dollars a week as a collector. He would also collect money from the Teamsters Union, which would pay to obtain contracts from Daddano at McCormick Place, where Daddano worked. Gio had also begun doing "heavy work" (intimidation and assault) at the time he was arrested.

Although the lives of Frank Cullotta and Nick Gio provide colorful examples of the relationship between professional theft and organized crime, the importance of professional theft for the Outfit has diminished. Gambling is now the main activity of the Chicago Outfit. Virtually every member of the Outfit is involved in some form of gambling today.[44]

In the Chicago underworld, wannabes are people who want to be associated with the Outfit. They will do anything to ingratiate themselves with Outfit members. A guy could be a working stiff or a man in business who just wants to be around them. Wannabes are distinct from gamblers and thieves, though gamblers and thieves can also want to be part the Outfit. What distinguishes wannabes is that they generally have some other job not connected to organized crime.[45]

Wannabes are people who like to be where the action is. They gamble, buy stolen property, and can be heard discussing news reports about the latest arrests of crime syndicate figures. They like the excitement, the atmosphere. They are attracted by the aura of secrecy and the romanticized version of organized crime that is glorified in such movies as *The Godfather*. They are into the organized crime lifestyle. They also believe they are important because they associate with Outfit guys. A Chicago bookie pointed out, "It is clout to be known by wise guys." However they get to know them, whether it is from the neighborhood or by some other means, legitimate people befriend gangsters because it gives them status.[46]

Most wannabes are content just hanging around with Outfit guys. However, the term *wannabe* is generally considered to be a derogatory designation. Some wannabes do become Outfit guys. If someone likes you and you do a good job, then you might be given the chance to move up. You would begin by being a "gofer," a person regulated to menial tasks such as running errands, running a wire room, or stealing a truck.[47]

The concept of an organized public as it pertains to the Chicago Outfit is supported by the fact that in modern times innocent people are rarely the victims of organized crime activity. Historically, union officials were kidnapped and threatened with violence, but that appears to be a thing of the past. Innocent people do become the victims of robberies and burglaries perpetrated by the Outfit, but by and large they are never the victims of extortion or violence perpetrated by the organization. A Chicago bookie argued that there must be some type of obligation in order to be a victim. This obligation is created through voluntary participation in gambling, loan sharking, participation in connected burglary crews, and other involvement with organized crime.[48]

The idea that the Outfit operated under some sort of rules has been expressed on several occasions. For example, Jake Guzik told Lieutenant Joseph Morris of the Scotland Yard detail in 1953, "We never shot or hurt a policeman . . . because we knew it was a copper's job to make arrests." Twenty-six years later, during the trial of two men charged in the 1979 murder of jeweler Robert Brown, mobster Frank Cullotta testified that the Outfit had a rule against hurting innocent people. In a conversation recorded by the FBI between Frank Calabrese Jr. and his father, Frank Calabrese Sr., as part of the Family Secrets investigation, the senior Calabrese told his son that the "real model" of the Outfit since the beginning was not to hurt innocent people. Although fellow Syndicate members are not innocent people, Frank Cullotta testified that it was also against the Outfit's rules to steal from each other.[49]

Success as a result of past involvement in organized crime activities can also create an obligation. For example, five gangsters associated with Lenny Patrick were found guilty of extorting money from various Chicago-area businesses, a number of which had past ties to organized crime. Two of the victims, Myron and Philip Freedman, owners of Myron and Phil's Restaurant in Lincolnwood, Illinois, reportedly had been bookies before opening their restaurant, which is a popular hangout for gamblers and organized crime figures. If an organized crime figure extorts a legitimate person, it is said that he will "lose his edge." Innocent people go to the police. The same theory applies to the juice loan business. People don't get juice loans to buy a house. They usually get juice loans to cover gambling debts and other illegal activity.[50]

The Contingency Model

This review, using Chicago as a model, has sought to determine the true organizational nature of traditional organized crime in American society. The data gathered here indicate that the Outfit, the traditional organized crime group in Chicago, has exhibited elements of both the bureaucratic and patrimonial models of complex organizations. The division of labor within the Chicago Outfit—made guys and Outfit guys—suggests that the organization has a hierarchical structure. At the same time, connected guys, gamblers, thieves, and to some extent, wannabes appear to be in patron-client relationships with individual members of the Outfit. As such, it would seem that the contingency argument best describes the organization of the Chicago Outfit. It is an open system that adapts to the external circumstances that it confronts.

The establishment of the Lake County faction of the Taylor Street Crew supports the contingency argument. The organizational structure of the Chicago Outfit has changed as people moved from city to suburban areas, as is evidenced by the Cicero and Elmwood Park Crews. Contingency theory may also provide a suitable explanation for the emergence of traditional organized crime. The conditions that gave rise to organized crime are rooted in the environment, and not in the rational decisions of a group's members. Organized crime as we know it came about because Prohibition fostered an alliance between vice entrepreneurs, machine politicians, and the criminal underworld. In short, organized crime could not have been invented until the structure of society was ready to accommodate it. If organized crime is a rationally organized phenomenon, any group setting about to "do" organized crime would be able to similarly organize. We know that this is not the case. Traditional organized crime has never been duplicated in this country.

Although support for the contingency argument is an important finding, probably the single most important finding that has been revealed by this research is that there are people who order their lives according to their beliefs about organized crime. The members of this criminal organization, and its organized public, defer to the Outfit and look upon organized crime as part of the legitimate structure of Chicago society. Whether a made guy, Outfit guy, or connected person; whether a gambler, thief, or wannabe, they are all part of organized crime.

8

STREET CREW NEIGHBORHOODS

The connection between neighborhood areas and organized crime is well established in the criminology literature. Delinquency areas, racket subcultures, and defended neighborhoods have all been found to contribute to the continuation of traditional organized crime in American society. In the Chicago metropolitan area five communities have historically been associated with organized crime. These neighborhoods have served as racket subcultures in Chicago. This chapter tests the hypothesis that members of traditional organized crime come from select community areas by determining the communities of origin of a sample of 191 members of the Chicago Outfit. If the works reviewed in chapter 1 are correct, these neighborhoods should be overrepresented in this analysis. This chapter also reviews the history of each of these areas in order to explicate the relationship between these communities and organized crime.

The Chicago Police Department named the street crews of the Chicago Outfit after the five neighborhoods in which they evolved: Taylor Street, Grand Avenue, Twenty-sixth Street, the North Side, and the suburb of Chicago Heights. In addition to these areas, a number of other Chicago communities have had a reputation of being associated with organized crime, including the suburbs of Cicero, Elmwood Park, and Melrose Park. These communities differ, however, in that they were not the locations of the original indigenous organized crime crews. The groups that have been present in each of these other Chicago areas began because gangsters from the five original street crew neighborhoods relocated there. For example, in the 1960s many people left the Taylor Street neighborhood and moved to Melrose Park, just as they later moved to the suburb of Elmwood Park. As a result, these towns received an infusion of people associated with organized crime.[1]

With the exception of Chicago Heights, Chicago's street crew neighborhoods are all located in what were once described as Chicago's river wards. The Chicago River with its north and south branches set the basis for the industrial topography of Chicago. The river's twenty-four miles of shoreline provided access to both water transportation and waste disposal for the city's nascent industries. As a result, an industrial belt emerged, hugging the course of the river.[2] With these new factories came a demand for labor, which was filled by the rising tide of immigration.

The river wards rose from farmland to centrally located urban real estate within one generation. The area's unpaved streets and wooden cottages were unfit for urban living. As a result, property owners saw no reason to undertake improvements, especially since the property, which was located on the very edge of the central business district, would soon be redeveloped for industrial purposes. Immigrants drifted to the river wards because rent was cheap. In addition, they found themselves within walking distance of their places of employment. Because of the careless disregard of property by absentee landowners, there was little resistance to the invasion of criminal gangs, bootleggers, and people with lower standards of living. The immigrants themselves, not being citizens, were politically impotent but spent their time working to improve their lot and move from the district.

Taylor Street

The most prominent of Chicago's Street Crew neighborhoods was the Taylor Street community. Taylor Street is contained within the Near West Side community area of Chicago.[3]

The Taylor Street area currently extends from Morgan Street to Ashland and from Roosevelt Road to Harrison Street. Historically, however, Taylor Street was much larger. Every block from the Chicago River to Western Avenue was part of Taylor Street. Although not generally recognized as part of Taylor Street, it could be argued that the neighborhood once extended all the way east to State Street. Italians lived on Plymouth Court and Taylor and on nearby Ewing Street as early as 1893. In 1916 Jane Addams reported that ten thousand Italian immigrants lived in the blocks surrounding Taylor Street between Halsted and the Chicago River.[4]

Much of the Taylor Street neighborhood was annexed to the city of Chicago in 1851 when the boundaries of the city were extended to Western Avenue. Immigrants from Germany, Ireland, and Scandinavia first settled the area. In the decades that followed the Great Chicago Fire of 1871, new immigrants arrived, including Italians and Russian and Polish Jews. By 1895 the Near West Side was completely settled, though the inhabitants were poorly housed and the buildings were badly overcrowded. The poverty and condition of the area led to the establishment of Chicago's first settlement house by Jane Addams in 1899. Mother Cabrini, the first American saint of the Catholic Church, also labored among the poor in the area until her death in 1917.

Taylor Street was located in the "Bloody Maxwell" police district. The southern portion of the Maxwell Street district was called the "Valley," named for the steep embankment of railroad tracks that formed the southern boundary of the district. Most of the Valley was razed to make way for Chicago's South Water Market fruit and vegetable terminal, which was relocated there from Chicago's riverfront in 1925. Maxwell Street was known as the toughest police district in the world. Stretching from the Chicago River on the east to Wood Street on the west, and from Harrison Street on the north to Sixteenth Street on the south, Maxwell Street was home to two hundred thousand people from countries as far away as Ireland, Russia, Italy, and Poland. Concentrated in an area less than two miles long and one mile wide, the district was believed to harbor more murderers, robbers, and thieves than any similar district in the world. Two blocks from the Maxwell Street police station was the corner of Fourteenth and Sangamon, where more policemen were killed by criminals, and more criminals by police, than at any other location in Chicago. The Maxwell Street district spawned a number of criminal gangs, including the Henry Street Gang, led by stickup man John McGrath; the Johnson Street Gang, led by burglar and holdup man Buff Higgins; and the Valley Gang. The Valley Gang, however, was the only one to make it into big-time bootlegging. Its early leaders included saloon keeper Paddy "The Bear" Ryan and Red Bolton.[5]

A 1915 investigation by the Chicago School of Civics and Philanthropy reported that 10,125 people lived within the Taylor Street district and that 72 percent of the families who lived within the area were Italian.[6] The community extended from Harrison Street on the north to Taylor Street on the south, and from Morgan Street on the west to Des Plaines Street on the east. Despite the number of residents, a large portion of the district was dedicated to manufacturing, leaving only sixteen square blocks for residential housing. As a result, the area was densely overcrowded, with an average of 265 residents per acre. Most of the houses in the area were comparatively old, two-story frame cottages containing two to four small apartments. Fearing further expansion of the manufacturing area, property owners were often unwilling to expend even a small sum for the repair of a house that might soon be replaced by a factory. Deteriorating housing, poor sanitation, unpaved alleys, and the presence of horses and other livestock all led to unsanitary living conditions, which researchers believed led to low educational standards, high mortality and morbidity, industrial inefficiency, and crime.

The poor condition of the area eventually led to a number of urban renewal projects, including the creation of the Medical Center District in 1941 and the Chicago campus of the University of Illinois in 1961. As they improved their lot, or were displaced by urban renewal efforts, the early immigrants moved from the Near West Side to other growing areas of the city. By the end of the Second World War, the Near West Side was largely made up of African Americans, who had recently emigrated from the rural areas of the South, and a small Italian ethnic neighborhood along Taylor Street.

The Taylor Street neighborhood was the setting for Solomon Kobrin's 1967 study of adolescent street corner groups. In describing the Taylor Street community, Kobrin wrote that a firmly established integration of legitimate and illegitimate elements had existed in the community for some length of time. This integration of deviant and conventional lifestyles manifested itself in a locally acknowledged alliance between the political leadership and the leadership of the city's gambling and vice rackets. The Taylor Street neighborhood also served as the model for Gerald Suttles's 1972 conceptualization of the "defended neighborhood." Although it appears that Suttles did not intend his theory to specifically refer to racket subcultures, the defended neighborhood concept does accurately describe Chicago's four inner-city racket neighborhoods.[7]

The political-criminal alliance in the Taylor Street area predated the turn of the last century. Irish machine boss John Powers originally controlled the Taylor Street neighborhood, which at the time was part of Chicago's Nineteenth Ward. The Municipal Voters League described Powers as the leader of the "Grey Wolves," a group of aldermen recognized as the worst element in the city council. Powers was elected to office in 1888 when the ward was predominantly German and Irish. Over the years the ethnic composition of the Taylor Street area changed. The earlier residents moved away and were replaced by newly arriving Italian immigrants. By 1916 the ward consisted largely of Italians and Eastern European Jews. Because of the change in the ethnic makeup of the area, the Italian community sought to elect one of its own, Anthony De'Andrea, to the office of alderman. The effort to unseat "Johnny de Pow," as Powers was called by the Italians, resulted in an "Alderman's War" in the Nineteenth Ward. Before it was over, thirty men had died in the war to control the "Bloody Nineteenth." Many were murdered after their name had been tacked to the "Dead Man's Tree," a poplar growing at 725 South Loomis Street.[8]

The Nineteenth Ward remained under Powers's control until it was reorganized in 1921 when the Chicago City Council increased the number of Chicago wards from thirty-five to fifty and changed the boundaries of the existing wards. The West Side Italian community was divided among four new wards—the Twentieth, Twenty-fifth, the Twenty-sixth, and the Twenty-seventh—forever diminishing the Italian vote. Powers retained control of the Twenty-fifth Ward.[9]

Republican ward committeeman Joseph Esposito, popularly known as "Diamond Joe" because of his penchant for wearing diamonds, dominated political efforts in Chicago's Near West Side Italian community. Esposito was born in Accera near Naples, Italy, in 1872. When he was twenty-three he immigrated to New York, where, after working as a laborer, he found employment in a Brooklyn bakery.[10] In 1905, at age thirty-three, he came to Chicago, where he opened his own bakery in the Near West Side. Within three years he had become the business agent of the International Hod Carriers Building and Construction Laborers Union. He also rose to president of the Circolo Accera, a social club composed of five hundred men and women from his native region in Italy. Like Big Jim Colosimo, Esposito had organized his followers into a voting bloc and eventually rose to the position of Republican committeeman in the (senator) Charles Deneen faction of the Republican Party. In 1917 he opened his now famous Bella Napoli restaurant at 850 South Halsted Street in the heart of the Taylor Street community.

Although Esposito had become an influential political figure and ward leader, he was also active in bootlegging. He had a license to distribute Cuban sugar, one that he claimed had been granted by President Calvin Coolidge in return for his assistance in delivering the Italian vote. Since sugar was critical to the distillation of alcohol, and Cuba was the major U.S. supplier of sugar, Esposito was in a position to influence bootlegging operations in Chicago and elsewhere during Prohibition. In fact, he operated his own one-thousand-gallon still at the Milano Café in south suburban Chicago Heights. Esposito's Bella Napoli restaurant was raided by Prohibition agents in 1923 and resulted in his receiving a one-year license suspension. A federal judge, however, unlocked the restaurant for one night on December 22, when Esposito staged his annual Christmas dinner for the children of his ward. Each Christmas, Esposito distributed baskets of food, coal, clothing, and even rent money to the poorest of his constituents.[11]

Diamond Joe Esposito was murdered on March 22, 1928, while walking home from a meeting of the Nineteenth Ward Republican Club. It is believed he was killed by Sam Giancana and members of the Forty-two Gang at the behest of Al Capone. Sam Giancana's nephew, Chuck Giancana, writes that

Capone recruited the Forty-two Gang to help him gain control of bootlegging activities in Chicago's Near West Side. Many members of the Forty-two Gang had served as apprentices to the Genna brothers and were familiar with their bootlegging activities.[12]

The remnants of the Forty-two Gang made up the cell that eventually became known as the Taylor Street Crew, playing an important part in the development of the crew and the evolution of organized crime in Chicago. After the fall of Al Capone, Frank Nitti took over the Syndicate, assisted by Paul "The Waiter" Ricca. Ricca was so named because he began his working years as a waiter in Diamond Joe's Bella Napoli restaurant. His familiarity with Giancana and his gang allowed many of the Forty-twos to join the Outfit. Their relationship with Ricca and their aggressive pursuit of illegal money-making enterprises, such as the eventual takeover of policy gambling in the black community, led to a transfer of power to the Taylor Street faction of the Outfit. After Nitti organized crime would no longer be dominated by the remnants of the First Ward Levee district but by the "West Side" of Chicago.[13]

Despite its history and formidable reputation, there is little organized crime activity in the Taylor Street area today. The neighborhood has been greatly changed because of the presence of the University of Illinois, rising property values brought on by the neighborhood's proximity to Chicago's central business district, and the demise of the power of the machine-dominated First Ward.[14]

Grand Avenue

Today, the Grand Avenue neighborhood extends from Halsted Street to California Avenue and north from Hubbard Street to Chicago Avenue with Grand Avenue running through the center. Like Taylor Street, Grand Avenue had different sections. According to a former Chicago bookmaker, each was made up of different people, but they were all connected in that many knew one another, and they all shared the same residential identity—they were from "Grand Avenue." There was Grand and Ogden, Grand and Damen, Grand and Western, Ohio and Leavit, Ohio and Western. All of these different little cliques, little neighborhoods, little corners, and every neighborhood had the same culture but with different guys.[15]

Grand Avenue is located in the West Town community area of Chicago. Grand Avenue itself follows the route of the old Whiskey Point Indian trail that ran from the center of Chicago to what became known as Western Avenue. The area was incorporated into the city in 1869. Large numbers of people began settling in the West Town area after the Great Chicago Fire, and the ever increasing size of the early Italian settlement near Grand and Orleans Streets added to the adjacent West Town's growth. By the turn of the century, twenty-five thousand Polish immigrants had also moved into the West Town community, settling in the area centering on Division Street and Milwaukee Avenue. Although the Poles became the area's largest nationality group, the Italian population gradually took possession of the entire district below Chicago Avenue and expanded west all the way to California Avenue.[16]

The Italian settlement that began near the corner of Grand Avenue and Halsted Street was a continuation of the Near North Side, which was connected to Grand Avenue by a bridge over the north branch of the Chicago River. The Grand and Halsted area received a large number of new residents as families began moving out of the Near North Side because of the influx of Negro migrants. Other Italians settled farther west on Grand Avenue in the triangle of land bounded by Grand, Chicago Avenue, and Western Avenue in order to work in the Chicago, Milwaukee, and St. Paul Railroad yards and the adjoining factories that dominated the area. Although West Town is largely Puerto Rican today, Polish, Ukrainian, and Italian sections still remain.[17]

Unlike Taylor Street, little has been written about the early criminal history of the Grand Avenue community. Frederic Thrasher writes that before being annexed to Chicago, West Town had become a refuge for criminal gangs. When Chicago's gangs first began to find life difficult within the city limits, they moved to West Town because of its ineffective municipal government. As a result, West Town became wide open with saloons, cabarets, gambling houses, and vice resorts.[18]

Anthony Accardo, the longtime senior statesman of the Chicago Outfit, was born in 1906 at 1353 West Grand Avenue. Accardo had once been a bodyguard and enforcer for Al Capone. He was recruited into the Capone mob by gangster Vincenzo De Mora, alias "Machine Gun" Jack McGurn. Accardo began his criminal career as a member of the Circus Café Gang, founded by John "Screwy" Moore, better known as Claude Maddox, a Missourian with a long criminal record. The Circus Café Gang was a group of young toughs who frequented a tavern called the Circus Café located at 1857 West North Avenue during the late 1920s. The Circus Café Gang and another Near Northwest Side gang, the Guilfoyle Gang, were subsidiaries of the Capone syndicate and served as counterforces to the O'Banion Gang in Chicago's Near North Side. It is believed that the Saint Valentine's Day Massacre was planned at the Circus Café.[19]

One of the most important early Grand Avenue gangsters was Anthony "Tough Tony" Capezio, the boss of the area. He ran a number of gambling operations in the Grand Avenue area, including one at 2439 West Chicago Avenue and at the Par Mar Club at 2410 West Chicago. In 1952 the Chicago Police Department's Scotland Yard detail raided Tough Tony Capezio's Grand Club, a bar at 1958 West Grand Avenue. Although Capezio was not present, twenty-seven known burglars, robbers, and hijackers were arrested, including current and future Outfit members James "Cowboy" Miro, Americo DePietto, John Di Fronzo, and James D'Antonio. The raid at the Grand Club was in response to threats made by the bar's patrons that any police officer who stuck his nose in the place would be beaten. The importance of the raid is that it clearly documented the integration of different age levels of offenders. Adult mobsters like Miro and DePietto were found interacting with neighborhood toughs. John Di Fronzo, the future head of the Outfit was twenty-three years old at the time of the raid. James D'Antonio was twenty-four.[20]

Crime syndicate activities continue in the Grand Avenue community today. However, the 1982 imprisonment of Grand Avenue Street Crew boss Joseph Lombardo had a detrimental effect on the Grand Avenue Crew. Lombardo's imprisonment seemed to leave the crew leaderless and without direction, resulting in a decline in their activities. Before going to jail, Lombardo and the Outfit are reported to have played a definite role in the Grand Avenue community. Lombardo acted as a Fagan and mentor to a number of young people in the area who eventually entered the ranks of the Outfit. A number of the members of the C-Notes street gang, centered at Ohio and Leavitt Streets, became Grand Avenue Street Crew members under the tutelage of Lombardo.[21]

Twenty-sixth Street

The Twenty-sixth Street area extends roughly from the Dan Ryan Expressway on the east to Halsted Street on the west and from Twenty-fourth Street on the north to Thirty-third Street on the south.[22] Twenty-sixth Street is contained within the Armour Square community area of Chicago and is named after the nearby Armour Institute of Technology, the original name of the Illinois Institute of Technology.[23] The Armour Square community is truly an interstitial space in that it is a one-half-mile-wide strip of land surrounded by a railroad yard and the Chicago River on the north and raised embankments of railroad tracks on two of the remaining sides.

Armour Square was first settled in the mid-1800s by Irish, German, and Swedish laborers. The northern half of the community was annexed to the city of Chicago in 1853. The southern half of the area was settled after the opening of the Union Stock Yards in 1865. By 1895 all of the vacant land in the area had been built upon. Italians, Yugoslavians, and Chinese began moving into the area during the early 1900s. As the Italian colony centered on the Polk Street Depot in the old Custom House Levee district began to expand, their southern movement was hampered by the presence of the New Levee district. The effect was to divert their march southwest along Archer Avenue and then south once more along Wentworth and Princeton Avenues into the Armour Square area.[24]

In 1912 Chicago's original Chinatown relocated from the area of Van Buren and Clark, on the south edge of the Loop, to the area of Twenty-second and Wentworth. This was the beginning of Chicago's current Chinatown. Blacks next began to move into the Armour Square area around the time of the First World War. By 1940 nearly one-half of Armour Square's population was African American. Much of the black population, however, was displaced with the building of the Dan Ryan and Stevenson Expressways beginning in the 1950s. Today the Armour Square community is made up largely of black, Chinese, and Italian residents, each occupying their own segment of the community.[25]

The Twenty-sixth Street area is called the "Patch." The term *patch* has increasingly been applied to other street crew neighborhoods as well. Traditionally, the word was used in Chicago to describe undesirable residential areas. For example, during the winter of 1860 many unemployed sailors settled in an area known as Conley's Patch, which ran from Madison Street south to Polk and from Wells Street west to the south branch of the Chicago River. Conley's Patch was described by one writer as a collection of hundreds of the "dirtiest, vilest, most rickety, one-sided, leaning forward, propped up, tumbled-down, sinking fast, low-roofed miserable shanties—the worst of several patches in the city of Chicago."[26]

There are also other explanations for the origin of the patch name. For example, an Armour Square resident told the Chicago Historical Society in 1927 that his father had established a successful cabbage farm in the area of Thirty-fifth and Wells during the late 1800s. As a result, the area became known as the "Patch." Local tradition holds that this cabbage patch was the setting for Kate Douglas Wiggin's famous book, *Mrs. Wiggs of the Cabbage Patch*. Another explanation for the origin of the patch name may be traced to 1888 when Italian immigrants were forced to move from the Sherman Patch neighborhood at Fourteenth and Indiana as the area became a more exclusive residential district. Those who were forced to leave the Sherman Patch settled in the current Twenty-sixth Street area, bringing their patch name with them.[27]

The Twenty-sixth Street neighborhood is adjacent to the site where the New Levee, the birthplace of the Capone syndicate, once stood. The Twenty-sixth Street community originally reached into the Levee district, but much of the area has been replaced by an interstate roadway and public housing. In fact, some consider the Twenty-sixth Street Crew to be the direct descendant of the original Torrio-Capone syndicate, the forerunner of today's Outfit.[28] Many of the people who worked for Colosimo, and later Torrio and Capone, lived in the nearby Twenty-sixth Street Italian neighborhood.

The first leader of what would become known as the Twenty-sixth Street Crew was Bruno Roti. A Prohibition-era gangster and Black Hand extortionist, Roti had been a suspect in several murder investigations, including that of labor leader Maurice "Moss" Enright. When Roti died in 1957, his son-in-law Frank "Skids" Caruso took control of the Twenty-sixth Street Crew. Caruso reportedly concentrated on illegal gambling and provided juice loans to those in debt; he also ran an illegal craps game in the neighborhood. Over the years, many members of the Roti clan held city patronage jobs. A 1959 newspaper exposé found eleven members of the Roti family employed by the city of Chicago.[29]

Angelo "The Hook" La Pietra led the Twenty-sixth Street Crew in the 1970s, collecting revenue from back-room betting parlors and dice games. Street tax was also collected from Fan Tan and mahjong games in nearby Chinatown. In 1994 the On Leong Chinese Merchants Association was found guilty of paying a total of $747,000 in street tax for the privilege of running illegal gambling in their Chinatown casino. La Pietra's reign ended in 1986 when he pled guilty to skimming money from a Las Vegas casino and was sentenced to sixteen years in federal prison.[30]

Fred Roti Jr. became the alderman of the First Ward in 1968. The Twenty-sixth Street Crew has historically been aligned with Chicago's First Ward and, as a result, has exerted influence on city contracts and jobs within the city's Bureau of Streets and Sanitation. Contracts for hauling frequently went to mob-connected trucking companies, such as the one owned by Roti's nephew Fred Barbara. So extensive was the influence of the Twenty-sixth Street Crew that nine (22 percent) of the forty members of the Twenty-sixth Street Crew in 1987 held jobs with the city. Roti remained alderman until 1990, when he failed to seek reelection after his arrest by the Justice Department. Roti was widely regarded to be organized crime's representative in city government and a made member of the Outfit.[31]

The Twenty-sixth Street neighborhood continues to be a street crew area today. It is the strongest street crew neighborhood in metropolitan Chicago. Unlike Taylor Street and the North Side, there have been no major urban renewal efforts in this community. The homes are well cared for and the neighborhood is racially stable. While gangsters from other street crew areas have moved to the suburbs, people from Twenty-sixth Street have remained in the neighborhood. The neighborhood is characteristically a defended neighborhood. It is an interstitial space, geographically surrounded by railroad tracks, the Dan Ryan and Stevenson Expressways, and Chicago's black South Side.[32]

In 1997 a young black youth named Leonard Clark was severely beaten because he walked through the white Twenty-sixth Street neighborhood. One of the assailants was Frank Caruso Jr. the grandson of mob boss Frank "Skids" Caruso. After a jury found the younger Caruso guilty, Cook County judge Daniel Locallo sentenced him to eight years in prison. The guilty boy's father, Frank "Toots" Caruso, told the sentencing judge that the neighborhood where they lived had standards that were so archaic that they were out of a B movie and that he would have moved away sooner but did not want to leave his aging mother. The next November there was an organized attempt to have Judge Locallo recalled from the bench. The FBI also received word that there could be an attempt on his life.[33]

Angelo La Pietra and his brother James are reported to have contributed to the building of the Old Neighborhood Italian American Club at Thirtieth and Shields in the heart of the Twenty-sixth Street neighborhood. After having spent ten years in a federal penitentiary on the Las Vegas skimming case, Angelo La Pietra reportedly wanted to give something back to the community, so he funded the club. Although the club started in the early 1980s, it moved into a new two-million-dollar building in 1991. The new facility includes a racquetball court, boxing ring, workout rooms, steam room, kitchen, poolroom, dining room, library, and computer lab—all for the benefit of neighborhood residents and children. The building is sometimes referred to as "Angelo's Dream" in honor of La Pietra. It was the target of FBI telephone taps in the 1980s, because the government suspected that it was the nerve center for Twenty-sixth Street gambling and juice loan collections.[34]

The North Side

In its heyday the North Side neighborhood ran from the Chicago River on the south to North Avenue and roughly from Clark Street on the east to the Chicago River on the west. It is included in the Near North Side community area of Chicago. The Near North Side area was included in the original incorporation of the city in 1837. In 1856 a bridge was constructed across the Chicago River, bringing settlers to the area. By 1860 large numbers of

Irish, German, and Swedish immigrants settled in their own sections of the community. The Irish section, known as Kilgubbin, was infamous for its lawless element. So many German immigrants originally settled in the Near North Side that it was commonly known as the "*Nord Seite*."[35]

Although most of the Near North Side was destroyed by the Great Chicago Fire, the area was quickly rebuilt. The section along the North Branch of the Chicago River became known as Smokey Hollow because of the smoke generated from the activities of riverboats, trains, and factories. By the turn of the century, a portion of the Near North Side was already being referred to as the Gold Coast because of the large numbers of luxurious homes being built along the lakefront. The turn of the century also brought large numbers of Italians, and in particular Sicilians, to the area, eventually replacing earlier immigrant groups. The "dark people," as they were called, soon dominated a portion of the area. By 1910 the Italian community extended from Chicago Avenue to Division Street and by 1920 across North Avenue into the Lincoln Park community area. Little Sicily or Little Hell, as the Sicilian community was known, was centered on Sedgwick Street from Division to North Avenue. The name Little Hell predated Sicilian immigration and was derived from the frequent rows and disturbances that occurred in the area. As early as 1875, knifings were common and the police often traced burglars and their plunder to the neighborhood.[36]

The natural clash between the well-to-do families of the east and the immigrant families of the western portion of the Near North Side resulted in the central area becoming progressively less desirable as a residential district.[37] As a result, many of the wealthier families and businesses moved from the area. During the 1920s many of the residential hotels and large homes that had been left behind were transformed into boarding houses in order to make them profitable for their owners. These rooming houses brought a large transient element to the area as well as a population of lower economic status. Soon the once fashionable district became a center for dance halls, prostitution, nightclubs, and other forms of illegal activity and the beginning of the Clark Street and later Rush Street vice districts in Chicago.

The North Side was the focus of Harvey Zorbaugh's prominent community study, *The Gold Coast and the Slum*. In his writings Zorbaugh described the North Side as a community that was in the process of "disintegration," where the church, school, family, and government had ceased to bear any influence upon community life. Existence there, he stated, was "without the law and without the mores of the larger society," a classic case of social disorganization. Zorbaugh's findings, however, were challenged by William

Foote Whyte, who argued that portions of the North Side, particularly the Italian settlement, were highly organized. Noting the writings of Dr. Anthony J. Lendino, one of the leaders of the Chicago Area Project's North Side Civic Committee, Whyte argued that although the area was characterized by congested population, poor housing, and low family income, people there lived in family groupings and built up elaborate social networks reminiscent of Italian village life.[38]

The connection between the North Side community and the Chicago Outfit can be traced to Prohibition, Al Capone, and the Unione Siciliana. In 1929 Tony Lombardo, Capone's handpicked successor to the leadership of the Unione, was murdered by the Aiello brothers allied with Bugs Moran. Capone responded by sending a number of his men, led by Frank Nitti, into Little Sicily.[39] Nitti's men established their headquarters at the nearby Circus Café on West North Avenue and bombed Aiello-Moran alcohol stills and speakeasies all over the North Side. The blasting continued until February 14, 1929, when the St. Valentine's Day Massacre ended the Aiello-Moran axis forever. The fall of Aiello and Moran left the Capone syndicate firmly in control of Chicago's Near North Side.

Just as they had done on Taylor Street, Capone gangsters turned to local Italian toughs to handle crime syndicate business in other parts of the city. In the Near North Side the Capone mob recruited members of the Gloriana Gang, a notorious group of burglars and holdup men. The gang derived its name from its leader, Charles Gloriana. Deputy Police Commissioner John Alcock described the Gloriana Gang as the most dangerous band of criminals to ever infest Chicago. Three of its members—Dominick Nuccio, Dominick DiBella, and Dominick Brancato, collectively known as the "Three Doms"—worked to bring much of the Near North Side's illegal gambling under Syndicate control.[40]

Once the Capone syndicate had taken control of bootlegging activities in the Near North Side, it was a simple matter for them to dominate other vice activities as well. The control of illegal liquor also facilitated the control of prostitution and gambling, which were centered in the nightclubs and taverns that dotted Clark Street. The proximity of Clark Street to Little Sicily also provided the Capone organization with access to recruits for his criminal organization. Ross Prio ran the North Side neighborhood for the Capone Syndicate. There was, however, an attempt in the 1940s to buck Syndicate control of the North Side when Prio, Thomas Neglia, and Vincent Benevento attempted to establish the "Little Outfit" independent of Syndicate control. Neglia and Benevento were murdered for their treachery, but Prio was spared after making peace with Tony Accardo. Through his political connections,

Prio controlled gambling in the Forty-second and Forty-third Wards, which included Chicago's Gold Coast, Rush Street, Old Town, New Town, and the Uptown nightlife districts. Prio, assisted by Dominick DiBella and Vince Solano, eventually became the boss of the whole North Side of Chicago.[41]

Prio's counterpart in city government was Mathias "Paddy" Bauler. Bauler ran the Forty-third Ward, which governed the Lincoln Park community area, located immediately above the Near North Side, and ran his political activities from his tavern at 403 West North Avenue. In 1933 Bauler was tried, and acquitted, for shooting police officer John Ahearn in front of his former saloon at 343 West North. Responding to repeated attacks by the press, Bauler once showed reporters a thick wad of money and stated, "This is what elects me."[42]

The Near North Side was often called "Honky Tonk USA." Saloons, cabarets, and rialtos marked every block on Clark Street, its main thoroughfare, from Grand Avenue to Division Street. Clark Street was the site of the Sands, one of Chicago's original turn-of-the-century tenderloin districts. The area was also featured in the stage play and movie *Show Boat*. It was to North Clark Street that Gilbert Ravenal, the gambler in Edna Ferber's story, brought his young bride.

In 1953 the Chicago Crime Commission reported that the Clark Street area was home to 165 "clip joints, burlesque bars, assignation houses, and gambling joints" where scantily clad "26 girls" hustled drinks from out-of-town conventioneers and local men seeking a good time. The game "26" involved a board about three feet square at which customers were encouraged to throw dice, gambling for drinks. In 1953 the Chicago City Council's "Big Nine" Emergency Crime Committee found a direct connection between ward committeeman Bauler and gambling in his district.[43]

After the demise of Clark Street, neighboring Rush Street soon took up the slack. Just one mile in length, Rush Street is sometimes referred to as "Glitter Gulch." Gambling arrived on Rush Street as early as 1920, when the Club Alabam speakeasy at Rush and Chicago Avenue was raided by Chicago police. Although the Chicago City Council passed an anti-nudity ordinance in 1978, nude entertainment continued for many years in such Rush Street spots as the Cabaret at Rush and Walton Streets and the Candy Store at 874 North Rush. The eventual demise of Rush Street can be attributed to changes in the real estate market as well as enforcement actions of the police. The condo craze of the 1970s also turned renters into owners, who were against the noise and congestion of the Rush Street nightlife, and the entertainment district that was once centered on Rush Street ended with the gentrification of the neighborhood.[44]

The North Side racket community does not exist today. Most of the members of the original Sicilian community moved away when the neighborhood was torn down between 1941 and 1962 during the successive stages of the construction of the Cabrini-Green housing complex. Many North Side migrants resettled in the far West Side Chicago Avenue community and the suburb of Melrose Park.

Chicago Heights

Although it is not part of the city, the suburb of Chicago Heights has played a significant role in the history of organized crime in Chicago. Chicago Heights was first incorporated as a city in 1901. Its name is derived from the fact that the area is located on the Valparaiso Moraine, 694 feet above sea level, one of the highest elevations in Cook County, Illinois. Migrants first began to settle in the area in 1833 after the resolution of the Black Hawk War. The first settler, Absolum Wells, made his home along the banks of Thorn Creek at Hubbard's Trail, which was also known as the Vincennes Trace. The Vincennes Trace was an important route connecting Fort Dearborn on the banks of the Chicago River at Lake Michigan and the fort at Vincennes, Indiana on the Wabash River.[45]

In 1838 the federal government auctioned preempted Indian land, which attracted settlers to the area. These early pioneers were of Scotch, Irish, and German descent. They made their way to the area, which was known at that time as Thorn Grove, by way of the Sauk Trail from Detroit. Because Thorn Grove was located at the intersection of the Sauk and Hubbard Trails, the town quickly grew in importance. The name Thorn Grove was changed to Bloom in 1849 in honor of German patriot Robert Blumh. In 1890 the Chicago Heights Land Association, led by Chicago industrialist Charles Wacker, began promoting the development of industry in the area. Soon after, large numbers of Italian immigrants were recruited to work in the new factories that were being constructed in the area. Drawn there by the availability of work, Italians settled in two areas: the East Side and the "Hill." Both neighborhoods developed into well-established Italian communities, each with a strong political and economic base.[46]

The development of organized crime in Chicago Heights parallels the development of organized crime in Chicago. The saloon was an integral part of the Chicago Heights scene. When the city had a population of ten thousand residents, it boasted ninety saloons and ten uniformed police officers to maintain law and order. By 1908 Chicago Heights had a reputation for being overrun with gamblers, and many of its saloons supported prostitution. That same year, Mayor Lee Hooks was arrested, along with five other people, on gambling charges as crime became a recurrent theme in Chicago Heights politics. In 1915 mayoral candidate Craig Hood promised to crush commercialized vice and clean out the police department if elected. In 1929 John Thomas swore that, if elected, he would see that commercial gambling and vice did not exist in Chicago Heights while he was mayor.[47]

During Prohibition, Chicago Heights was famous for its bootlegging activities. Two major raids—one at Diamond Joe Esposito's Milano Club in 1925, and the other on a variety of booze and slot machine holdings in 1929—brought national attention. George Golding of the U.S. Treasury Department announced that Chicago Heights was one huge distillery and that there was nothing in the United States equal to it. Conditions in Chicago Heights were so scandalous that the chief of police Leroy Gilbert was murdered in his own home on December 6, 1928, because he had been scheduled to testify before a grand jury investigating two local bootleggers.[48]

The 1929 raid demonstrated the complex nature of organized crime in Chicago. On January 7, 1929, more than one hundred federal agents and Chicago police seized the Chicago Heights City Hall and fanned out across the city seizing bootleg stills and slot machine warehouses.[49] More than 423 slot machines were seized along with 10 double-barreled shotguns, 16 revolvers, and 500 rounds of ammunition. The raids were directed by the U.S. Attorney's Office and carried out with the cooperation of Deputy Police Commissioner John Stege and Captain William Schoemaker of the Chicago Police Department. Despite the rampant corruption in Chicago, both Stege and Shoemaker had gained notoriety as honest and effective law enforcement officials. No matter the political power of the underworld, each generation of the Chicago police has produced a cadre of officers who were willing to work against Chicago's politically organized underworld.

With the advent of Prohibition, a number of politicians and businessmen joined forces with local criminal elements to take advantage of the new business opportunities. Bootleggers were major sugar buyers and employers of truck drivers and plumbers (to construct stills), which brought a measure of prosperity to the community. In addition, bootleggers dabbled in both Democratic and Republican politics in order to protect their illegitimate activities just as in Chicago.[50]

Of the three major gangland factions in Chicago Heights in the early 1920s, two were Sicilian. The Costello brothers—Sam, Nick, Tony, and Charlie—owned Costello Brothers Inc., a wholesale candy business. Their access to sugar provided the Costellos with an important commodity that was also needed to produce illegal alcohol. Former Chicago Heights alderman Antonio Sanfilippo, nightclub operators Phil Piazza and Jim Lamberta, and drugstore and poolroom owner Joe Martino led the second Sicilian group, which was tied to the Unione Siciliana. Both the Costello and Sanfilippo organizations were headquartered in the East Side. The third faction was made up of non-Sicilian, Italian gangsters headed by nightclub owners Dominic Roberto and Jimmy Emery (Vincenzo Ammeratto). Roberto had been a member of the "Corporation Gang," a group of burglars who were active in the area.[51]

After the 1924 murder of Antonio Sanfilippo, Philip Piazza emerged as the leader of their group. In typical gangster fashion, Sanfilippo's funeral involved a two-hundred-car procession led by two automobiles filled with beautiful floral arrangements. Piazza, however, soon ran into trouble; he had accepted protection payments from other bootleggers but allowed them to be raided anyway. This treachery touched off a violent gang war during which the Roberto-Emery faction joined forces with the Costellos and turned to Al Capone for assistance. Capone offered the warring bootleggers a better deal: little or no protection money in exchange for doing business only with him. With Capone's support the Roberto and Emery forces eliminated all competition and became the undisputed lords of the Chicago Heights underworld.[52]

Elderly residents told the Italians in the Chicago Oral History Project that they remembered Al Capone's frequent visits to the city, especially his Robin Hood–like performance at a 1931 baptismal reception at the Mount Carmel School during the Great Depression. As well-wishers filed past, Capone handed out one-, five-, ten-, and twenty-dollar bills to the guests. They also reported that underworld leaders conducted "court" from a bakery at Twenty-second and Butler, where everything from domestic squabbles to territorial disputes among bootleggers were adjudicated.[53]

Prohibition also brought an increase in violent crime as mobsters fought for control of the illegal liquor business. Dozens of gangland killings occurred in Chicago Heights, mostly in the East Side Italian neighborhood. In February 1929 the *Shanghai (China) Times* reported that there were sixty-five murders in a two-year period in Chicago Heights, calling it the most lawless community in the United States. This legacy of lawlessness gave rise to the permanent establishment of traditional organized crime in the town of Chicago Heights, a presence that remained until the 1990s.[54]

Dominic Roberto was deported to Italy in 1935 following charges that he made false statements on his petition for citizenship. Jimmy Emery then became the undisputed boss of Chicago Heights, assisted by Roberto's cousin Frank La Porte. La Porte is believed to be the man most responsible for the development of a sin strip in nearby Calumet City on the site of the old

Torrio speakeasies and cathouses. Two blocks along State Street were home to approximately one hundred taverns, striptease joints, and honky-tonks. For the serious gambler there were skillfully concealed back rooms that contained slot machines, roulette wheels, birdcage dice games, and dozens of poker games. By 1955, however, Calumet City had lost its luster. The *Chicago Daily Tribune* reported that Calumet City was growing "tired," although State Street still had fourteen rialtos where women disrobed in public some 350 times a day. Its clientele were no longer party seekers from Chicago, but factory workers from Gary.[55]

Jimmy Emery ruled the southern suburbs of Cook County until his death in 1957. He was succeeded by La Porte. Later, La Porte's driver, Al Pilotto, assumed control of the area. Pilotto ruled until 1981 when he was murdered while playing golf at the Lincolnshire Country Club in south suburban Crete. Pilotto and Tony Accardo had been indicted on charges of defrauding the health and welfare benefit fund of the Laborers' International Union, which may have been the reason for his death. Pilotto was president of Local 5 of the laborers' union and vice president of the union's Chicago area council. Upon his death, Albert Caesar Tocco took control of the Chicago Heights Crew.

Tocco attempted to gain control of the stolen auto racket in Chicago Heights and the surrounding area. There were a number of automobile salvage yards in southern Cook and Will Counties operating as fronts for car thieves that he brought under Outfit control. The real profit in auto theft came from stripping stolen autos and selling the parts. It is estimated that it would cost $125,000 to build a $20,000 car today solely from parts.[56] Tocco was indicted on federal charges in 1988 and fled overseas to Greece but was eventually captured by the FBI and convicted on multiple counts of racketeering. In a first for the Chicago Outfit, Tocco's wife, Betty, testified against her own husband, implicating him in several killings, including the brutal 1986 murders of Anthony Spilotro and his brother Michael.[57]

Tocco was succeeded as the boss of the Chicago Heights Crew by Dominick "Tootsie" Palermo, field representative of the Laborers' International Union. In 1990 Palermo was the target of a twenty-nine-count racketeering indictment charging that he ran a sports betting operation, organized a barbooth dice game, and used terror tactics to enforce collection of street taxes. Eleven people testified that they paid extortion money to Palermo's men rather than risk harm to themselves or the members of their families. He was sentenced to thirty-two years and fined $250,000. He died in federal prison at the age of eighty-eight.[58]

Organized crime activity in the Chicago Heights community has ended. The 1989 conviction of Chicago Heights mob boss Albert Tocco was devastating to the Chicago Heights Street Crew. The card rooms and social clubs are gone, and it is now difficult to locate organized crime figures in the Chicago Heights area. However, the influence of the Chicago Heights Crew was felt as recently as 1992 when Chicago Heights mayor Charles Panici and two former city councilmen were indicted for extorting money from numerous contractors who wanted to do business with the city. Among the contractors who gave money to the mayor was crime boss Albert Tocco, who also held the city's garbage hauling contract.[59]

The decline of the Chicago Heights Crew has coincided with other changes that have taken place in the community. The post–World War II period saw the creation of new suburban areas and the development of regional shopping centers that hastened the end of Chicago Heights' once bustling downtown business district. In addition, the decline of the railroads and the demise of heavy industry in the area have added to the deterioration of the town. Chicago Heights is experiencing what Pierre de Vise has called "socioeconomic obsolescence."[60] This gritty, blue-collar town is also undergoing extensive demographic change. As the town ages, many of the children of the original Italian settlers have moved to other suburban areas. They are being replaced by blacks and Hispanics who have begun moving into the Chicago Heights area.

The Neighborhood

Being from one of Chicago's neighborhoods tells something about the person. Your address tells where your grandparents came from, how much money you have, and what color your skin is. People who are from street crew or so-called patch areas are said to be from "the neighborhood." Being from the neighborhood tells the trained eye that you are likely to share a secret knowledge of organized crime; being from the neighborhood means you have something in common with or at least an understanding of the Outfit. The idea of being from the neighborhood is important for the continuation of organized crime in Chicago. Take, for example, the response of a Chicago bookie when asked about the influence of street crew neighborhoods upon organized crime: "The Outfit is in trouble. People who are not brought up in the neighborhood do not understand. You must have the neighborhoods, which are migrating. This will hurt the Outfit. Because the neighborhoods are no longer strong, beliefs about organized crime are wearing down. The neighborhood provided the rearing and conditioning necessary to become a wise guy."[61] Chicago neighborhoods have always been a kind of a halfway house for urban immigrants. The old neighborhoods allowed newcomers to get their feet on the ground amid friends and then move on to better homes in newer areas of the city and suburbs. Although they moved to other areas, many neighborhood emigrants continue to hold sentimental ties to the old neighborhood after they leave. They remember the good times, and the bad, that they shared with their neighbors and the urban realities that they learned there. Included in the realities that are learned in street crew neighborhoods is an understanding of organized crime.

This familiarity with organized crime allows people from street crew areas to see themselves as different from residents of other communities. As described by a past member of the Chicago Outfit, people from the neighborhood see themselves as "a little wiser, a lot stronger, a wise guy, a guy that has been around." Being from the neighborhood also provided a sense of status, one that they were proud of; being from the neighborhood meant you "knew people." There was a power there, an unforeseen power. And the neighborhood was the source of this power. Accompanying this power was the expectation that people from the neighborhood would act in a certain manner. They were required to be "stand-up guys"—people who kept their mouth shut, were loyal, dignified, and not to be pushed around. There may have been a slight variance between the neighborhoods, but the people were very much alike. They were all similar, no matter if they were from Taylor Street, Grand Avenue, or Twenty-sixth Street.[62]

Being from the neighborhood also created certain obligations. A police officer who testified in court against Outfit boss Rocco Infelise regarding his participation in the theft of silver from a metal processing plant reported that Infelise asked him how he could testify against him, because "they were both from the same neighborhood."[63] This obligation also applied to the victims of organized crime. According to one former mob figure, it was best to victimize your own, because they did not call the police, for fear of being called a stool pigeon. People from the neighborhood were concerned about what others would think of them. What would their relatives and neighbors say if they talked to the police?[64]

Even if they move to suburban communities, emigrants from street crew areas are still from the neighborhood. When making new acquaintances, "Where are you from?" is a common question that is asked by residents and former residents of street crew neighborhoods. For members of the Chicago Outfit, finding out where an individual is from is the key to being able to verify who you are and what you stand for. It acts as a test. If they know somebody is from the neighborhood, they can go back and check up on them. See what kind of guy they were—check their references, so to speak. Finding out where you are from is a background check. It is a verbal background check that is easily traceable. Everybody knew everybody in the old neighborhood.[65]

This background check is important because of the illegal nature of the activities of the Outfit. Can this person be trusted not to expose the organization's activities to the police? Demographic changes in street crew areas, however, have had an effect on determining one's pedigree. As the neighborhoods slowly disintegrated and people moved out, the background check system no longer functioned. This is important for the continuation of the Outfit. The decline of street crew neighborhoods has made recruitment more difficult. It is harder for the Outfit to determine whether one can be trusted. Today it is much more difficult for them to find someone who knows your parents, your aunts and uncles, and your cousins, someone who knows whether you were a good burglar or cartage thief and whether or not you would talk if arrested.[66]

Linking Individuals to Racket Subcultures

The records of the Chicago Police Department indicate that there were 191 members of the Chicago Outfit in 1987. Of these, 146 (76 percent) had Italian surnames. In 1936 only 75 (41 percent) of the then 181 members had Italian surnames. Organized crime in Chicago had become largely an Italian phenomenon. Where gangsters were once recruited from Levee criminals and various ethnic gangs, they were now being recruited from Italian neighborhoods. The year 1987 was chosen to analyze because it was the last year that the original neighborhood street crew designations were used. Changing demographic conditions and shrinking size led the Outfit to reorganize into North, South, and West Side Crews in later years.[67]

The communities of origin of 98 (51 percent) of these individuals have been identified. Of these, 59 (60 percent) were born in one of the five street crew communities. Forty (41 percent) still resided there at the time the sample was taken. These data are consistent with the racket subculture argument that gangsters come from select neighborhood areas. A review of the data for each of the individual communities, however, indicates that rates of nativity and residence varied among the different neighborhoods examined.

The majority of the members of the Grand Avenue and Twenty-sixth Street Crews were raised in these two areas. Of the 33 members of the Grand Avenue Crew, the communities of origin of 27 (82 percent) were determined.

Of these, 23 (85 percent) were raised in the Grand Avenue neighborhood. Of the 40 members of the Twenty-sixth Street Crew, the communities of origin of 27 (67 percent) were identified. Of these, 24 (89 percent) were identified as having been raised in the Twenty-sixth Street neighborhood.

There were also large numbers of gangsters living in both the Grand Avenue and the Twenty-sixth Street neighborhoods. Seventeen (63 percent) of the identified members of the Grand Avenue Crew resided in the Grand Avenue neighborhood. Fifteen (55 percent) of the 27 identified members of the Twenty-sixth Street Crew resided in that community. The position that these neighborhoods were racket areas is also supported by interview data. Respondents maintained that street crew activities were still visible in both the Grand Avenue and Twenty-sixth Street areas well into the 1990s, when organized crime figures could be seen frequenting social clubs and spending large portions of their time in these communities.[68] As recounted by a Chicago police detective:

> You go to the neighborhood and everybody is standing on the corner like at the old Italian American Social Club at Twenty-sixth and Princeton. You got Angelo's Dream over there. It is on the other side of Princeton. On Shields, north of Thirty-first Street. Those guys are wannabes, they honor these people. They all stand on the corner and go to the clubs. You see them hanging around with all the bookmakers and all the made guys, you know, the guys with the bent noses. You see the young guys twenty to twenty-five years old. They are all sitting out there doing the same thing. And that holds true around Grand Avenue. You know, you go west on Grand Avenue from Halsted to, like, Ogden and that area in there. There are four to five social clubs in there. You go by there and you see all the young kids in there. Talking, hanging around with all the guys that are fifty to sixty years old. Taking their cars to get washed and running out and getting donuts and bringing them lunch.[69]

An analysis of the residency data for the Taylor Street and the North Side neighborhoods, however, indicated different findings. There were 49 members of the Taylor Street Crew in 1987. The communities of origins of 25 (51 percent) were identified. Of these, only six were raised in the Taylor Street Community. Only two still resided there. The remaining 19 identified members came from various other Chicago communities. Of the 35 members of the North Side Crew, the communities of origin of 11 (31 percent) were identified. Of these, only 3 were raised in the area and 3 continued to reside there at the time of the analysis. Both of these communities have undergone extensive social and economic change, which would explain why they no longer produce recruits for organized crime. Few crime syndicate members resided in either area, and those that are part of both street crews were probably recruited from outside the neighborhood.

Of the 29 members of the Chicago Heights Crew, the communities of origin of 8 (28 percent) were identified. Of these, 3 were identified as having been raised in the Chicago Heights community, and 3 continued to live there. It should be noted that community nativity and residence information concerning the Chicago Heights Crew was particularly difficult to obtain since, because of its suburban location, the Chicago Police Department did not keep extensive records of this crew's activity.

The fact that most of the members of the Grand Avenue and Twenty-sixth Street Crews were raised in these two areas and that a significant number still resided there at the time the data were collected supports the conclusion that racket areas existed in Chicago. These data are particularly significant when one considers that there are a total of 207 community and suburban areas in metropolitan Chicago where these people could have come from. These findings suggest that neighborhood areas are important to organized crime recruitment.

There is evidence that there are communities in Chicago other than the traditional street crew neighborhoods that have also been tied to organized crime. Another community that respondents frequently mentioned is the Chicago Avenue neighborhood, particularly the intersection of Chicago and Hamlin Avenues. Chicago Avenue is located within the Humboldt Park community area of Chicago. It got its name from the 207-acre park that lies, surprisingly, just outside its eastern boundary. Most of the Humboldt Park community was annexed to the city in 1869 when the Illinois legislature extended Chicago's boundaries north to North Avenue and west to Crawford Avenue (now Pulaski Road). An influx of Italians and Poles from the Near North Side and the West Town communities stimulated residential construction in the area from 1900 to 1920. By 1960 Italians had become the largest foreign-born group living in the area. Within the next twenty years, a mass out-migration of European-descended whites occurred, leaving the area almost completely black and Hispanic today.[70]

During the years following World War II, Chicago Avenue was known as the Alamo community. Massive urban renewal efforts and the influx of blacks led many Taylor Street and North Side residents to move to other parts of the city, and in particular Chicago Avenue. Chicago Avenue became associated with the Outfit because a number of members of the Taylor Street Crew moved there. A 1979 study found twelve gangsters living in the area. Their headquarters was Moon's Restaurant at Chicago and Hamlin, where gangsters like Joseph "Joe Gags" Gagliano and William "Wee Willie" Messina carried out gambling and juice loan activities.[71]

The influence of organized crime in the Chicago Avenue neighborhood was made evident during the 1951 aldermanic elections. Chicago Avenue is located within the Twenty-eighth Ward, which was the headquarters of Pat Nash who controlled the Democratic machine that ruled Chicago from 1933 to 1947. George Kells, a protégé of Nash, was the ward's alderman and democratic committeeman until the underworld decided that he should retire.[72] Kells left Chicago in 1951 because of threats on his life. He was replaced by Patrick Petrone, brother of state representative Robert "Happy" Petrone, a close friend of crime syndicate leader Tony Accardo. Both Petrones were members of the West Side Bloc, a group of elected officials who were under the control of the Chicago Outfit.

Just as changing demographic factors had prompted many residents to move from the Taylor Street and North Side areas to the Chicago Avenue neighborhood, these same influences soon drove many Chicago Avenue residents to move to other parts of the city and to western suburbs such as Elmwood Park and Melrose Park. Included among these urban emigrants were people who held values that were sympathetic to organized crime and retained these attitudes as they moved from one community to another. As expressed by a Chicago gambler, "They brought their ideas with them."[73]

It is interesting to note how the boundaries of Chicago's organized crime neighborhoods correspond to the city's recognized community areas as they are listed in the *Local Community Fact Book for Chicago*.[74] The boundaries of the Armour Square/Twenty-sixth Street, the (Near) North Side, and the Chicago Heights communities generally correspond, though there are some minor differences. Taylor Street and Grand Avenue, however, are not individually recognized but are contained within larger community areas.

Chicago community areas, except for the two communities added in the 1980 edition of the *Fact Book*, have been drawn the same since the original 1938 publication. This was done in order to provide constant subareas within the city that could be compared in studying changes in social, economic, and residential conditions. Recognizing that the *Fact Book* did not identify all Chicago communities, Albert Hunter attempted in 1984 to catalog all of Chicago's identifiable community areas. The result of this work, *Symbolic Communities*, identified 206 recognizable Chicago communities. Neither Taylor Street nor Grand Avenue, however, are mentioned by Hunter, who locates these areas within the Near West Side and West Town community areas respectively.

Suttles's conceptualization of the defended neighborhood may provide an answer to the absence of Taylor Street and Grand Avenue in Hunter's work.[75] He argues that one structural characteristic of the defended neighborhood is the fact that it may be divided into levels, or orbits, which radiate from an "egocentric to a sociocentric" frame of reference. People living in the area may have a different sense of the neighborhood's boundaries from those who do not. Even if this is true, it is almost incredible to think that neither the *Fact Book* nor Hunter's research identified two of Chicago's most famous neighborhoods.

Closely related to the concept of the neighborhood is that of the "West Side." Being from the West Side of Chicago historically has had a certain meaning for a person's identity. Just as people from the South Side are assumed to be White Sox fans and people from the North Side are expected to by Cubs fans, people from the West Side were assumed to possess a certain character. People do not always agree on the boundaries of Chicago's West Side. Generally speaking, it runs from North Avenue to Cermak Road and from the Chicago River into the western suburbs. Although the area is made up of many different ethnic and socioeconomic groups, the people who live there are all from the West Side. The West Side, however, is more than a geographical place; it is also a state of mind. Included in the collective representation of the West Side is a reputation for organized crime. According to Chicago writer Bill Granger, "The West Side was always a melting pot of convenience: No matter your race or nationality, you were brothers with your eye on the main chance. Books have been written about the brotherhood of crime that accepted Jews, Irish, and Italians into neat gangs that controlled popular vices such as prostitution, gambling, and booze."[76]

Evidence of the West Side's connection to organized crime can be traced as far back as the 1920s when the *West Side Times* announced that the mission of the upcoming Great West Side Pageant of Publicity was to counteract the area's bad reputation. The *Times* stated that there were more than one million people living in the West Side of Chicago, and not all of them were involved in racketeering. In studying the Near West Side during the 1970s, Gerald Suttles also found that the area had a reputation for organized crime. According to Suttles, "The area has long had an enduring reputation for juvenile gangs and organized crime, included among its alumni Frank the 'Enforcer' Nitti and the Forty-two Gang." Taylor Street and Grand Avenue are both located in Chicago's West Side, which has also contributed to its reputation for organized crime. Although most of the West Side is black today, these two areas are, and have long been, Italian neighborhoods. Another factor contributing to the West Side's reputation for organized crime was its domination by the West Side Bloc.[77]

The representation of the West Side and its connection to organized crime also carried over into Chicago's near western suburbs. As explained by Granger:

> The lords of the Outfit, as Chicagoans call the thing that is called the crime syndicate or the Mafia in other locales, are said to sleep in places like Oak Park, River Forest, and Elmwood Park, they do. They can afford it. Sam Giancana, who once ran the Outfit, was permanently put to sleep in the basement of his house in south Oak Park. Oak Park is part of the West Side too, though not the city part—the West Side, remember, is a state of mind.[78]

The top leadership of the Chicago Outfit has historically been referred to as the West Side. Most of the bosses after Al Capone lived in a western suburb; hence the term *West Side* referred to the top leadership of the mob.[79] When gangsters had to see the top guys, they would have to "see the guy out west." The term *West Side*, when used to refer to the hierarchy of the Outfit, also refers to the fact that organized crime in Chicago has been dominated by the Taylor Street Crew since the 1950s and the emergence of the Outfit as we know it today.

Being from the West Side of Chicago means different things to different people. Obviously, being from the Austin community today means something different than being from the Taylor Street neighborhood twenty years ago, although both are located in the city's West Side. An individual's sense of community will vary depending upon his position in the social structure of society and the demographic characteristics of the community itself.[80] When a member of the Outfit or a resident of a street crew neighborhood says he is from the West Side, he means Taylor Street or Grand Avenue. When a *former* resident of a street crew neighborhood says he is from the West Side, he is also referring to Taylor Street or Grand Avenue—or maybe Chicago Avenue, even though the Chicago Avenue community no longer exists. He does not mean Austin or Humboldt Park. They were not part of his symbolic definition of the West Side.

The early development and formation of organized crime in each of Chicago's street crew neighborhoods generally followed the familiar pattern set in the Levee district. This is especially true in the Taylor Street, North Side, and Chicago Heights areas. Both the Taylor Street and the North Side communities were dominated by corrupt political organizations. Each had their own equivalent of boodlers Bathhouse John Coughlin and Hinky

Dink Mike Kenna. Alderman and saloonkeeper John Powers controlled the vote in the Near West Side Taylor Street area and was an avid supporter of gambling king Mike McDonald. Alderman "Hot Stove" Jimmy Quinn, also a saloon operator, was in political control of the Near North Side and promoted gambling boss Mont Tennes.

Just as Big Jim Colosimo dominated the Near South Side Levee, other Italian gang leaders existed in Chicago's remaining street crew neighborhoods. Diamond Joe Esposito and the Genna brothers ruled in the Taylor Street neighborhood, and Antonio Lombardo and the Aiellos were in charge of the city's North Side. In Chicago Heights the Costello brothers and the Sanfilippo gang fought for control of the bootlegging business. It was Prohibition and the determination of the Capone mob that turned these local ethnic criminals and their followers into organized crime. Conquering rival saloon and Prohibition gangs, the Capone syndicate established itself throughout the Chicago area by setting up cells in each of Chicago's major southern Italian districts. Those areas that were once under the control of the Unione Siciliana and its alky-cooking activities were a particularly important target of the Capone expansion. These cells eventually became the source of fresh recruits for the Outfit and the organized crime neighborhoods of Chicago.

The data examined here suggest that organized crime in America is in decline because of demographic changes in urban neighborhoods. The physical destruction of the North Side community and its replacement by the Cabrini-Green housing complex virtually spelled the end of the North Side Street Crew. Similarly, socioeconomic and racial change in the town of Chicago Heights has contributed to the decline of organized crime activity in this suburban community. The decline of organized crime activity in these two areas highlights the importance of community contexts for the continuation of traditional organized crime in Chicago and other urban centers.

The logic of these findings suggests that traditional organized crime cannot exist without accompanying community support. This would be a convenient place to end this argument but for the fact that the Taylor Street Crew continued to attract new members even though it was no longer centered in the Taylor Street community. The factors that explain how organized crime can continue to successfully recruit new members, regardless of the demise of street crew neighborhoods, are found within the symbolic dimensions of community life. The symbolic value of being from the "neighborhood" has allowed recruitment to continue despite the fact that the ecological dimensions of these community areas have declined in importance.

CONCLUSION

This study has demonstrated that traditional organized crime in America is not the result of a transplanted Sicilian Mafia but is directly related to the social conditions that were found in American society during the early years of the twentieth century. This argument is supported by the fact that Italian-dominated organized crime does not exist in Brazil or Argentina, other countries that experienced major southern Italian immigration, nor did it exist in the north of Italy until the advent of the *nuova mafia* after World War II. This difference can be attributed to the fact that in the United States and Chicago, in particular, social and political conditions were favorable to the rise and spread of organized crime. Historian Humbert Nelli writes: "Chicago displayed and continued into the twentieth century to possess many characteristics of a frontier town, some commendable and others execrable. It was vigorous, brash, lusty, optimistic, and energetic. It also contained labor violence, corruption in civic and business affairs, apathy toward poverty, inadequate housing, unsanitary living conditions, vice, and organized crime."[1]

It was into this environment that increasing numbers of southern Italian and Sicilian immigrants began to arrive after 1880. And it was within this environment that organized crime was born. Organized crime did not evolve in linear fashion beginning with the Mafia in Sicily, emerging in the form of the Black Hand in America's immigrant colonies, and culminating in the development of the Cosa Nostra in America's urban centers. Organized crime was born in the slums of the new world and was the result of the social structure of American society. This position is highlighted by the fact that the overwhelming majority of the early members of the Capone syndicate were either American born or raised. Most were not even Italian. Further, the Italian government protested the deportation of Italian-born American criminals, arguing that most of the deportees had left Italy when they were babies and that it was the American urban environment, not their Italian birth that was responsible for their criminality.[2]

Additional evidence against the alien conspiracy theory is provided by sociologist William Chambliss. In his study of "Rainfall West," a pseudonym given to the city of Seattle, Washington, Chambliss found that a vice cabal had been operating there since the early 1900s.[3] Chambliss attributed the success of this cabal to an alliance between the business, political, and law enforcement communities and not simply the members of any particular criminal society. This syndicate provided all the services of traditional organized crime—corruption, gambling, prostitution, and usurious loans—without the participation of Italian Americans or any mention of the Mafia.

Ethnic Succession and the Crooked Ladder

One of the major theoretical constructs flowing through much of the scholarly research on organized crime is the ethnic succession thesis. Based upon Daniel Bell's functionalist argument that crime serves as a means of social mobility, the ethnic succession thesis sees organized crime as a vehicle for social advancement.[4] Deprived of traditional opportunities for achievement, newly arriving immigrant groups, it was hypothesized, used crime as a means of acquiring wealth and gaining status in society. This hypothesis is reminiscent of the observation attributed to French novelist Honoré de Balzac that "behind every great fortune is a great crime."

Although it appears that the urban rackets continue to be a means of economic and social mobility for newly arriving immigrant groups such as rural blacks, Puerto Ricans, and Mexicans in the form of their participation in the distribution of illegal drugs, there has been relatively little ethnic succession when it comes to traditional organized crime. Although minority numbers bankers and bookies have been employed by organized crime groups such as the Outfit, Francis Ianni's predicted takeover of Italian American organized crime by black and Hispanic urban immigrants simply has not occurred.[5] This is not to say, however, that Italian American organized crime is not in decline. It is. What has changed is the very nature of organized crime itself.

The decline of traditional organized crime can be related to a number of important changes in the structure of American society. The demise of big-city political machines, the increasing middle-class character of American life, state-sponsored gambling, increased sophistication on the part of law enforcement, suburbanization, and the breakup of the old ecological patterns of slum and tenement settlement have all contributed to the end of traditional organized crime as we have come to know it today. When we talk about organized crime in the traditional sense, we must remember that we are referring to a method of crime that is related to a definite period in American history, a period that was characterized by corrupt government administrations and differentially organized urban areas.

It is precisely because the conditions that brought traditional organized crime into being no longer exist that other ethnic groups will not follow Italian Americans into traditional organized crime. There will be organized drug cartels and other criminal enterprises, but because of the absence of deep-rooted official corruption, these groups will not qualify as "organized crime" as our society has come to know it. In addition, areas that have been characterized as racket subcultures in the past, such as the organized crime neighborhoods of Chicago, are disappearing from the American experience.

Adherents of the ethnic succession hypothesis argue that there are striking parallels between the era of Prohibition and the proliferation of drug trafficking in society today, particularly due to the wholesale movement of street gangs into the distribution of illicit narcotics. Like traditional organized crime, drug trafficking within street gangs provides for the integration of different age levels of offenders. But unlike traditional organized crime, adult offenders within the street gangs of today are not associated with the established political structure, although there have been efforts to initiate such ties. For example, Gangster Disciple (G. D.) leader Wallace "Gator" Bradley redefined G. D. to mean "Growth and Development" and ran for alderman in Chicago. However, increased sophistication on the part of law enforcement will prevent such efforts from obtaining true political power.

Moreover, it is not likely that modern government will ever again allow organized criminal groups to gain the political power they have held in Chicago since the late 1800s. Even if a criminal group were to corrupt the local political structure and influence local police efforts, such an organization would still have to face an awesome array of federal law enforcement agencies. There are checks and balances in place today that did not exist at the time of the emergence of Mike McDonald's Democrats and the Capone syndicate. The FBI, as we have come to know it, did not exist during Prohibition. In fact, the establishment of the Prohibition Bureau within the Justice Department, and the dispatch of Elliot Ness and his "Untouchables" to Chicago in 1930, was literally the beginning of modern federal law enforcement.

Alien Conspiracy and the Myth of the Mafia

Italian historian Humbert Nelli argues that what set the Italians apart in their struggle to dominate organized crime in Chicago and elsewhere was their cultural heritage. Their group solidarity and cultural distrust of government uniquely prepared many for entrance into the secret world of organized crime. The single most important factor of life in the south of Italy was the weakness of the state, even in the elemental provision of police protection for the individual. The consequence of this weakness was the development of a culture that stressed family ties above all else as the source of mutual aid, protection, and the practice of taking justice into one's own hands. A man trained to work outside the law was a natural recruit to sell bootleg booze and to carry out the violent acts that were required to distribute it. The idea that southern Italians were uniquely positioned to participate in organized crime is supported by the American FBI, who argue that significant numbers of *mafiosi* fled Italy in the early 1920s, during the purges of prefect Cesare Mori, and helped to establish what is known today as the Cosa Nostra or the American Mafia.[6]

The idea that southern Italian culture lent itself to organized crime has its critics. Recent research has called into question the diffusion of southern Italian culture outside of its original territory. This point is well taken considering the fact that most of Al Capone's men were not Italian. Some may have come from Italy (Capone appointed only Italians to his bodyguard detail), but what about in later years? The National Origins Act of 1924 severely restricted Italian immigration. These restrictions remained in effect until 1965. So where did Italian gangsters come from? By the 1950s the Capone syndicate had evolved into the Chicago Outfit, whose street crews were neighborhood based. Was it southern Italian culture that allowed organized crime to prosper in certain areas of Chicago, or was it the differential organization of Chicago's inner-city neighborhoods?[7]

The patterns of land use within a city are largely determined by economic considerations that lead each part to be inevitably stained with the peculiar sentiments of its population. The effect of such economic segregation is to convert a geographical space into a community with its own sentiments, traditions, and history. The effects of culture and sentiment were most likely to be found in areas where deviations from zonal and sectoral patterns of land use occurred. These departures were often found in the immigrant and racial colonies of the so-called urban ghettos, where population segregation preserved and intensified the intimacies and solidarity of the local neighborhood group.[8]

It was in the southern Italian enclaves of Chicago that the effects of the racket subculture were most often felt. This does not mean Mafia subcultures that valued organized crime were established in these areas. There is absolutely no evidence that the Italian immigrant community as a whole supported organized crime. There is evidence, however, that the young men who were recruited by the Chicago Outfit were delinquents from socially disadvantaged community areas who had already proven their criminal abilities before being recruited into the underworld. John Landesco's study of the Forty-two Gang documented the fact that the Capone syndicate recruited Italian street toughs to fill the ranks of its emerging street crews. Landesco demonstrated for the first time that organized crime had its roots in the social organization of American society.

Community Social Structure and Organized Crime

This book has sought to explain the importance of community social structure for the emergence and continuation of traditional organized crime in American society. Organized crime in Chicago began during the early years of the twentieth century in the city's Levee district, where local vice entrepreneurs formed a powerful criminal alliance with elected government officials. The power of the Syndicate, as it was originally called, grew with the advent of Prohibition. The demand for illegal alcohol was surpassed only by the profits that it produced. Saloon and criminal gangs from throughout the Chicago area entered into violent competition to dominate the liquor trade. One group emerged victorious: the Capone syndicate. Once in power, the Outfit, as it was eventually known, became the supreme overlord of vice and crime in Chicago.

The conditions that led to the emergence of the Levee syndicate were directly related to the social organization of Chicago society. Gambling interests cooperated in electing politicians who were sympathetic to their activities and would not interfere with their operations. At the same time, the communities where vice was rampant were fraught with the social ills that accompanied industrialization and urban immigration. As a result, the people in these areas were not able to organize against vice interests and control their own communities. The control of government by criminal interests also had a direct influence upon the police, who were prevented from enforcing the law and ensuring the moral order in these areas.

The very values that distinguished the United States from much of the world—universal suffrage and the guarantee of self-determination for every man—also contributed to the development of organized crime. Proximity and neighborly contact are the basis for the simplest and most elementary form of association in the organization of city life.[9] Local interests and associations breed local sentiment, and under a system that makes residence the basis for participation in government, the neighborhood became the basis of political control. The ability of ethnically and territorially based political groups tied to saloon and gambling interests to gain political power through the use of the popular ballot allowed criminal elements to gain substantial influence in the affairs of local government at the beginning of the twentieth century.

The eventual domination of vice activity by the Capone syndicate created a need for personnel. As the Syndicate grew in territory, its leaders looked for people they could trust to govern their newly expanded activities. As the Outfit had come to be dominated by men of Italian descent, it was only natural for them to look among their own kind for recruits. All organized criminals, whether Italian Cosa Nostra groups, Jamaican posses, or Chinese triads, depend upon trust and loyalty to operate and survive. The basis for such trust is usually found in the primary blood culture. Thus, kinship patterns, ethnicity, and place of family origin and birth all become important factors in the selection of personnel.

The search for trustworthy recruits by the Chicago Outfit led them to the southern Italian colonies of Chicago. In each of the five major southern Italian enclaves, a street crew was formed to carry out organized crime activity in that portion of the city. Just as the inception of organized crime was related to the organization of Chicago society, the inception of organized crime activities in each of these areas was also related to the social structure of the neighborhoods in which they emerged. The Levee, Taylor Street, Grand Avenue, and the North Side could all be characterized as slum districts, where poverty, unemployment, disease, and delinquency were common. In addition, the often rough-and-tumble politics of most of these tenement districts had led to the election of political leaders who were sympathetic to gambling interests and other forms of political boodling. The same conditions were found in the town of Chicago Heights, whose history is replete with political scandals and vice activities.

The conditions of a socially disorganized society in each of these areas, coupled with the presence of organized crime, led to the establishment of differentially organized community areas. The presence of the Outfit in each of these areas contributed to this organization, and as a result the Outfit became an important element in the social construction of these communities. Because of the manner in which these communities were organized, they became exceptions to the zonal hypothesis of Robert Park and Ernest Burgess. Taylor Street, Grand Avenue, Twenty-sixth Street, and the North Side are among the oldest communities in the city of Chicago. Although many residents moved to more affluent areas of the city as these communities aged, sufficient numbers remained in most of them to allow the culture that had been established there to continue. Because the areas surrounding these communities did not fare as well, neighborhoods such as Taylor Street became islands of stability in a sea of impoverished community areas.

The need to segregate itself from the surrounding area led to the establishment of a defended neighborhood in the Taylor Street area. Both Grand Avenue and Twenty-sixth Street also fit the defended neighborhood model. The Outfit became an important element in the construction of the defended neighborhood in that the Outfit helped to protect the community, through the threat of violence, from the uncertainties that surrounded it. The defended neighborhood as a mechanism of social control was used to further differentiate racial and cultural groups. It is also a cognition that gives an important sense of identity to its members. Because most of the neighborhoods in Chicago that fit the defended neighborhood model were also street crew areas, the residential identity associated with each of these communities took on a specialized meaning. People who are born and raised in these areas are said to be "from the neighborhood" and as a consequence are accepted as members of a trusted in-group. This specialized status has allowed organized crime to continue beyond the borders of these street crew areas and has allowed the Outfit to continue today.

A Reconceptualization of the Racket Subculture

The increasing scale and complexity of modern urban society has altered the social structure of urban communities. Greater social stratification and geographic mobility have marked the end of many ethnically defined neighborhoods. As such, racket subcultures and street crew neighborhoods began to vanish from the American social scene as their residents became educated, found jobs, and moved to the suburbs. For example, the North Side and Chicago Heights are no longer street crew neighborhoods. These changes suggest that traditional organized crime is in decline because of demographic changes in racket areas and the integration of the Italian American population into mainstream American life.[10]

The fact that community areas that support the pursuit of a life in organized crime still exist in the Chicago area is also supported by the data. Many organized crime figures were born and continued to reside in both the Twenty-sixth Street and Grand Avenue neighborhoods. The Twenty-sixth Street neighborhood in particular bears a number of the markings of a racket community. Racket subcultures are communities of local interest where ascriptive ties are based upon ethnicity and kinship. They also serve a number of important community functions. Characteristically, these neighborhoods have protected their inhabitants from the invasion of alien minority groups and have provided employment in the enterprises that were dominated by the criminal organization.

The fact that racket areas have continued, however, is not the major finding of this book. The major finding of this research is that recruitment into traditional organized crime has continued, in the case of the Taylor Street Crew, without its being physically present in the Taylor Street community. The history of organized crime indicates that recruitment is related to the social structure of community areas. In Chicago these racket subcultures have manifested themselves in the form of five street crew neighborhoods. Just as these communities occupy a physical space, they also exhibit a normative dimension consisting of culture, social structure, and the symbolic elements that characterize the community. The collective representation of the neighborhood highlights the fact that racket subcultures, like other local communities, are symbolic as well as ecological entities.

The symbolic dimension of the racket subculture allowed immigrants from street crew neighborhoods to take their ideas about organized crime with them when they moved to other city and suburban communities. As explained by a former resident of the West Side when asked about the effects of emigration from these areas: "The Patch loses its thing, but it will always be in their mind." The fact that people took their ideas about organized crime with them when they left street crew neighborhoods has helped keep the Chicago Outfit alive.[11]

Evidence of the presence of organized crime activities in suburban areas manifested itself in the 1990s with the existence of the Elmwood Park Social Athletic Club (SAC), which for all practical purposes was the headquarters of the Taylor Street Crew. The Elmwood Park SAC was the center of west suburban organized crime activity for many years. It is where gangsters met in the daytime to conduct business and play cards. Does this mean a racket subculture was reestablished in the suburb of Elmwood Park? The residency data examined here clearly indicate that neither Elmwood Park nor Melrose Park have produced many recruits for the Outfit. Only six of the ninety-eight members of the Chicago Outfit whose nativity and residency have been established in this analysis came from Elmwood Park and Melrose Park. Nineteen of these same people lived in these two towns, fifteen in Elmwood Park. All but four originally came from the Taylor Street and Grand Avenue neighborhoods.

If people take their ideas about organized crime with them, why haven't the suburbs of Elmwood Park and Melrose Park produced substantial numbers of recruits for the Outfit? The answer may be that suburbs by their very nature are different from urban areas. When questioned about the difference between city and suburban areas, a Chicago police officer and former resident of the West Side recounted that certain activities are tolerated in the Patch that would not be tolerated in other places. For example, the police allow white kids to congregate on the corner in the Patch. This would not be tolerated in the suburbs or in the better residential areas of the city. People in the Patch feel safe and secure when they look out and see young toughs on the corner because of the proximity of blacks to their neighborhoods.[12]

When asked about the difference between city and suburban areas and beliefs about organized crime, a former resident of the North Side pointed out that in the old neighborhood everyone was close and trusted one another, but when one moved to the suburbs such relationships were "diluted." People were different. They were more "aloof," or as a former member of the Grand Avenue Street Crew stated: "They get a little bit more highfalutin. In the neighborhood, houses are built one on top of the other, right down the street. Everybody knew everybody else and they were all related. On one street you probably had three aunts, four brothers, a nephew, and a cousin. You move to the suburbs, you buy a house on a block where they are all strangers."[13]

Not only are people's beliefs about organized crime watered down in suburban areas, but so is their commitment to local community life. The hypothesized eclipse of the urban community has resulted in the advancement of the theory of the "community of limited liability" in which ascriptive ties and local community orientations still exist, but commitment is partial and varied.[14] The centerpiece of the limited liability theory suggests that an individual's sense of community varies with the status he occupies, within both the local community structure and in the larger society and the demographic and social characteristics of the community itself. As such, an individual's ties to his local community will often be less important than his occupational status and his position within the wider society.

Although the position that an individual holds within the larger society and the ecological characteristics of suburban areas generally do not lend themselves to the creation of a traditional racket neighborhood, a semblance of a racket subculture does exist in some suburban communities. A gambler familiar with the west suburban scene explained that in the old neighborhood, you could look at a bookmaker driving a big Lincoln and say, "Boy, I would like to be a bookmaker." Young people don't see much of this in the suburbs, but they see some of it.[15]

What little organized crime that is seen in suburban areas supports recruitment and has allowed the Outfit to continue. The presence of organized crime in suburban areas, however, takes a different form from that of the inner city. Besides places like the Elmwood Park SAC, the only places where organized crime figures can be seen in suburban areas are a few restaurants and bars. They are virtually unknown in the communities where they reside. They are not seen walking the streets or standing on the corner socializing with community residents as in Patch neighborhoods. A number of crime syndicate members have lived in the wealthy suburbs of Oakbrook and Barrington, yet these towns do not have a reputation for organized crime. The structure of these communities simply does not lend itself to organized crime activities.

The fact that members of the Taylor Street Crew were found in the Elmwood Park SAC and a few suburban restaurants and bars is important for the continuation of the Chicago Outfit. These types of locations served the same purpose as the old street crew neighborhoods in that they provided places for crime syndicate figures to congregate and be seen. The Outfit has to be visible someplace in order to attract new people. If members of the Chicago Outfit generally came from street crew neighborhoods, who are the people recruited today by the Outfit, and where do they get the idea that they want to be gangsters?

People who are recruited by the Outfit today are people who are attracted to the gangster lifestyle. Just as people once saw real-life examples of organized crime in street crew neighborhoods, today they are seeing organized crime in the mass media. There is virtually no one in the United States who has not been exposed to Italian American organized crime. Gangsters have become part of American culture and folklore. People can see organized crime today without ever leaving their home just by turning on the television. People whose parents once lived in street crew neighborhoods also get information about organized crime from their families. When questioned about people's familiarity with organized crime, a former gambling investigator stated, "It's probably something that has been handed down from generation to generation. Grandpa always told stories to the kids about Al Capone. Somebody knows somebody whose uncle probably got killed somewhere along the line, and I think there is still a certain amount of respect for all that."[16]

Although information about organized crime is available to the public, not everyone is eligible to join the Outfit. A recruit still must be known. His family must have come from one of the street crew neighborhoods where they were known to the underworld, or he must have proven himself trustworthy, as is evidenced by the case of Nick Gio. He must still withstand the background check. Salvatore "Sollie" DeLaurentis provides a good example of how the Taylor Street Crew continued to recruit members. An Internal Revenue Service agent explained the following about DeLaurentis:

> This guy wanted to be a mobster from day one. His family grew up on Taylor Street and he got fucked. His family moved out to Lake County, and he couldn't be a mobster, because there was nobody to be a mobster with. So he gradually made connections back in the old neighborhood. Sollie always had it in his mind that he was a gangster. People knew him before he was a real gangster. He always acted like a real gangster. He needed that to fit into his life. So that is how he became one.[17]

The fact that recruitment, in the case of the Taylor Street Crew, continued without its physical presence in the Taylor Street community does not necessarily signal the end of the importance of the community for organized crime. Despite the fact that increasing urban differentiation has contributed to the decline of ecological communities, groups of people sharing a common life and rules of conduct continue to exist. In essence, people who seek a life in the rackets, or people who have had traditions of organized crime handed down from family and friends, today make up the community of the Taylor Street Crew—no matter their place of residence. This is not to say that physical locations are unimportant to the Taylor Street Crew. I believe they are. The neighborhood of today's Taylor Street Crew may simply be a "roving neighborhood."

The roving neighborhood is the area where an individual strays in search of friends, of somewhat specialized recreational activities, and for membership in voluntary associations.[18] Each individual conceives of the roving neighborhood in many different ways according to that segment of activities that temporarily looms in the foreground of his mind. For example, a suburban homeowner might work in a nearby city's downtown area, seek recreation in the city's nightclub district, shop at a suburban regional shopping mall, and belong to a country club or voluntary association in a totally different town. This individual's neighborhood consists of the people he meets in each of these areas. The concept of the roving neighborhood may be used to locate the street crew neighborhood of the Taylor Street Crew. Today a member of the Taylor Street Crew may live in Oakbrook, attend "business" meetings in Elmwood Park, and frequent restaurants and bars on Taylor Street for recreation.

The importance of the Taylor Street neighborhood to the Taylor Street Crew, and the Outfit in general, lies in the fact that Taylor Street has become the collective representation of the neighborhood and the West Side of Chicago. This neighborhood has become an artifact of an earlier period, one that represents the embodiment of the racket subculture as well as the history of Italian immigration and settlement in Chicago. Taylor Street is referred to as "Little Italy," despite the fact that many of the residents are students at the nearby University of Illinois campus. Stories about the Forty-two Gang and Al Capone, as an icon of ethnic mobility, abound, and the name Taylor Street continues to be synonymous with organized crime.

Whether centered in a street crew neighborhood or in a roving neighborhood, many Chicagoans express definite attachment to the Chicago Outfit as is evidenced by the following statements:

> I believe in them. I believe in them and I respect them. They never hurt me. I am sure they hurt people. I know the police have hurt a lot more people than the Outfit, and I have been around the Outfit all my life. It's a part of life. It's a group of people with a belief. It's a culture. It's a way of life for many people, for a big part of society in our area. It's a way of life to many people, to many families.[19]

> The Outfit guys never bothered anybody except their own. If you'd cross them, they would take care of you. But as far as hurting innocent people, that just never happened. You could even say they protected the neighborhood. Nobody came on Taylor Street to do robberies or to break into houses—they'd be dead if they tried anything like that. We didn't have to lock our doors or windows; the Outfit made us feel safe. And from Capone's days till now, you know, the Syndicate has been known to help people out with hospital bills and whatnot. It burns me up when I see police picking on them and letting the real crooks go free.[20]

Such sentiments suggest that the Outfit has a community base not only in the ecological sense but also in the normative sense. For example, when street crew boss Joseph Lombardo was tried in federal court during the early 1980s, many Grand Avenue residents came to court and testified as character witnesses on his behalf. One neighbor testified that Lombardo could be depended on to settle petty disputes between neighbors, to help children stay out of trouble, and to protect older citizens from harassment. In a separate organized crime prosecution, a group called the Committee Against Government Oppression held a fund-raiser in 1989 through which they raised more than two hundred thousand dollars for the defense of Rocco Infelise and members of the Taylor Street Crew who had been arrested by the federal government. These same people later gathered in front of the Dirksen Federal Building in downtown Chicago on July 2, 1992, to protest the methods used by the government in prosecuting Infelise and his associates.[21]

The fact that the Taylor Street Crew continued to exist beyond the boundaries of the Taylor Street community demonstrates that the Outfit, as an organization, has been able to adapt to change. Will the Outfit be able to continue to adapt and recruit new members when people "from the neighborhood" no longer exist? How many generations will be able to pass on the collective representations and moral sentiments that have facilitated recruitment in street crew areas?

The implication of this analysis is that demographic change alone will not defeat traditional organized crime. This is not to say that demographic change has not had a monumental effect on the Outfit in Chicago. Indeed there has been a significant impact, as evidenced by the decline of many organized crime neighborhoods and their accompanying street crews. Yet in the case of the Taylor Street Crew, organized crime continued without its physical presence in the Taylor Street community. This finding underscores the need for continued law enforcement pressure against organized crime in Chicago and other urban areas.

The Failure of Social Control

Traditional organized crime in America followed the precedent established by early saloon and gambling interests; it was strongly influenced by the culture of corruption existing in big-city America; and it seized upon the opportunities created by Prohibition. Its ties to the established political structure not only prevented the swiftness and certainty of sanction but also gave the underworld a quasi-legitimate place in the structure of urban society. An elderly Chicago barber and onetime bookie for the old North Side Street Crew told me, "There was no such thing as organized crime; it was called the Democratic Party." His statement is an obvious referral to the fact that for many years the Outfit in Chicago was intimately tied to the established political structure.

Responsibility for the failure of elected officials to come to grips with organized crime must be shared at all levels of government. The *Chicago Daily Tribune* reported in 1959 that no big shot in the Syndicate had ever been sentenced to a major prison term by local authorities in Chicago and that only 17 of the 926 gangland murders occurring since the 1920s had been solved.[22] For many years neither the federal government nor the states had effective organized crime control programs. At the federal level, the Federal Bureau of Investigation was not created until 1935, and even then its longtime director, J. Edgar Hoover, denied the existence of traditional organized crime. It was not until the 1961 election of Robert Kennedy as attorney general of the United States that the FBI was finally forced into the effort against organized crime in Chicago and other cities. Hoover knew that attacking organized crime meant attacking the big-city political machines that had tremendous influence in national affairs because of the large numbers of votes that they delivered for elected officials. At the state level, Illinois has never had an effective organized crime control program except for a short seven-year period between 1970 and 1977 when Governor Richard Ogilvie established the now defunct Illinois Bureau of Investigation.

Another problem with the control of organized crime was the decentralized nature of American government. Historically, organized crime control was seen as a problem best handled by local authorities. This insistence on local control, combined with the tendency to regulate public and private morality by law, created huge problems for state and municipal law enforcement. Gambling and other vices provided revenue that was used to corrupt the very politicians who controlled the agencies of criminal justice.

Even when action was taken against the Outfit and other organized criminal groups, the code of silence practiced by its members and the organization's ability to perpetuate itself prevented law enforcement from having a detrimental effect on the organization. If a boss or high-ranking member was sent to jail, someone simply rose through the ranks to take his place. A better control strategy would have been to attack political corruption and the social conditions within the racket subculture that were sources of gang recruitment. The street crews of the Chicago Outfit weakened as the old organized crime neighborhoods of Chicago disappeared.

The control perspective is further supported by the recent success of law enforcement in its efforts against organized crime. The enactment of the RICO Act and its effective utilization by federal law enforcement, in particular the FBI, has had a devastating effect upon the Outfit and other traditional organized crime groups across the nation. Although enacted in 1970, the RICO law was not widely used until the 1980s when then President Ronald Reagan declared war on organized crime in America. The end result has been a sweeping array of indictments against organized crime figures across the nation.

What makes the RICO law so effective is that it is directed against the organization. Whether a bookmaker or contract killer, anyone convicted of violating the RICO statute may be subject to twenty years' imprisonment for participating in the criminal enterprise. The government now is able to arrest whole street crews at one time, thus preventing lower-ranking members from filling the void created by the arrest of a prominent organized crime figure. Such a law has proven to be particularly effective when used against criminal groups, like the Taylor Street Crew, that have been able to replicate themselves in nontraditional settings.

It is especially interesting to note that the state of Illinois tried to pass a RICO law in 1983. Sponsored by the Chicago Crime Commission, this legislation was soundly defeated in the Illinois General Assembly. The Illinois RICO law and accompanying wiretap legislation was opposed by the American Civil Liberties Union and, astonishingly enough, by executives of some of the very corporations who sat on the board of directors of the Chicago Crime Commission itself![23] The total neglect of organized crime control at the municipal and state level continues today. Neither the city of Chicago nor the state of Illinois has any type of dedicated organized crime control program.

Looking beyond the myth of the Mafia, the story of traditional organized crime in Chicago is really the story of the failure of American institutions to work for the good of all men. It was political corruption that allowed organized crime to grow, and it was political expediency that allowed it to continue. I can think of no better explanation for the development of organized crime than Thrasher's 1927 classic statement that gangs were the result of the failure of the normally directing and controlling institutions of society to function effectively.

NOTES

The following abbreviations are used for frequently cited sources:

CA	*Chicago American*
CD	*Chicago Defender*
CDN	*Chicago Daily News*
CDT	*Chicago Daily Tribune*
CR-H	*Chicago Record-Herald*
CS	*Chicago Sun*
CST	*Chicago Sun Times*

Preface

1. Jerald E. Caiden, "What Should be Done about Organized Crime," in *The Politics and Economics of Organized Crime,* ed. Alex N. Caiden (Lexington, MA: D. C. Heath, 1985), 149.

2. John Landesco, *Organized Crime in Chicago* (1929; Chicago: University of Chicago Press, 1968); James T. Carey, *Social and Public Affairs* (Beverly Hills: Sage, 1975), 148.

3. Howard Abadinsky, *The Mafia in America* (New York: Praeger, 1981); Donald Cressey, "The Functions and Structures of Criminal Syndicates," *Task Force Report: Organized Crime* (Washington, DC: U.S. Government Printing Office, 1967); Annelise G. Anderson, *The Business of Organized Crime: A Cosa Nostra Family* (Stanford, CA: Hoover Institution, 1979); Francis A. J. Ianni and Elizabeth Reuss-Ianni, *A Family Business* (New York: Russell Sage Foundation, 1972).

4. Francis A. J. Ianni, *Black Mafia* (New York: Simon and Schuster, 1974), 17.

5. Illinois Institute of Technology, *A Study of Organized Crime in Illinois* (Chicago: Chicago Crime Commission, 1971), v–vi.

6. Barney G. Glaser and Anselim L. Strauss, *The Discovery of Grounded Theory* (New York: Aldine, 1967), 163.

7. President's Commission on Law Enforcement and the Administration of Justice, *Task Force Report: Organized Crime* (Washington, DC: U.S. Government Printing Office, 1967), 34.

8. Norman Denzin, *The Research Act* (Chicago: Aldine, 1970).

Introduction

1. Hearings before the Permanent Subcommittee on Investigations of the Committee on Government Operations, 83rd Congress, 1st session, 1953; Estes C. Kefauver, *Crime in America* (Garden City, NY: Doubleday, 1951), 1.

2. Hearings before the Select Committee on Improper Activities in the Labor and Management Field, 85th Congress, 1st session, 1957; "Police Nab 67 Mafia Chiefs," *CDT*, 14 November 1957.

3. Donald Cressey, "The Functions and Structures of Criminal Syndicates," in President's Commission on Law Enforcement and the Administration of Justice, *Task Force Report: Organized Crime* (Washington, DC: U.S. Government Printing Office, 1967), 1.

4. Ibid.

5. Donald R. Cressey, *Theft of the Nation: The Structure and Operations of Organized Crime in America* (New York: Harper and Row, 1969); Ralph F. Salerno and John S. Tompkins, *The Crime Confederation* (Garden City, NY: Doubleday, 1969).

6. Federal Bureau of Investigation, "La Cosa Nostra Chicago Division," File 92-6054, 16 July 1964.

7. Federal Bureau of Investigation, "La Cosa Nostra," Italian Organized Crime, FBI.gov, http://www.fbi.gov/hq/cid/orgcrime/lcn/lcn.htm (accessed 14 July 2006).

8. Walter Lippman, "The Underworld as Servant," in *Organized Crime in America: A Book of Readings*, ed. Gus Tyler (1962; Ann Arbor: University of Michigan Press, 1967), 59; Frederic D. Homer, *Guns and Garlic: Myths and Realities of Organized Crime* (West Lafayette, IN: Purdue University Press, 1974), 63.

9. Kefauver, *Crime in America*, 1.

10. William H. Moore, *The Kefauver Committee and the Politics of Crime* (Columbia: University of Missouri Press, 1974), x.

11. Daniel Bell, *The End of Ideology: On the Exhaustion of Political Ideas in the 1950s* (New York: Free Press, 1960), 117; Francis A. J. Ianni, *Black Mafia: Ethnic Succession in Organized Crime* (New York: Simon and Schuster, 1974), 13; Eric McKitrick, "The Study of Corruption," *Political Science Quarterly* 122 (December 1957): 502–14.

12. Jackson Toby, "Hoodlum or Businessman: An American Dilemma," in *The Jews*, ed. Marshall Sklare (Glencoe: Free Press, 1958), 548.

13. Bell, *End of Ideology*, 128

14. Herbert Asbury, *The Gem of the Prairie: An Informal History of the Chicago Underworld* (1928; DeKalb: Northern Illinois University Press, 1986), 105.

15. John D. Buenker, *Urban Liberalism and Progressive Reform* (New York: Scribner, 1973), 2.

16. Madison Grant and Charles Davidson, eds., *The Alien in Our Midst* (New York: Galton Publishing, 1930), 53, 204.

17. Joseph R. Gusfield, *Symbolic Crusade: Status, Politics, and the American Temperance Movement* (Champaign: University of Illinois Press, 1986).

18. Mark H. Haller, "Organized Crime in Urban Society: Chicago in the Twentieth Century," *Journal of Social History* 5 (1971–1972): 210–34.

19. Humbert S. Nelli, *The Business of Crime: Italians and Syndicate Crime in the United States* (New York: Oxford Press, 1976), 25.

20. Cressey, "Functions and Structures," 54.

21. Irving A. Spergel, *Racketville, Slumtown, Haulburg* (Chicago: University of Chicago Press, 1964), 44; Francis A. J. Ianni and Elizabeth Reuss-Ianni, *A Family Business: Kinship and Social Control in Organized Crime* (New York: Russell Sage Foundation, 1972), 133.

22. Cressey, "Functions and Structures," 55.

23. Gerald D. Suttles, *The Social Construction of Communities* (Chicago: University of Chicago Press, 1972).

24. Dwight C. Smith, and Richard D. Alba, "Organized Crime and American Life," *Society* 16 (March/April 1979): 32–38.

25. John Landesco, *Organized Crime in Chicago* (1929; Chicago: University of Chicago Press, 1968).

Chapter 1. Explaining Organized Crime

1. Clifford R. Shaw and Henry D. McKay, *Juvenile Delinquency and Urban Areas: A Study of Rates of Delinquency in Relation to Differential Characteristics of Local Communities in American Cities* (Chicago: University of Chicago Press, 1942).

2. Mario Puzo, *The Godfather* (New York: G. D. Putnam's Sons, 1969).

3. Thorsten Sellin, *Culture Conflict and Crime* (New York: Social Science Research Council, 1938), 29.

4. William F. Whyte, *Street Corner Society: The Social Structure of an Italian Slum* (Chicago: University of Chicago Press, 1943).

5. Francis A. J. Ianni and Elizabeth Reuss-Ianni, *A Family Business: Kinship and Social Structure in Organized Crime* (New York: Russell Sage Foundation, 1972), 89.

6. Salvatore Lupo and Anthony Shugar, trans., *History of the Mafia* (New York: Columbia University Press, 2009).

7. Robert M. Lombardo, *The Black Hand: Terror by Letter in Chicago* (Champaign: University of Illinois Press, 2010).

8. Ruth R. Kornhauser, *The Social Sources of Delinquency: An Appraisal of Analytic Models* (Chicago: University of Chicago Press, 1978).

9. Emile Durkheim, *Suicide: A Study in Sociology* (New York: Free Press, 1951).

10. Robert K. Merton, "Social Structure and Anomie," *American Sociological Review* 3 (1938): 672–82.

11. Robert K. Merton, *Social Theory and Social Structure* (Glencoe: Free Press, 1957), 146.

12. Daniel Bell, *The End of Ideology* (New York: Free Press, 1964), 117.

13. Kornhauser, *Social Sources of Delinquency,* 165; Durkheim, *Suicide.*

14. Frederic M. Thrasher, *The Gang: A Study of 1,313 Gangs in Chicago* (Chicago: University of Chicago Press, 1927), 33.

15. Bell, *End of Ideology*; Alan Block, *East Side, West Side: Organizing Crime in New York, 1930–1950* (New Brunswick, NJ: Transaction Books, 1983); John Gardner, *The Politics of Corruption: Organized Crime in an American City* (New York: Russell Sage Foundation, 1970).

16. Robert Park, Ernest Burgess, and Roderick McKenzie, *The City* (Chicago: University of Chicago Press, 1967), 64.

17. Albert Hunter, *Symbolic Communities* (Chicago: University of Chicago Press, 1974), 20.

18. Park, Burgess, and McKenzie, *City,* 64; Sophonisba P. Breckinridge and Edith Abbott, "Chicago Housing Conditions IV: The West Side Revisited," *American Journal of Sociology* 17, no. 1 (1911): 1–34.

19. Park, Burgess, and McKenzie, *City,* 77.

20. Robert Bursik, *Neighborhoods and Crime: The Dimensions of Effective Community Control* (New York: Lexington Books, 1993); Robert E. L. Faris and H. Warren Dunham, "Natural Areas of the City," in *Theories of Deviance,* ed. Stuart H. Traub and Craig B. Little (Itasca, IL: F. E. Peacock, 1980).

21. Clifford R. Shaw and Henry D. McKay, *Juvenile Delinquency and Urban Areas* (Chicago: University of Chicago Press, 1969), 316; Shaw and McKay, *Juvenile Delinquency* (1942), 14.

22. Shaw and McKay, *Juvenile Delinquency* (1942), 186–88.

23. National Commission on Law Observance and Enforcement, *Report on the Causes of Crime Vol.* 2 (Washington, DC: U.S. Government Printing Office, 1931), 62.

24. Shaw and McKay, *Juvenile Delinquency* (1942), 172.

25. Edwin H. Sutherland and Donald R. Cressey, *Principles of Criminology* (Chicago: Lippincott, 1955), 160.

26. Louis Wirth, *The Ghetto* (Chicago: University of Chicago Press, 1928), viii.

27. Park, Burgess, and McKenzie, *City,* 45; Thrasher, *Gang,* 284–85.

28. John Landesco, *Organized Crime in Chicago* (1929; Chicago: University of Chicago Press, 1968), x, 207, 221.

29. John Landesco, "Crime and the Failure of Institutions in Chicago's Immigrant Areas," *Journal of the American Institute of Criminal Law and Criminology* 23, no. 2 (1932): 238–48.

30. Landesco, *Organized Crime in Chicago* (1929), 6.

31. Whyte, *Street Corner Society,* 273.

32. Ibid., 38.

33. Shaw and McKay, *Juvenile Delinquency* (1942), 2.

34. Solomon Kobrin, "The Conflict of Values in Delinquency Areas," in *Juvenile Delinquency,* ed. Rose Giallombardo (New York: John Wiley and Sons, 1966), 151–60.

35. Richard A. Cloward and Lloyd E. Ohlin, *Delinquency and Opportunity: A Theory of Delinquent Gangs* (New York: Free Press, 1968), 153.

36. Irving Spergel, *Racketville, Slumtown, and Haulburg: An Exploratory Study of Delinquent Subcultures* (Chicago: University of Chicago Press, 1964), 35, 44.

37. Irving Spergel, "An Exploratory Research in Delinquent Subcultures," *Social Service Review* 35, no. 1 (1966): 33–47.

38. James F. Short and Frank L. Strodtbeck, *Group Process and Gang Delinquency* (Chicago: University of Chicago Press, 1966); Albert Cohen, *Delinquent Boys* (Glencoe: Free Press, 1955).

39. Cloward and Ohlin, *Delinquency and Opportunity,* 169.

40. Mary Pattillo, *Black Picket Fences: Privilege and Peril among the Black Middle Class* (Chicago: University of Chicago Press, 1999), 68.

41. Sudhir Venkatesh, *Off the Books: The Underground Economy of the Urban Poor* (Cambridge: Harvard University Press, 2006), 322.

42. Gerald D. Suttles, *The Social Construction of Communities* (Chicago: University of Chicago Press, 1972), 21; Donald Tricarico, *The Italians of Greenwich Village: The Social Structure and Transformation of an Ethnic Community* (New York: Center for Migration Studies of New York, 1984).

43. Tricarico, *Italians of Greenwich Village,* 41.

44. Suttles, *Social Construction of Communities,* 21, 38.

45. Park, Burgess, and McKenzie, *City,* 23.

46. Suttles, *Social Construction of Communities,* 35.

47. Ibid., 25, 252.

48. Ibid., 35; Gerald D. Suttles, *The Social Order of the Slum: Ethnicity and Territory in the Inner City* (Chicago: University of Chicago Press, 1968), 25–26; Emmett H. Buell, "Busing and the Defended Neighborhood South Boston, 1974–1977," *Urban Affairs Quarterly* 16, no. 2 (1980): 161–87.

49. Suttles, *Social Construction of Communities,* 36–37.

50. Ibid., 37.

51. Tricarico, *Italians of Greenwich Village,* 43.

52. Suttles, *Social Construction of Communities,* 35.

53. Roderick D. McKenzie, *The Neighborhood* (New York: Arno Press, 1970), 348, 607.

54. Suttles, *Social Order of the Slum,* 25–26.

55. Ibid., 20.

56. Spergel, *Racketville, Slumtown, and Haulburg,* 19.

57. Nicholas Pileggi, *Wiseguy* (New York: Pocket Books, 1985), 37–38.

58. Suttles, *Social Order of the Slum*, 231.

59. Ibid., 175, 220.

60. Ibid., 107.

61. Anthony J. Sorrentino, *Organizing against Crime: Redeveloping the Neighborhood* (New York: Human Sciences Press, 1977), 130, 142.

62. Tricarico, *Italians of Greenwich Village*, 70.

63. Park, Burgess, and McKenzie, *City*, 104; Frank Tannenbaum, "The Professional Criminal," *Century* 110 (1925): 577–88.

Chapter 2. The Gem of the Prairie

1. H. L. Schroeder and C. W. Forbich, *The Men Who Have Made the Fifth Ward* (Chicago: Forbich and Schroeder, 1895), 37.

2. "A Little Engine Takes Off," *CDT*, 12 January 1997.

3. Emmett Dedmon, *Fabulous Chicago* (New York: Random House, 1953), 32; "City Responds to Plight of the Union," *CDT*, 12 April 1861; "'Hog Butcher for the World' Opens Shop," *CDT*, 30 January 1997; United States Census Reports, 1840–1890.

4. Jack McPhaul, *Johnny Torrio: First of the Gang Lords* (New Rochelle, NY: Arlington House, 1970), 56–57.

5. Delos Avery, "Swatter of Squatters," *CDT*, 18 July 1943; "The Dens of the Sands Broken Up," *CDT*, 21 April 1857.

6. Jay R. Nash, *People to See* (Piscataway, NJ: New Century, 1981), 57–59; "The Scarlet Sisters Everleigh," *CDT*, 19 January 1936.

7. Dedmon, *Fabulous Chicago*, 74; Virgil F. Peterson, *Barbarians in Our Midst: A History of Chicago Crime and Politics* (Boston: Little, Brown, 1952), 35.

8. John H. Lyle, *The Dry and Lawless Years* (Englewood Cliffs, NJ: Prentice Hall, 1960), 25.

9. "Do You Remember?" *CDT*, 21 February 1960; *New Scholastic Dictionary* (New York: Scholastic Publishers, 1981), 492.

10. Carter H. Harrison, *The Stormy Years: The Autobiography of Carter H. Harrison, Five Times Mayor of Chicago* (New York: Bobbs-Merrill, 1935), 42; "Gamblers Alley Pool-Rooms," *CDT*, 29 June 1879; "Gamblers Alley," *CDT*, 7 February 1887.

11. "Great Fire Survivor," *CDT*, 8 October 1995; Henry Chafetz, *Play the Devil: A History of Gambling in the United States from 1492 to 1955* (New York: Potter, 1960), 417.

12. Peterson, *Barbarians in Our Midst*, 39–40; Dedmon, *Fabulous Chicago*, 137; John J. Flinn, *History of the Chicago Police: From the Settlement of the Community to the Present Time* (1887; Montclair, NJ: Patterson Smith, 1973), 153–201.

13. "Who Is Mike McDonald?" *CDT*, 28 October 1992; Alson J. Smith, *Syndicate City: The Chicago Crime Cartel and What to Do about It* (Chicago: Henry Regnery, 1954), 28.

14. "Mike McDonald at Death's Door," *CDT*, 8 August 1907; "A King Who Had Us in His Pocket," *CDT*, 20 October 1988.

15. "Dog Eat Dog," *CDT*, 20 August 1873; "What Mike McDonald Is After," *CDT*, 2 November 1889.

16. William T. Stead, *If Christ Came to Chicago: A Plea for the Union of All Who Love in the Service of All Who Suffer* (1894; Evanston, IL: Chicago Historical Bookworks, 1990), 233; L. O. Curon, *Chicago Satan's Sanctum* (Chicago: C. D. Phillips, 1899), 26; "panel house," *Webster's New American Dictionary* (New York: Random House, 1994), 1042; "badger house," Jonathan Green, *Casell's Dictionary of Slang* (London: Orion Publishing, 1998), 53.

17. Smith, *Syndicate City,* 30; "Death of Harry Varnell," *CDT*, 13 September 1898.

18. "Big Jim O'Leary," *CDN*, 25 January 1925; Richard T. Griffin, "Big Jim O'Leary: Gambler Boss iv th' Yards," *Chicago History* 5 (1976–1977): 213–22.

19. "O'Leary through with Gambling Game," *Chicago Examiner*, 12 August 1904; "Will Wake up Tom Barrett," *CDT*, 3 March 1905; "O'Leary Closes Up, Car Service Ends," *CDT*, 4 March 1905.

20. Smith, *Syndicate City,* 31; Richard C. Lindberg, *To Serve and Collect* (New York: Praeger, 1991), 99.

21. Commission of the Review of National Policy toward Gambling, *Gambling in America: Final Report of the Commission on the Review of the National Policy toward Gambling* (Washington, DC: U.S. Government Printing Office, 1976), 107.

22. Harrison, *Stormy Years,* 158; "From Bath to Beer," *CDT*, 24 July 1895; "Hilarity Reigns along the 'Levee'," *CDT*, 7 April 1897.

23. "Share in the Booty," *CDT*, 27 August 1894.

24. Harrison, *Stormy Years,* 85.

25. Ibid., 86; Lloyd Wendt and Herman Kogan, *Bosses in Lusty Chicago: The Story of Bathhouse John and Hinky Dink* [Originally published as *The Lords of the Levee,*1943] (Bloomington: Indiana University Press, 1967), 28, 146; "Police Will Let Crime Run Wild," *CDT*, 5 November 1894.

26. Wendt and Kogan, *Bosses in Lusty Chicago*, 104; "Fewer Crimes on the West Side," *CDT*, 6 June 1891; "Shot by an Officer," *CDT*, 11 July 1892.

27. Stead, *If Christ Came to Chicago,* 308; Andrew Bruce, "The Criminal Underworld of Chicago in the '80s and '90s," *Journal of Criminal Law, Criminology, and Police Science* 25 (1935): 344; John Landesco, "Chicago's Criminal Underworld of the '80s and '90s," *Journal of Criminal Law, Criminology, and Police Science* 25 (1935): 932.

28. Stead, *If Christ Came to Chicago* 124, 129; "Local Geography," *CDT*, 21 May 1882; Neta Candella, "Trinkets from Bawdy House Excite Collectors," *Alton Telegraph*, 26 June 1968; "Harrison's Headquarters," *CDT*, 29 March 1883.

29. Viva Divers, *The Black Hole* (No publisher, 1891–1892), 10.

30. John Kelly, "History of the Near South Side," Document 1b, Chicago History

Museum; Herbert Asbury, *The Gem of the Prairie* (1940; DeKalb: Northern Illinois University Press, 1986), 106.

31. "May Segregate Vice," *CRH*, 6 November 1903; *CDN*, "War on Chinese Dens," 11 May 1904.

32. Kelly, "History of the Near South Side," 7; Women's Christian Temperance Union, *Chicago's Dark Places* (Chicago: Craig Press, 1891), 65, 119.

33. Kelly, "History of the Near South Side," 7; Harrison, *Stormy Years*, 312; "Levee Crusade on in Earnest," *CDT*, 29 June 1901.

34. Lloyd L. Wendt and Herman Kogan, *Big Bill of Chicago* (New York: Bobbs-Merrill, 1953), 43.

35. Douglas Bukowski, *Big Bill Thompson: Chicago and the Politics of Image* (Urbana: University of Illinois Press, 1998), 13; Wendt and Kogan, *Big Bill*, 31–41.

36. "The Scarlet Sisters Everleigh," *CDT*, 19 January 1936; "Death Claims Ike Bloom, Old Red Light Host," *CDT*, 16 December 1930.

37. "Starts Vice War," *CDT*, 25 October 1911; Edward J. Zulkey, "The Ladies Everleigh," *CDT* 21 January 1979; Harrison, *Stormy Years*, 309; "The Scarlet Sisters Everleigh," *CDT*, 19 January 1936.

38. Lloyd Wendt, "When Hoodlums Made Whoopee," *CDT*, 8 December 1940; Lloyd Wendt, "John the Bath and the First Ward Ball," *CDT*, 15 December 1940.

39. Dedmon, *Fabulous Chicago*, 256; Kelly, "History of the Near South Side," 7; Wendt and Kogan, *Bosses in Lusty Chicago*, 94; Charles Washburn, *Come Into My Parlor* (New York: National Library Press, 1936), 117.

40. "Sell the Gospel!" *CDT*, 1 November 1942; Walter E. Reckless, *Vice in Chicago* (Montclair, NJ: Patterson Smith, 1933), 33.

41. "Public Indignation Stirs Officials to Close Area," *CDT*, 2 February 1936; Vice Commission of Chicago, *The Social Evil in Chicago: A Study of Existing Conditions* (Chicago: American Vigilance Association, 1911), 70; "Says Vice Will Be 1915 Issue," *CDT*, 31 October 1911.

42. Lincoln Steffens, *The Shame of the Cities* (1902; New York: Sagamore, 1957), 163.

43. "Expose Vote Sale Science in First," *CDT*, 16 September 1910; "The Scarlet Sisters Everleigh," *CDT*, 19 January 1936.

44. Vice Commission of Chicago, *Social Evil in Chicago*, 70; "Heitler Called Vice Trust Head," *CDT*, 20 January 1911; "Mayor Planning Three Levees," *CDT*, 7 November 1903.

45. "The Scarlet Sisters Everleigh," *CDT*, 19 January 1936; Vice Commission of Chicago, *Social Evil in Chicago*, 42.

46. "Wayman Men Raid Resorts; Levee in Panic," *CDT*, 5 October 1912; "Closed Levee Wide Open," *CDT*, 13 July 1913; "Tells Vice War," *CDT*, 6 December 1913; "Old Vice District Being Cleaned Up," *CDT*, 7 December 1913; "Death Claims Ike Bloom, Old Red Light Host," *CDT*, 16 December 1930.

47. "Inside Story of Vice's Grip on Chicago," *CDT*, 18 July 1914.

48. Virgil Peterson, "Inside the Crime Syndicate," *CDT*, 14 October 1956; "Who Killed Big Jim?" *CDT*, 7 February 1954.

49. Robert M. Lombardo, *The Black Hand: Terror by Letter in Chicago* (Chicago: University of Illinois Press, 2010), 1; "Torrio Is Shot; Police Hunt for O'Banion Men," *CDT*, 25 January 1925.

50. "Wayman Closes Levee in 1912," *CDT*, 17 July 1914.

51. "Inside Story of Vice's Grip on Chicago," *CDT*, 18 July 1914; "Rival Vice Police Duel; One Dead; Four Hurt," *CDT*, 17 July 1914; "Wayman Closes Levee in 1912," *CDT*, 17 July 1914; "Duel in Levee Gangster Job; Ended Wrong," *CDT*, 19 July 1914; "Disgusted Police Head Ends Levee Rule," *CDT*, 20 July 1914; "Transfer Capt. Ryan; Jim Colosimo Prisoner," *CDT*, 21 July 1914.

52. "Police Bow to Prince Arthur," *CDT*, 18 July 1914; "New Vice List Names 72 Places Throughout the City," *CDT*, 2 March 1914; "Vice Resorts Reduced a Half by Levee Lid," *CDT*, 14 January 1916; "Bundesen and Negro Fight in Morals Court," *CDT*, 28 August 1923.

53. Wendt and Kogan, *Bosses in Lusty Chicago*, 328; John Kobler, *Capone* (New York: Collier Books, 1971), 56.

54. "Colosimo's Arrowhead Inn," dinner menu, *Hammond Times*, 17 August 1918; "Jim Colosimo Beats Reporter on Vice Inquiry," *CDT*, 19 May 1919; "Colosimo 'The Immune' Fined $300 and Costs," *CDT*, 29 May 1919; "Death Claims Ike Bloom, Old Red Light Host," *CDT*, 16 December 1930.

55. "Hint 'Pull' Aids Jim Colosimo Death Suspect," *CDT*, 17 December 1920; "Boss Carrozzo Wafted to Fame by White Wings," *CDT*, 15 April 1940; Arthur J. Bilek, *The First Vice Lord* (Nashville, TN: Cumberland House, 2008), 250.

56. "Courts, Opera, Underworld to Bury Colosimo," *CDT*, 14 May 1920.

57. "$13,900 Chief's Share in Graft, Costello Says," *CDT*, 19 December 1917.

Chapter 3. The Black Mafia

1. St. Claire Drake and Horace R. Clayton, *Black Metropolis: A Study of Negro Life in a Northern City* (1945; Chicago: University of Chicago Press, 1993), 111; Francis A. J. Ianni, *The Black Mafia: Ethnic Succession in Organized Crime* (New York: Simon and Schuster, 1974); Rufus Schatzberg and Robert J. Kelly, *African-American Organized Crime: A Social History* (New York: Garland, 1996), 11.

2. Robert J. Kelly, "African-American Organized Crime," in *Organized Crime: Uncertainties and Dilemmas,* ed. Stanley Einstein and Menachem Amir (Chicago: University of Illinois Press, 1999), 273.

3. Ianni, *Black Mafia,* 12; Daniel Bell, *The End of Ideology: On the Exhaustion of Political Ideas in the Fifties* (New York: Free Press, 1960); James O'Kane, *The Crooked Ladder: Gangsters, Ethnicity, and the American Dream* (New Brunswick, NJ: Transaction, 1992), 84.

4. Drake and Clayton, *Black Metropolis,* 32, 39, 62; Franklin E. Frazier, *The Negro*

Family in Chicago (Chicago: University of Chicago Press, 1932), 93; Thomas L. Philpott, *The Slum and the Ghetto: Immigrants, Blacks, and Reformers in Chicago, 1880–1930* (Belmont, CA: Wadsworth, 1991), 134.

5. Drake and Clayton, *Black Metropolis*, 58, 8; Chicago Commission on Race Relations, *The Negro in Chicago: A Study of Race Relations and a Race Riot* (Chicago: University of Chicago Press, 1922), 137.

6. Allan H. Spear, *Black Chicago: The Making of a Negro Ghetto, 1890–1920* (Chicago: University of Chicago Press, 1967), 129.

7. Ibid.; James R. Grosman, "African-American Migration to Chicago," in *Ethnic Chicago: A Multicultural Portrait*, ed. Melvin G. Holli and Peter d'A. Jones (Grand Rapids: W. B. Eerdmans, 1995), 303–40.

8. Drake and Clayton, *Black Metropolis*, 12, 80; John Allswang, *A House for All Peoples* (Lexington: University Press of Kentucky, 1971), 205.

9. Drake and Clayton, *Black Metropolis*, 76.

10. "Mushmouth Gets Better," *CA*, 24 August 1907; "Mushmouth Johnson Is Dead," *CDN*, 14 September 1907; "Mushmouth Johnson," *CRH*, 24 August 1907.

11. Harold F. Gosnell, *Negro Politicians: The Rise of Negro Politics in Chicago* (1935; Chicago: University of Chicago Press, 1967), 127; "Lid Off at Mushmouth's," *CDT*, 3 April 1905; "May Segregate Vice," *CRH*, 6 November 1903.

12. "Den License Is Gone," *CDN*, 16 November 1903; Spear, *Black Chicago*, 76; "Thrives as Police Wink," *CDT*, 15 June 1903.

13. "Through the Recommendation of the Chief of Police Revokes the License of Col. 'Pony' Moore," *Broad Ax*, 18 November 1905; "Pony Loses Glitter Can't Pay His Dues," *Broad Ax*, 10 August 1907; Charles Washburn, *Come Into My Parlor* (New York: National Library Press, 1936), 90.

14. "Robert T. Motts, Owner and Manager of the Pekin Theatre," *Broad Ax*, 15 July 1911; "Noted Lawmakers of Early Chicago," *CD*, 2 April 1933; Gosnell, *Negro Politicians*, 128.

15. "Robert T. Motts," *Broad Ax*, 28 December 1907.

16. Gosnell, *Negro Politicians*, 128; Spear, *Black Chicago*, 77.

17. Alan Lomax, *Mister Jelly Roll: The Fortunes of Jelly Roll Morton* (New York: Pantheon Books, 1950), 185.

18. "Healy Admits Bribes from De Priest Aide," *CDT*, 5 June 1917; "Capt. Healy and De Priest to Be Arrested Today," *CDT*, 19 January 1917; "Teenan Jones to Turn against Ex-Ald. De Priest," *CDN*, 2 June 1917.

19. "Teenan Jones Bares Huge Graft Levies," *CDN*, 23 January 1917; "Healy Admits Bribes from De Priest Aide," *CDT*, 5 June 1917; "De Priest Names Harding as Boss in Black Belt," *CDT*, 6 June 1917; "How Roe Moved in on Fabulous Jones Brothers," *CD*, 23 August 1952.

20. "De Priest Names Harding as Boss in Black Belt," *CDT*, 6 June 1917.

21. Kenneth Allsop, *The Bootleggers: The Story of Prohibition* (New York: Arlington House, 1961), 182; Chicago Commission on Race Relations, *Negro in Chicago*, 323.

22. William H. Kenny, *Chicago Jazz: A Cultural History, 1904–1930* (New York: Oxford University Press, 1993), 13; Allsop, *Bootleggers,* 179–81.

23. Eddie Condon, *We Called It Music: A Generation of Jazz* (Westport, CT: Greenwood Press, 1947), 19, 23; Lomax, *Mister Jelly Roll*, 96.

24. Condon, *We Called It Music,* 27.

25. Lomax, *Mister Jelly Roll,* 219.

26. Condon, *We Called It Music,* 103; "Patronize Worthy Race Enterprises along the Stroll," *CD*, 8 May 1915.

27. Langston Hughes, *The Big Sea* (New York: Hill and Wang, 1940), 30.

28. Kelly, "African-American Organized Crime," 1999, 16; Kenny, *Chicago Jazz,* 17, 5.

29. Frazier, *Negro Family in Chicago,* 98; James R. Grossman, "African-American Migration to Chicago," in Holli and Jones, *Ethnic Chicago*, 331.

30. "Scattered City Vice Beats Segregation," *CDN*, 25 May 1915; John Landesco, *Organized Crime in Chicago* (1929; Chicago: University of Chicago Press, 1968), 852.

31. "$10,000 Graft Paid Politicians Weekly by Second Ward Vice Dens," *CDN*, 15 August 1921.

32. "Syndicate Crosses 2D Ward Gamblers," *CDN*, 16 August 1921.

33. "$10,000 Graft Paid Politicians Weekly by Second Ward Vice Dens," *CDN*, 15 August 1921.

34. Ibid.; "2nd Ward Dems. Reopen as Graft Ring Revives," *CDN,* 12 October 1921; "Police Raid Exposed 2nd Ward Gambling Dens," *CDN*, 13 October 1921.

35. "Graft Men Defiant, Order Gaming Lid Off," *CDN*, 21 October 1921.

36. "Fortunes Won, Lost in Big Gaming House" *CDN*, 5 June 1922; "Jackson Ring Again Menaces South Side," *CDN*, 29 December 1922.

37. Douglas Bukowski, *Big Bill Thompson, Chicago, and the Politics of Image* (Urbana: University of Illinois Press, 1998), 15; Spear, *Black Chicago,* 188; Allswang, *House for All Peoples,* 146.

38. Spear, *Black Chicago,* 188.

39. "Vice Dens Run by Police, Jury Is Told," *CDN*, 9 January 1923.

40. "Jackson Ring Again Menaces South Side," *CDN*, 29 December 1922; "Lueder Seen Victor as the Polls Close, Litsinger Is 2nd," *CDN*, 27 February 1923.

41. "Raid Dan Jackson Den," *CDN*, 30 April 1923; "Official Swears Thompson Bartered Privilege for South Side Votes," *CDN*, 8 March 1928.

42. "Wide-Open Town Seen as Scourge," *CDN*, 6 March 1928; Travis J. Dempsey, *Black Politics* (Chicago: Urban Research Press, 1987), 79.

43. "Official Swears Thompson Bartered Privilege for South Side Votes," *CDN*, 8 March 1928; "Wide-Open Town Seen as Scourge," *CDN*, 6 March 1928; "Push Inquiry into South Side Slush," *CDN*, 18 August 1928; "Gamblers Verify Vice Fund Tales," *CDN*, 13 September 1928.

44. Ianni, *Black Mafia,* 115; "Second Ward Committeeman Stricken on Eve of Plot Trial," *CDN* 17 May 1929; Gosnell, *Negro Politicians,* 132.

45. "Special Jury Hunts Slush in Colored Belt," *CDT*, 17 August 1928; "Hold De Priest, Jackson, 9 Aides," *CDN*, 29 September 1928; "Grand Jury Indicts Politicians," *New York Times*, 30 September 1928.

46. "Henchman Turns on Dan Jackson, Boss of 2D Ward," *CDT*, 24 September 1928; Drake and Clayton, *Black Metropolis,* 351; "Opens War on Policy Game," *CD*, 12 July 1931.

47. "Arrest Sons of Minister in Vice Raid," *CD*, 21 September 1931; Roger Biles, *Big City Boss in Depression and War* (DeKalb: Northern Illinois University Press, 1984), 89; "Policy Games Ready to Quit, Says Cermak," *CDN*, 11 August 1931; "Lucrative Racket," *CDT*, 16 January 1955.

48. "Links Skidmore to Policy," *CDN*, 6 September 1938.

49. Biles, *Big City Boss,* 90–92; Gosnell, *Negro Politicians*, 267.

50. Mark H. Haller, "Organized Crime in Urban Society: Chicago in the Twentieth Century," *Journal of Social History* 5 (1971–1972): 210–34.

51. Drake and Clayton, *Black Metropolis,* 472; "Policy! Racket Bleeding City over the Years," *CDT*, 16 January 1955; "15 Racket Kings Enriched by Poor," *CDN*, 29 August 1938.

52. Illinois Writers Project: Negro in Illinois, Policy Sam, Box 35, Number 18:3, undated, Woodson Library, Chicago, Illinois.

53. Drake and Clayton, *Black Metropolis,* 485; "Hard Blow to Graft," *CRH*, 9 November 1903; "Roe Murder Spells End to Lush Racket and Men It Made Famous," *CD*, 16 August 1952.

54. Illinois Writers Project, Box 35, Number 18:4; "Dooms Policy Game in Chicago," *CDT*, 21 April 1905.

55. Illinois Writers Project, Box 35, Number 18:1, 5–6; "Policy Sam Young Rites Held Friday," *CD*, 22 May 1937.

56. Dennis Nordin, *The New Deal's Black Congressman* (Columbia: University of Missouri Press, 1997), 105; U.S. Congress, Senate, Special Committee to Investigate Organized Crime in Interstate Commerce, *Third Interim Report, May 1, 1951,* 82nd Congress, 1st session, 195. S. Rpt. 307: 56.

57. "Roe Murder Spells End to Lush Racket and Men It Made Famous," *CD*, 16 August 1952.

58. Illinois Writers Project, Box 35, Number 18:6; "Vice Dens Run by Police, Jury Is Told," *CDN*, 9 January 1923; "Chicago Raids Dan Jackson Den," *CDN*, 30 April 1923.

59. "Wide-Open Town Seen as Scourge," *CDN*, 6 March 1928.

60. Ibid.

61. "Bury Walter Kelly in Pomp and Splendor," *CD*, 14 January 1939; "Inside Facts on How Gang Paid Gunmen," *CD*, 21 January 1939.

62. "Cops Guard Man Who Saw Killers," *CD*, 30 August 1952.

63. "How Roe Moved in on Fabulous Jones Brothers," *CD*, 23 August 1952; "Cops Guard Man Who Saw Killers," *CD*, 30 August 1952.

64. "Roe Murder Spells End to Lush Racket and Men It Made Famous," *CD*, 16 August 1952; "Arrest Sons of Minister in Vice Raid," *CD*, 21 September 1931; "Kings of Policy in City Named," *CDN*, 30 August 1938.

65. "Roe Murder Spells End to Lush Racket and Men It Made Famous," *CD*, 16 August 1952; "Rackets Now Flourish in All Quarters," *CD*, 24 September 1932.

66. "Kings of Policy in City Named," *CDN*, 30 August 1938.

67. "15 Racket Kings Enriched by Poor," *CDN*, 29 August 1938; "Policy Swindle Nets WPA Cash," *CDN*, 31 August 1938.

68. "Jury Indicts 26 in Policy Rings," *CDT*, 31 January 1942.

69. Gosnell, *Negro Politicians*, 125; Albert N. Votaw, "Chicago: Corrupt and Contented?" *New Republic* 127–28 (1952): 13–14.

70. Illinois Writers Project, Box 35, Number 11:3; 'Policy Lid Off," *CDN*, 15 March 1928.

71. Chicago Crime Commission, "Policy Racket in Chicago," unpublished, 3 June 1946:5.

72. Illinois Writers Project, Box 35, Number 11:10; "Unscrupulous Matt Bivens Was the Playboy of Policy," *CD*, 6 September 1952.

73. Illinois Writers Project, Box 35, Number 11:13.

74. Ibid., Box 35, Number 23:3; "Policy Swindle Nets WPA Cash," *CDN*, 31 August 1938.

75. Kelly, "African-American Organized Crime," 21.

Chapter 4. The Syndicate

1. Increase Mather, *Wo to Drunkards* (Boston: Marmaduke Johnson, 1673); Herbert Asbury, *The Great Illusion: An Informal History of Prohibition* (New York: Greenwood), 106.

2. Benjamin Rush, *An Inquiry into the Effects of Ardent Spirits upon the Human Body and Mind* (Boston: James Loring, 1823).

3. Asbury, *Great Illusion*, 27.

4. Joseph R. Gusfield, *Symbolic Crusade: Status Politics and the American Temperance Movement* (Champaign: University of Illinois Press, 1963), 5; "Dirty Work at Dearborn," *Time*, 24 March 1930.

5. John Landesco, *Organized Crime in Chicago* (Chicago: University of Chicago Press, 1968), 180; Frederic M. Thrasher, *The Gang: A Study of 1,313 Gangs in Chicago* (Chicago: University of Chicago Press, 1927), 141; "Gilhooley Gang All Free," *CDT*, 4 October 1909; "Questioned," *CDT*, 17 April 1945; Guy Murchie Jr., "Capone's Decade of Death," *CDT*, 9 February 1936.

6. John Lyle, "The Beginning: The Dry and Lawless Years," *CDT*, 12 November 1960; *American College Dictionary* s.v. "bootleg booze."

7. Humbert S. Nelli, *The Italians in Chicago, 1880–1930: A Study in Ethnic Mobility* (New York: Oxford Press 1970), 148; Lloyd Wendt and Herman Kogan, *Big*

Bill of Chicago (New York: Bobbs-Merrill, 1953), 239; Robert J. Schoenberg, *Mr. Capone: The Real—and Complete—Story of Al Capone* (New York: Wm. Morrow, 1992), 96.

8. John Kobler, *Capone: The Life and World of Al Capone* (New York: Collier Books, 1971), 114; Fred D. Pasley, *Al Capone: The Biography of a Self-Made Man* (Salem, NH: Ayer Publishing, 1930), 40.

9. Lyle, "Beginning," 171.

10. Charles Gregston, "Crime in Chicago Now on Business Basis," *CDN*, 15 November 1924; Chicago Commission on Race Relations, *The Negro in Chicago: A Study of Race Relations and a Race Riot* (Chicago: University of Chicago Press, 1922), 12, 13, 54, 55.

11. "O'Banion Gang Like Pirates of Old Days," *CDT*, 11 November 1924; "Girl on O'Banion's Death Clue," *CDT*, 11 November 1924; "Senator Moike Dies; Once King of Little Hell," *CDT*, 16 October 1916.

12. James O'Donnell Bennett, "Gangland: The True Story of Chicago Crime," *CDT*, 3 February 1929.

13. Norman Mark, *Mayors, Madams, and Madmen* (Chicago: Chicago Review Press, 1979); "Rid City of Gunmen—Dever," *CDT*, 14 November 1924; Pasley, *Al Capone*, 43; "Girl on O'Banion Death Clue," *CDT*, 11 November 1924.

14. "Extent of Genna Gang's Alcohol Trade Revealed," *CDT*, 17 June 1925; "Gennas in Terror; Tony Dies," *CDT*, 9 July 1925; "Death Marked for Three More of Genna Family," *CDT*, 10 July 1925; Jane Addams, "A Decade of Prohibition," in *Eighty Years at Hull House*, ed. A. F. Davis and M. L. McCree (Chicago: Quadrangle Books, 1969), 158–62; Donald A. Pacyga and Ellen Skerrett, *Chicago* (Chicago: Loyola University Press, 1986), 214.

15. "Genna Gunmen Fire First, Two Survivors Say," *CDT*, 28 October 1925; "Collins Shifts 36 Police out of Genna Land," *CDT*, 15 November 1925; James O'Donnell Bennett, "Chicago Gangland," *CDT*, 10 March 1929.

16. Bernard P. Barasa, "The Unione Siciliana," *CDT*, 19 June 1925; "320 Seized in Gang Raids," *CDT*, 15 June 1925.

17. John R. Schmidt, *The Mayor Who Cleaned Up Chicago: A Political Biography of William E. Dever* (DeKalb: Northern Illinois University Press, 1989), 132; Schoenberg, *Mr. Capone*, 112; John Lyle, "Kill O'Banion—The Mob Says," *CDT*, 26 November 1960; "Ganglands Whose Who—O'Banion Warfare," *Chicago Examiner*, 22 September 1926.

18. James Doherty, *CDT*, "Thousands at Funeral," 15 November 1924.

19. "Torrio Is Shot; Police Hunt for O'Banion," *CDT*, 25 January 1925; Jack McPhaul, *Johnny Torrio: First of the Gang Lords* (New Rochelle, NY: Arlington House, 1970), 224–38.

20. "New Rich Rum Chief Slain by Gunmen in Car," *CDT*, 26 May 1925; "Kill Two Cops; City Aroused," *CDT*, 14 June 1925; "Gennas in Terror; Tony Dies," *CDT*, 9 July 1925.

21. Giovanni Schiavo, *The Italians in Chicago: A Study in Americanization* (Chicago: Italian American Publishing, 1928); "Gunmen Bury Lombardo with Kingly Pomp," *CDT*, 12 September 1928.

22. Landesco, *Organized Crime,* 1073, 1079; "Police Accuse Joe Aiello as Lolordo Slayer," *CDT*, 10 January 1929.

23. "Seize Five in Assassination Plot," *CDT*, 21 November 1925; John H. Lyle, "O'Banion's Successors Learn Revenge Is a One Way Ride," *CDT*, 27 November 1960; "U.S. Uncovers True Story of Capone's Rise," *CDT*, 14 June 1931; "Two Are Shot When Bullets Rake Bakery," *CDT*, 29 May 1927.

24. "Kill Lombardo, Mafia Chief," *CDT*, 8 September 1928; "Police Accuse Joe Aiello as Lolordo Slayer," *CDT*, 10 January 1929; Pasley, *Al Capone*, 227, 228.

25. "Panic Grips 'Little Sicily'," *CDT*, 9 September 1928.

26. Chicago Police Department Internal Memorandum, "Murder of Seven Men at 2122 N. Clark Street," 14 February 1929; "Slay Doctor in Massacre," *CDT*, 15 February 1929; "Accuse Al's Aids of Tip Off in Bremer Case," *CDT*, 28 January 1935.

27. James O'Donnell Bennett, "Chicago Gangland," *CDT*, 17 February 1929; "Beer Sold Here in Week Put at 25,000,000 Pints," *CDT*, 26 February 1931.

28. John H. Lyle, "'Public Enemy'—A Weapon Becomes a War Cry," *CDT*, 16 December 1960; "Police Drive Adds Word to Gang Jargon," *American Tribune*, 26 September 1930.

29. "Capone Takes Cover in Jail," *CDT*, 18 May 1929; "Capone Starts Fight to Regain Lost Freedom," *CDT*, 19 May 1929; "Capone Sealed in Prison Gloom; Predict Release," *CDT*, 20 May 1929; "Capone's Story by Himself," *CDT*, 22 March 1930.

30. "Machine Gun Slugs Riddle Gang Leader," *CDT*, 24 October 1930; "Hunt Assassins and Partner of Dead Gangster," *CDT*, 25 October 1930.

31. Dennis Hoffman, *Business vs. Organized Crime: Chicago's Private War on Al Capone, 1929–1932* (Chicago: Chicago Crime Commission, 1989), 29; Virgil Peterson, "Inside the Capone Syndicate," *CDT*, 21 October 1956; "Charges Capone Put up $260,000 to Aid Thompson," *CDT*, 17 February 1931.

32. Wendt and Kogan, *Big Bill*, 351; Nelli, *Italians in Chicago*, 191.

33. Wendt and Kogan, *Big Bill*, 280; Virgil Peterson, "Inside the Crime Syndicate," *CDT*, 21 October 1956; "Big Gamblers Not Worried; Small Fry Hit," *CDT*, 23 September 1931.

34. Hoffman, *Business vs. Organized Crime,* 21, 33; John H. Lyle, "The Mighty Capone Muscles in on Labor Unions," *CDT*, 4 December 1960.

35. "Capone's Purchase of Second-Hand Beer Truck in 1922 First Link in Evidence of 5,000 Dry Law Charges," *Frederick [Virginia] Post*, 29 June 1931.

36. Hoffman, *Business vs. Organized Crime,* 16; John H. Lyle, "The Mighty Capone Muscles in on Labor Unions," *CDT*, 4 December 1960.

37. "The War in Chicago," *CDT*, 16 March 1931; National Commission on Law

Observance and Enforcement, *Final Report* (Washington, DC: U.S. Government Printing Office, 1931); James Doherty, "Curtains for Capone," *CDT*, 15 April 1951.

38. "Gangs to Fight for Share in Beer Business," *CDT*, 29 March 1933. Oral history respondent Al "Wallpaper" Wolf (1990) worked with Eliot Ness and his Untouchables.

39. "Capone's Decade of Death," *CDT*, 9 February 1936.

40. Louis Wirth, *The Ghetto* (1928; Chicago: University of Chicago Press, 1998), 153–55, 169–71, 227; Ron Grossman, "From Pushcarts to Prosperity," *CDT*, 16 April 2000, Magazine Section.

41. Wirth, *Ghetto*, 225, 238; "Manny Shakes Up Police," *CDT*, 6 June 1913.

42. "Morton, Miller Tell How They Killed Police," *CDT*, 7 January 1922; "Nails Morton Gang Is Blamed for Booze Theft," *CDT*, 7 May 1922; "Nails Morton Killed by Horse," *CDT*, 14 May 1923.

43. Grossman, "From Pushcarts to Prosperity," 16, 18; Irving Cutler, "The Jews of Chicago: From Shtetl to Suburb," in *Ethnic Chicago: A Multicultural Portrait*, ed. Peter d'A. Jones and Melvin G. Holli (Grand Rapids: Wm. Eerdmans, 1995), 122–72; "The Vote Crop in the 24th Ward Has High Yield," *CDT*, 17 February 1946; "Jake Arvey and His Mr. Kennelly," *CDT*, 18 May 1947; "Report Income to Rosenberg from Gambling," *CDT*, 16 March 1934.

44. Capone biographer John Kobler attributes the name "Greasy Thumb" to *Tribune* reporter James Doherty. "Man Killed by Gunman," *CDT*, 9 May 1924.

45. "Frank Nitti," *CDT*, 19 October 1940; "Jack Guzik Now Is No. 1 Man of Gang Overlords," *CDT*, 25 October 1941.

46. "Sumner Reveals Humphreys' Plot against Union," *CDT*, 11 May 1953; "City's Debts Pile Up," *CDT*, 6 February 1930.

47. Gus Tyler, *Organized Crime in America: A Book of Readings* (Ann Arbor: University of Michigan Press, 1962), 181.

48. "U.S. Indicts 23 Capone Men," *CDT*, 2 May 1931.

49. "46 Species of Rackets Still Active, Charge," *CDT*, 6 April 1928; "How Carrozzo Got Power to Seize Unions," *CDT*, 27 March 1943; "Raid Unions; Racket War On," *CDT*, 18 September 1930.

50. "Pinball Machine Operators Ordered to Buy Licenses," *CS*, 26 September 1946; "William J. Block, "Gangland's Juke Box Empire," *CS*, 11 November 1946.

51. "Warn Cleaners Terrorism Is Periling Trade," *CDT*, 13 January 1932; "Swanson Told Story of Wars in Dyeing Trade," *CDT*, 17 January 1932; "Gang Big Shots, Heads of Truck Racket, Freed," *CDT*, 5 November 1932.

52. "Bioff, Browne Convicted of Extortion," *CDT*, 7 November 1941; "Browne, Bioff, Leaders in Film Racket, Paroled," *CDT*, 23 December 1944.

53. "Syndicate Attempt to 'Muscle In' on Service Told," *CDT*, 25 June 1946; "Victim's Own Story of Capone Gaming Control, Bared," *CDT*, 26 June 1946; "Ragen Poison Amount Called Considerable," *CDT*, 1 September 1946; "U.S. Cities Fear Vote Coup by Crime Combine," *CDT*, 24 September 1949.

54. "Thompson's Boxes Yield 1½ Millions," *CDT*, 31 March 1944; James Doherty,

"Big Bill Thompson," *CDT*, 29 April 1951; James Doherty, "End of an Era, the Last Days of Big Bill," *CDT*, 6 May 1951.

55. Fletcher Dobyns, *The Underworld of American Politics* (New York: Fletcher Dobyns, 1932), 36, 42, 47.

56. Ibid., 111.

57. Ibid., 147.

58. "Cermak and Courtney Join Forces to Drive Out Gangs," *CDN*, 6 December 1932; "Nitti Long Held Business Chief of Underworld," *CDT*, 20 March 1943; "Capone Gang Chief Sinking," *CDT*, 20 December 1932; "Nitti Shot in Loop Fight," *CDN*, 19 December 1932; "Mayor's War on Dens Keeps Judges Busy," *CDT*, 20 December 1932.

59. Alex Gottfried, *Boss Cermak of Chicago: A Study of Political Leadership* (Seattle: University of Washington Press, 1962), 320–22.

60. John T. Flynn, "These Our Rulers," *Colliers* (6 July 1940); Virgil Peterson, "The Mob Grows Fat," *CDT*, 4 November 1956.

61. James Doherty, "P. A. Nash Dies, Aged 80; Long Party Chief," *CDT*, 7 October 1943; James Doherty, "Courtney Acts against Three Policy Leaders," *CDT*, 14 August 1942.

62. Virgil W. Peterson, "The Myth of the Wide-Open Town," *Journal of Criminal Law and Criminology* (September 1948): 288–97; Roger Biles, *Big City Boss in Depression and War: Mayor Edward J. Kelly of Chicago* (DeKalb: Northern Illinois University Press, 1984), 107. FBI file #62–34299-24A quoted in Mars Eghigian Jr., *After Capone: The Life and World of Chicago Mob Boss Frank "The Enforcer" Nitti* (Nashville: Cumberland House, 2006), 323.

63. "Courtney Only Rival in Kelly's Political Path," *CDT*, 28 October 1943.

64. "Police Reveal 2 Judges Clash on Corruption Charges at Club," *CDT*, 18 October 1938; "Chicagoans Pay for a Safe City but Don't Get It," *CDT*, 9 June 1946; "Politics Keep Police Cliques in Their Jobs," *CDT*, 2 June 1946; "They Are Just Political Tools," *CDT*, 30 May 1946.

65. Arnold R. Hirsch, "Martin Kennelly," in *The Mayors: The Chicago Political Tradition*, ed. Paul M. Green and Melvin G. Holli (Carbondale: Southern Illinois University Press, 1987), 129; "Deny Political Angle in Ragen Case Arrest," *CDT*, 14 March 1947; Clayton Kirkpatrick, "Chicago's Cops More Honest since Repeal," *CDT*, 13 April 1953.

66. Virgil Peterson, *Barbarians in Our Midst: A History of Chicago Crime and Politics* (Boston: Little Brown, 1952), 228; "Kennelly Life Story Tribute to His Mother," *CDT*, 5 April 1951; "Hunter Lashes Kennelly; GOP Vote Held Vital," *CDT*, 7 January 1951.

67. "Nitti Kills Himself!" *CDT*, 20 March 1943; "Frank Nitti," *CDT*, 19 October 1940.

68. William Leonard and Sandy Smith, "How the Gang Operates," *CDT*, 25 October 1959; "The Mob Speaks Softly Today but It's Bigger Than Ever," *Oakland Tribune*, 29 January 1961.

Chapter 5. The Forty-two Gang

1. "Captive to Face Trial in Holdup of Mayor's Wife," *CDT*, 10 October 1930.

2. Frederic M. Thrasher, *The Gang: A Study of 1,313 Gangs in Chicago* (1927; Chicago: New Chicago Press, 2000), 145; Herbert Asbury, *The Gem of the Prairie* (1940; De Kalb: Northern Illinois University Press, 1986).

3. "Fewer Crimes on the West Side," *CDT*, 6 June 1891; "Pardon for a Thug," *CDT*, 26 October 1894; "De Luxe Troupe of Highwaymen All Convicted," *CDT*, 3 November 1919.

4. Thrasher, *Gang*, 145.

5. John Landesco, *Organized Crime in Chicago* (1929; Chicago: University of Chicago Press, 1968).

6. John Landesco, Papers, Box 4, Folders 1–4, Special Collections Research Center, University of Chicago Library.

7. John Landesco, "Crime and the Failure of Institutions in Chicago's Immigrant Areas," *Journal of the American Institute of Criminal Law and Criminology* 23, no. 2 (1932a): 238–48; John Landesco, "The Life History of a Member of the Forty-two Gang," *Journal of the American Institute of Criminal Law and Criminology* 23, no. 6 (1933): 964–98; Landesco, "Formation Consolidation, and Dissolution," Box 1, Folder 4; Landesco, "Diffusion of a Criminal Culture," Box 1, Folder 3.

8. "Sixth Police Killer Guilty; Gets 199 Years," *CDT*, 23 September 1933.

9. Landesco, "Life History of a Member," 970; Sam Giancana and Charles Giancana, *Double Cross* (New York: Warner Brothers, 1992).

10. Landesco "Life History of a Member," 973; Landesco, "Formation, Consolidation, and Dissolution," Box 4, Folders 1–4, 1–2, identifies them as Patsy Pargoni, Hank, Jitty Pargoni, "Fat" Riccio, Vito Pelletieri, Ned Rooney, Red O'Brien, Joe Roberti, John Bolton, Catrina, Monk Pupillo, Nick Muscato, Louie "Cadoodles" De Christoforo, Frank Gallichio, "Fat" Carpanelli, Frank "Chudaback" De Luca, the two De Millio brothers, and the two Schiulo brother.

11. Landesco, "Formation, Consolidation, and Dissolution," Box 4, Folders 1–4, 3; "42 Gang Recruits Boys of 6, Says Police Captain," *CDT*, 10 December 1932.

12. Landesco, "The Origin and Formation of the Criminal Gang," Box 1, Folder 1; "Mitchell Gem Gang Guilty," *CDT*, 17 January 1932.

13. Landesco, "Experience with Police," Box 1, Folder 3; Landesco, "Formation, Consolidation, and Dissolution," Box 4, Folders 1–4, 6.

14. Landesco, "Experience with Police," Box 1, Folder 3, 5, 12.

15. Ibid., 4.

16. "Seize 3 Boys; Two Confess Auto Thefts," *CDT*, 12 April 1932; "Survey Shows Gangs at Work Stripping Autos," *CDT*, 25 November 1932; "Cars Recovered Exceed Thefts for Second Year," *CDT*, 26 November 1932; Landesco, "Life History of a Member," 980; "Baby Bandit Caught in Stolen Car after Chase," *CDT*, 13 August 1929.

17. "Seize Alleged Thief with Two Shotguns in Car," *CDT*, 6 July 1933; "42 Gang Recruits Boys of Six," *CDT*, 10 December 1932; Landesco, "Experience with Police," Box 1, Folder 3, 14.

18. "4 Men Quizzed as Suspects in Dozen Robberies," *CDT*, 14 June 1930; Landesco, "Experience with Police," Box 1, Folder 3, 13; "Diligent Bandit Finds a Victim in Prison Cell," *CDT*, 11 April 1932; "Try Two '42' Gangsters for $3,000 Robbery," *CDT*, 31 December 1930; "Two Indicted for Threatening Robbery Victim," *CDT*, 28 October 1932; "Second Bandit Is Killed in Store Holdup," *CDT*, 26 November 1931; "Bouncer in Dance Hall Shot by Gang He Ejected," *CDT*, 30 December 1929; "Gangster Admits Holdup; Given Term in Prison," *CDT*, 6 August 1931; "Police Arrest 3 Suspects in Mail Robbery," *CDT*, 17 January 1934; "Ride Slaying Laid to War of Alky Dealers," *CDT*, 23 October 1932; "Youth, Freed in Robbery, Talks Self into Jail," *CDT*, 17 November 1933.

19. "Wounding of 5 in Café Battle Laid to Rum War," *CDN*, 2 January 1931.

20. Landesco, "Life History of a Member," 977; "Lay Gunfight in Cabaret to Robbers' Raid," *CDT*, 3 January 1931; Landesco, "Experience with Police," Box 1, Folder 3, 8, 20.

21. "Gunmen Shoot Police Chief; 1 Caught," *CDT*, 26 May 1929; "Policeman Slain and 9 Wounded in Holdup Battles," *CDT*, 2 January 1931.

22. "Two Members of '42' Gang Found Guilty of Attacking Girl," *CDT*, 25 November 1927; "Police Capture Pair Who Tried to Kidnap Girl," *CDT*, 19 September 1928; "Kills Gangster, Who, He Charges, Insulted Girl," *CDT*, 19 May 1927; "Death Penalty Law Is Sought for Gang Rape," *CDT*, 28 November 1928.

23. Landesco, "Diffusion of a Criminal Culture," Box 1, Folder 4.

24. "2 Youths Get 'Rides'; Police Hunt for Clews," *CDT*, 1 July 1930; "Laborer Is Ride Victim; Killing Puzzles Police," *CDT*, 2 July 1930; "42 Gangster Shot to Death in Automobile," *CDT*, 9 September 1930.

25. "Slain by Victim as Black Hand Plot Is Foiled," *CDT*, 22 February 1931.

26. "Clementi and 9 Aids Identified in Bank Holdup," *CDT*, 9 June 1933; "Father Slays 2 Bank Bandits to Avenge Son," *CDT*, 26 May 1934; "Coroner's Jury Praises Slayer of Bank Bandits," *CDT*, 27 May 1934.

27. "Judge Directs Capture; Four Confess," *CDT*, 17 January 1933; "Expect Jury to Indict Mitchell Jewel Robbers," *CDT*, 6 December 1931; "Hunt Mitchell Jewel Robbers in 'Valley' Raids," *CDT*, 25 November 1931; "Identify Tufano as Robber of Mitchell Gems," *CDN*, 27 November 1931; "Four Mitchell Jewel Robbers Are Sentenced," *CDT*, 23 January 1932; "Six Hoodlums in '42' Sentenced to Jail," *CDN*, 3 December 1931.

28. "Judge, Police in War on '42' Gang; Seize 65," *CDT*, 4 December 1931.

29. "Voice of the People," *CDT*, 12 December 1931; "Judge Directs Capture; Four Confess," *CDT*, 17 January 1933.

30. Landesco, "Experience with Police," Box 1, Folder 3, 16.

31. "Charges 'Sob Sister Policies' Would Wreck Saint Charles School for Boys,"

CDT, 29 July 1928; "Young Hoodlum Escapes in Auto at Saint Charles," *CDT*, 23 May 1932; "One of Kelly's Probationers Sent to Jail on Gun Charge," *CDT*, 18 August 1932.

32. "Insane Hospital Fugitive Hunted as Rape Suspect," *CDT*, 24 September 1935; "42 Gangster Gets Life Term in Theft Case," *CDT*, 8 March 1928; "Admit 'Special' Clemency for Gunman Robber," *CDT*, 20 October 1935; "135 Convicts Win Army O.K.; 4 '42' Bandits in Lot," *CDT*, 10 August 1943.

33. "Parole Abuses Laid to Politics in Penal Survey," *CDT*, 25 January 1928.

34. Landesco, "Life History of a Member," 964.

35. Landesco, "Crime and the Failure," 238; Clifford R. Shaw and Henry D. McKay, *Juvenile Delinquency and Urban Areas: A Study of Rates of Delinquency in Relation to Differential Characteristics of Local Communities in American Cities* (Chicago: University of Chicago Press, 1942).

36. Ray Baker, "Hull House and the Ward Boss," in *Eighty Years at Hull House*, ed. Allen Davis and Mary Lyn McCree (Chicago: Quadrangle Books, 1969), 62–65; "Kidnappers Free: Victims Suffer," *CDT*, 4 May 1914; Landesco, "Crime and the Failure," 239.

37. Landesco, "Crime and the Failure," 240–41.

38. Ibid., 244–45.

39. Ibid., 245–46.

40. Ibid., 246–47.

41. Ibid., 247; Landesco, "Experience with Police," Box 1, Folder 3, 14; Landesco, "Life History of a Member," 230.

42. James D. Vigil, *Barrio Gangs: Street Life and Identity in Southern California* (Austin: University of Texas Press, 1988); William J. Wilson, *The Truly Disadvantaged: The Inner City, the Underclass, and Public Policy* (Chicago: University of Chicago Press, 1990); Sudhir A. Venkatesh, *American Project: The Rise and Fall of a Modern Ghetto* (Cambridge: Harvard University Press, 2000); Landesco, "Formation, Consolidation, and Consolidation," Box 4, Folders 1–4, 9; "Slay Diamond Joe Esposito," *CDT*, 22 March 1928.

43. "Police Bullets Kill Two Thieves; One a Student," *CDT*, 25 November 1927; Landesco, "Formation, Consolidation, and Consolidation," Box 4, Folders 1–4, 8; Landesco, "Diffusion of a Criminal Culture," Box 1, Folder 3, 1.

44. Landesco, "Diffusion of a Criminal Culture," Box 1, Folder 3, 44. For a discussion of "thick description" in qualitative research, see Michael Q. Patton, *Qualitative Research and Evaluation Methods* (Thousand Oaks, CA: Sage, 2002), 437.

45. Landesco, "Diffusion of a Criminal Culture," Box 1, Folder 3, 5, 8, 10.

46. Ibid., 20, 21.

47. Ibid., 17.

48. John Landesco, "Prohibition and Crime," *Annals* 163 (1932b): 120–29, 125; Gerald D. Suttles, *The Social Construction of Communities* (Chicago: University of Chicago Press, 1972), 200.

49. Landesco, "Prohibition and Crime," 125; William Brashler, "Uncle Momo's World," *New York Magazine* (28 July 1975): 27–32.

50. Landesco, "Crime and the Failure," 247.

Chapter 6. The Outfit

1. William Leonard and Sandy Smith, "How the Gang Operates," *CDT*, 25 October 1959.

2. Outfit guy interview, Respondent 21, 1993, 3; Robert J. Schoenberg, *Mr. Capone: The Real—and Complete—Story of Al Capone* (New York: William Morrow, 1992), 77.

3. U.S. Congress, *Hearings before the Permanent Subcommittee on Investigations of the Committee on Government Operations*. 83rd Congress, 1st session, 1953, Exhibit 39; Memorandum, Office of the Independent Hearing Officer, Laborer's International Union of North America, In Re Trusteeship Proceeding of Local 1001 (Chicago, Illinois), 3 May 2003; "Mob Menace in Chicago," *CDT*, 3 September 1954.

4. "The Gambling Swag," *CDT*, 30 October 1934.

5. "How Roe Moved in on Fabulous Jones Brothers," *CD*, 23 August 1952; Alson J. Smith, *Syndicate City* (Chicago: Henry Regnery, 1954), 200.

6. Laurence Bergreen, *Capone: The Man and His Era* (New York: Simon and Schuster, 1994), 248; Allan H. Spear, *Black Chicago: The Making of a Negro Ghetto, 1890–1920* (Chicago: University of Chicago Press, 1967), 15; Ernest W. Burgess, "Residential Segregation in American Cities," *Annals of the American Academy of Political and Social Sciences* 140 (Nov. 1928): 112; Harvey W. Zorbaugh, *The Gold Coast and the Slum: A Sociological Study of Chicago's Near North Side* (Chicago: University of Chicago Press, 1929), 148.

7. "New Gang Chief Mobilizes Army," *CDN*, 28 April 1948; "Policy King's Release Seen as Kin Arrive," *CS*, 15 May 1946; "Is the 'Mob' an Equal Opportunity Employer?" *CD*, 3 May 1980.

8. "Police Fear Policy Baron Slain in Juke Box Racket," *CD*, 18 May 1946; "Negro Crime Baron Days Are Gone," *CD*, 14 November 1967.

9. "The Policy Racket in Chicago," *CD*, 3 June 1946; "Police Fear Policy Baron Slain in Juke Box Racket," 18 May 1946; "Policy Baron Facing Jury Quiz, Flees City," *CD*, 25 May 1946.

10. "Policy Baron Facing Jury Quiz, Flees City," *CD*, 25 May 1946; "Policy King's Ransom Is Believed Paid," *CS*, 16 May 1946; "Jones Kidnapping Followed Row," *CS*, 20 May 1946.

11. Chicago Crime Commission, Policy Gambling, 65-50C 2: 3–6; "Policy Racket Wheel Repairman Killed in Shop," *CDT*, 11 September 1946.

12. "Start Slow-Motion Probe in Murder of Policy Big Shot," *CST*, 11 September 1946; "Police Call Vague Clues Baffling," *CD*, 14 September 1946.

13. U.S. Congress, Senate Special Committee to Investigate Organized Crime in Interstate Commerce, *Third Interim Report, May 1, 1951*, 82nd Congress, 1st session, 195, S. Rpt. 307: 57.

14. "Jones Kidnap Starts Drive against Racket," *CD*, 1 June 1946.

15. "The Capone Gang Muscles into Big-Time Politics," *Colliers*, 30 September 1950; Arnold R. Hirsch, "Martin Kennelly," in *The Mayors: The Chicago Political Tradition*, ed. Paul M. Green and Melvin G. Holli (Carbondale: Southern Illinois University Press, 1987), 140; "Mayor Kennelly and Rep. Dawson," *CDT*, 2 February 1955; "Link Politics, Top Hoods to Policy Racket," *CDT*, 17 July 1960.

16. Chicago Crime Commission 65-50C 3: 8; "World Exposes Master Minds behind Vicious Policy Wheels," *Chicago World*, 29 March 1947; "World Faces $100,000 Suit in Dawson Libel," *Chicago Bee*, 6 April 1947; "Policy Probe to Have Aid of Tax Returns," *CDT*, 10 January 1955.

17. Chicago Crime Commission 65-50C 3: 20, 2: 3.

18. E. Franklin Frazier, *Negro Family in Chicago* (Chicago: University of Chicago Press, 1932), 93; "Chicago Business Man Defies Gang of Hoodlums and Bomb Terrorists," *CD*, 12 October 1940; Chicago Crime Commission 65-50C 1: 9.

19. "How Syndicate Grabbed Policy," *CDT*, 17 January 1955; "A Reproach to Mayor Kennelly," editorial, *CDT*, 23 January 1951; "Leaders of G.O.P. Fear Campaign by Terrorists," *CDT*, 8 February 1952.

20. "Cops Guard Man Who Saw Killers," *CD*, 9 August 1952.

21. Nathan Thompson, *The Murder of Policy King Ed Roe* (Chicago: Bronzeville Press, 2009); "How Roe Moved in on Fabulous Jones Brothers," *CD*, 23 August 1952.

22. "Roe Murder Spells End to Lush Racket and Men It Made Famous," *CD*, 16 August 1952; "Big Shot Tells Who's Who in Policy Circles," *CDT*, 20 December 1950.

23. "Court Claims Right to Claim Policy Treasure," *CA*, 28 February 1964.

24. "Mob Takes Wheel, Spineless Owner Flees, Crying I Don't Want to Die," *Crusader*, 29 November 1952; "Raid Hoodlum Wheels," *Crusader*, 25 April 1953; "Policy Wheel Manager Reputed to Have Sold Out Negro Owners," *Crusader*, 6 December 1952; "Notice," *Crusader*, 16 May 1953.

25. "Protest Dawson Activities," *CDN*, 31 March 1950.

26. Albert N. Votaw, "Chicago: Corrupt and Contented?" *New Republic* (25 August 1952), 13–14; "Guns Topple Old Policy Kings," *CDT*, 19 January 1955.

27. "The Mob Mourns South Side Empire," *CST*, 4 February 1973.

28. "List Hoodlums Ruling Flow of Graft," *CDT*, 23 February 1960; "The Mob Mourns South Side Empire," *CST*, 4 February 1973.

29. "Seized Photo Links Rackets with the Mob," *CST*, 21 January 1965; "Raid Dope Meeting, *CDT*, 25 October 1965.

30. U.S. Congress, Senate, Committee on Government Operations, *Organized Crime and Illicit Traffic in Narcotics,* 88th Congress, 1st and 2nd sessions, 1964: 890, 918, 931.

31. "Negroes on Outside Say Police," *CD*, 15 November 1967; "Negro Crime 'Barons' Days Gone," *CD*, 14 November 1967.

32. U.S. Congress, *Organized Crime,* 1064–65; "Seize $60,000 Dope Hoard in Raid by Police," *CDT*, 11 October 1951.

33. U.S. Congress, *Organized Crime,*1105; "Inside Story of Big Narcotics Raid Told," *CDT*, 31 October 1963; U.S. Congress, *Organized Crime,* 1072.

34. "5 Seized, 1 Hunted in Narcotics Probe," *CDT*, 3 November 1972; "Hood Gets 10 Years in Drug Case," *CDT* 20 December 1973.

35. U.S. Congress, *Organized Crime,* 1072; "Mob Slaying Linked to Taboo on Drugs," *CST,* 23 June 1974.

36. U.S. Congress, *Organized Crime,* 1072, 1088.

37. William J. Wilson, *When Work Disappears: The World of the New Urban Poor* (New York: Knopf, 1996); David Remnick, "Dr. Wilson's Neighborhood," *New Yorker* (29 April 1996), 102.

38. "The Mob Mourns South Side Empire," *CST*, 4 February 1973.

39. "This Lottery Makes State Big Losers," *CDT*, 16 June 1989.

40. "Senator Kefauver and the Chicago Underworld," *CDT*, 4 October 1950; Walter Trohan, "Kefauver Gains Power, Respect in Crime Probe," *CDT*, 30 March 1951; James Doherty, "What Can U.S. Crime Hunters Find in Chicago?" *CDT*, 22 January 1952.

41. "17 Hoodlums Called Heads of U.S. Crime," *CDT*, 21 February 1951; U.S. Congress, *Hearings before the Permanent Subcommittee on Investigations of the Committee on Government Operations,* 83rd Congress, 1st session, 1953: 148; *CDT*, 4 October 1950.

42. "List Hoodlum Tax Targets in Federal Probe," *CDT*, 9 June 1951; U.S. Congress, Testimony of Virgil W. Peterson, Operating Director, Chicago Crime Commission, *Hearings before the Permanent Subcommittee on Investigations of the Committee on Government Operations* (Washington, DC: U.S. Government Printing Office, 1950).

43. "Alcock Upsets Station; Sets Up Scotland Yard," *CDT*, 3 June 1931; "Chicago COPS Spark Senate Blast at Gang," *CDT*, 11 July 1958.

44. "Mob Menace in Chicago," *CDT*, 29 August 1954.

45. "Accardo, Guzik Run Gantlet of Jury and Police," *CDT*, 7 March 1953; "Hear Accardo Hopes to Move to California," *CDT*, 20 January 1953.

46. "Scotland Yard End Deplored by Peterson," *CDT*, 17 June 1956; "Seek Scotland Yard Gang Data; Find Folders Empty," *CDT*, 15 July 1958; "Illinois: Daley Life in Chicago," *Time*, 16 July 1956; "Disclose Rice Probed Bookie of Party Brass," *CDT*, 20 March 1955; "Morris Tells His Version of Wire Tap Tale," *CDT*, 4 April 1960; "Convict 5 in Vote Frauds," *CDT*, 8 January 1956; "The Election Fraud Conviction," *CDT*, 14 January 1956.

47. "What Can Angry People Do?" *CS*, 21 February 1952; "West Side Bloc," memorandum, Chicago Crime Commission, 19 December 1967.

48. "The Chicago Crime Commission's 1967 Legislative Program," memorandum,

Chicago Crime Commission; "West Side Bloc," memorandum, Chicago Crime Commission, 19 December 1967; "West Side Bloc: How it Decides Laws, Elections," *CDT*, 9 February 1952; "W. S. Block Has 30 Years of Influence," *CDT*, 6 May 1963.

49. John Gavin and Joe Egelhof, "The West Side Bloc and the Mob," *CDN*, 10 February 1964; "Skid Row Bums Pile Up Votes for Democrats," *CDT*, 23 January 1955.

50. "Bloc in Chicago Is a G.O.P. Issue," *CDT*, 13 April 1964; "A Short Road to a Clean City," *CDT*, 8 March 1952.

51. "Shotguns Kill G.O.P. Ward Chief," *CDT*, 7 February 1952; James Doherty, "Leaders of G.O.P. Fear Campaign by Terrorists," *CDT*, 8 February 1952.

52. George Tagge, "County G.O.P. Heads Decree Purge of Bloc," *CDT*, 9 February 1952; "Probe Slated for 49 Payrollers of 1st Ward on Political Sponsorship," *CDN*, 11 February 1964; "The Syndicate's Weapons: Muscle, Money, Manpower," *CDN*, 11 February 1964.

53. Aaron Kohn, ed., *The Kohn Report: Crime and Politics in Chicago* (Chicago: Independent Voters of Illinois, 1953), iii, 1; "Vote to Give Crime Report to Grand Jury," *CDT*, 16 January 1953.

54. "Big 19 Crime Foe Group to Hail 10th Year," *CDT*, 2 October 1961; "Bypass Boyle, 'Big 19' Urged Civic Leaders, Demand Jury," *CST*, 23 February 1952; "Big 19 Asserts It Did Not Urge City Income Tax," *CDT*, 16 September 1952.

55. "Mayoral Foes Agree Crime Is Organized," *CDT*, 6 March 1955; "G.O.P. "Endorses Merriam," *CDT*, 28 December 1954; "16,000 Hear Merriam Expose Plot," *CDT*, 30 March 1955.

56. "Richard J. Daley Tells about His Program for City," *Southtown Economist*, 27 March 1955; "Gamblers Find Chicago Down under Daley," *CDT*, 14 May 1956; M. W. Newman and Norman Glubok, "The Syndicate's Weapons: Muscle, Money, Manpower," *CDN*, 11 February 1964; "City Refuses to Give 'Big Nine' Files to Jury," *CDT*, 26 January 1960; "Vote to Give Crime Report to Grand Jury," *CDT*, 16 January 1953.

57. "Recall 1952 Pay Scandal in City, County," *CDT*, 8 November 1959; "Gambling King Hits Gold on City Payroll," *CDT*, 19 December 1959; "Reveal Barber Union Chief Draws City Pay," *CDT*, 16 December 1959; "Union Boss Is Fired from City Sewer Job," *CDT*, 17 December 1959; "Find Payroller Taking Bets," *CDT*, 28 December 1959; "Ballot Work Wins City Job for Gambler," *CDT*, 30 December 1959; Robert Wiedrich, "2 Daughters of Hoodlums on Public Pay," *CDT*, 21 July 1957.

58. "Summerdale Scandal Draws to Close," *CDT*, 31 October 1965.

59. "Chicago Mafia Chiefs Named," *CDT*, 4 March 1965; Andy Knott, "William Duffy," *CDT*, 20 April 1980; Robert Wiedrich, "Detectives Crack Mob Juice Arena," *CDT*, 26 July 1964; George Tagge, "Wire Tap Wins First Test," *CDT*, 5 June 1963.

60. "Ald. Lewis' Dramatic Career: From Georgia Boy to Big City Boss," 1 March 1963; "Hunt Ald. Lewis' Slayer," *CDT*, 1 March 1963.

61. Newman and Glubok, "The Syndicate's Weapons: Muscle, Money, Manpower,"

CDN, 11 February 1964; Gerald D. Suttles, *The Social Construction of Communities* (Chicago: University of Chicago Press, 1972), 210; Vince Romano, interview by author, 13 April 2010.

62. "Ogilvie's Record as a Crime Fighter," *CDT*, 19 March 1961; "Call Special U.S. Jury to War on Crime," *CDT*, 10 January 1959; "Set 11 Point Trap for Hoodlums," *CDT*, 24 January 1959; "FBI Crime Campaign Outdated: Ogilvie," *CA*, 28 March 1961; "Bribe Talk in Accardo Case Bared," *CDT*, 12 August 1965.

63. "Assails Crime Fighting Job Done by U.S.," *CDT*, 14 March 1961; "Ogilvie Rips into 7 Chief Crime Lords," *CDT*, 17 October 1962; *The FBI* (Washington, DC.: U.S. Government Printing Office, 2006), 53.

64. William Leonard and Sandy Smith, "The Capone Gang Today," *CDT*, 18 October 1959; William Leonard and Sandy Smith, "Gambling, The Mob's Biggest Racket," *CDT*, 27 December 1959.

65. George Tagge, "Mobster Tried to Block Me, Ogilvie Claims," *CDT*, 9 February 1962; "Find Gambling, Vice Wide Open Again in County," 28 February 1953.

66. "Ogilvie Beats Spencer," *CDT*, 7 November 1962; "Ogilvie to Give New Sheriff's COPS Lie Test," *CDT*, 20 November 1962.

67. "250 Arrested in 7 Raids by COPS, Sheriff," *CDT*, 16 December 1962; "Cicero's Night Life Stays at Subdued Pace," *CDT*, 14 January 1964; "Gaming Houses and Strip Joints Run under Babb," *CDT*, 13 April 1953; "Trap Auippa in Bribe," *CDT*, 19 August 1965.

68. "County Vice, Gambling Run Openly Again," *CDT*, 24 March 1955; "Gambling Hums in North End of County," *CDT*, 2 March 1953; "Reporters List Gambling Spots in Babb's Area," *CDT*, 12 April 1953.

69. "Heads County Board," *CDT*, 4 November 1966; "Nixon, Ogilvie Stars of Voting in Illinois," *CDT*, 7 November 1968; "House OK's Ogilvie Law, Order Bills," *CDT*, 30 June 1968; George Tagge, "Ogilvie Mentioned for a Possible Cabinet Post," *CDT*, 10 November 1972; "For Unified Law Enforcement," *CDT*, 4 April 1977.

70. Chicago Crime Commission, "Spotlight on Organized Crime: The Chicago Syndicate," October 1967; "New Crime Report Links 31 Companies to the Syndicate," *CST*, 7 November 1969.

71. Ray Brennan, "State Files Antitrust Suit against Mob's Jukeboxes," *CST*, 12 February 1970; Ray Brennan, "Jukebox Distributors Kick in $30,915 toward Mob's Fine," *CST*, 8 October 1971.

72. Illinois Institute of Technology Research Institute and the Chicago Crime Commission, *A Study of Organized Crime in Illinois* (Chicago: Illinois Law Enforcement Commission, 1972), 2–3.

73. Ibid., 9, 13.

74. Comptroller General of the United States, Report to Congress, *War on Organized Crime Faltering*, 17 March 1977.

75. Lyndon B. Johnson, 8 March 1965, Special Message to Congress on Law Enforcement and the Administration of Justice, *The American Presidency Project*; Omnibus Crime Control and Safe Streets Act of 1968, Public Law 90-351, 82

Stat. 197; Racketeer Influenced and Corrupt Organizations Act, 18 U.S.C. Sects. 1961–1968.

76. "Mob Generation Gap Endangers Tony Accardo and His Pals," *CDT*, 1 May 1977; Ronald Koziol and John O'Brien, "Rent-a-Racket' Is Mob's New Plan to Make Cash, Avoid Law," *CDT*, 29 November 1982.

77. George Bliss and Robert Davis, "Tie N.Y. Mob to Porn Here," 7 July 1977; "Chicago's Mob Figures Run Scared—to Death," *CDT*, 7 August 1983; Ronald Koziol and John O'Brien, "Gang Figures Tied to Bookie's Death," *CDT*, 12 February 1985.

78. Andrew Wang, "Infamous Outfit Hit Man Dies in Prison," *CDT*, 16 May 2010.

79. Andy Knott, "2 Top Byrne Aides Resign; Probe of Mob Clout Begins," *CDT*, 22 April 1980.

80. Ibid.; Robert Cooley and Hillel Levin, *When Corruption Was King: How I Helped the Mob Rule Chicago, Then Brought the Outfit Down* (New York: Carroll and Graf), 116; "Police Will Lose Years of 'Savvy' When Duffy Quits," 25 May 1980; "Mob Influence Reports Falsified, Brzeczek Says," *CDT*, 28 June 1980; Art Petacque and Hugh Hough, "Byrne's Inner Circle Keeps Growing," *CDT*, 21 October 1979.

81. "FBI and Police Raid Hit Chicago Chop Shop Racket," *CDT*, 2 December 1981; William Crawford, "Chop Shop Indictments List 16 People, 2 Firms," 20 July 1984; Mike Kennedy, "Flaw Cited in FALN Evidence," 10 January 1984.

82. Ronald Reagan, Executive Order 12435, President's Commission on Organized Crime, *The American Presidency Project,* 28 July 1983; Ronald Kozil, "Reagan Urged to Act on Mob-Union Ties," *CDT*, 7 March 1986.

83. Ronald Koziol, "5 Convicted of Mob Skimming," *CDT*, 22 January 1986; Ronald Koziol, "Spilotro Ran Sports Book, Loan Empire: Affidavit," *CDT*, 17 May 1979.

84. Dean Baquet and John O'Brien, "Organized Crime Caught in a 3-Way Squeeze," *CDT,* 12 February 1990.

85. *U.S. v. Rocco Ernest Infelise et al.,* 90 CR 87, U.S. District Court for the Northern District of Illinois, Eastern Division; John O'Brien and John Gorman, "20 Lined to Mob Indicted," *CDT*, 8 February 1990.

86. *U.S. v. Mario Rainone et al.,* 91 CR 727, U.S. District Court for the Northern District of Illinois, Eastern Division; John O'Brien, "An Aging Wise Guy Still Plays His Role to the Hilt," *CDT*, 18 September 1992.

87. "5 Indicted in 'Corruption Feast'; Stalwarts of 1st Ward Are Targeted," *CDT*, 20 December 1990.

88. *U.S. v. Anthony C. Zizzo et al.,* 92 CR 1034, U.S. District Court for the Northern District of Illinois, Eastern Division.

89. Peter Kendall and Steve Mills, "The New Mob, Lean but Still Mean," *CDT*, 1 October 1997; Steve Warmbir, "The New Outfit," *CDT*, 18 August 2002.

90. Steve Warmbir and Tim Novak, "Clout on "Wheels," *CST*, 25 January 2004.

91. *U.S. v. Nicholas Calabrese et al.,* 02 CR 1050, U.S. District Court for the

Northern District of Illinois, Eastern Division; P. J. Huffstutter, "The Outfit on Trial," *Los Angeles Times*, 28 September 2007.

92. Barb Markoff and Chuck Goodie, "'Large Guy' Sarno Found Guilty," *CDT*, 27 December 2010.

Chapter 7. The Outfit as a Complex Organization

1. President's Commission on Law Enforcement and the Administration of Justice, *Task Force Report: Organized Crime* (Washington, DC: U.S. Government Printing Office, 1967), 7.

2. Francis A. J. Ianni, and Elizabeth Reuss-Ianni, *A Family Business* (New York: Russell Sage Foundation, 1972), 108.

3. Joseph L. Albini, *The American Mafia: Genesis of a Legend* (New York: Irvington, 1979), 155, 229.

4. Howard Abadinsky, *The Criminal Elite: Professional and Organized Crime* (Westport, CT: Greenwood, 1983), 165, 108.

5. P. R. Lawrence and J. W. Lorsch, *Organization and Environment: Managing Differentiation and Integration* (Boston: Harvard University Press, 1967).

6. Annelise G. Anderson, *The Business of Organized Crime: A Cosa Nostra Family* (Stanford, CA: Hoover Institution, 1979), 34.

7. Chicago Crime Commission, *Spotlight on Organized Crime: The Chicago Syndicate*, October 1967; "Nobody Wants to Run the Mob Today," *CT*, 9 August 1970; Art Petacque and Jim Quinlan, "Mob Guns Signal a Changing of Guard," *CST*, 17 February 1985; "Chicago Outfit Organizational Chart," Chicago Crime Commission, unpublished, 1997.

8. "Chicago Crime Syndicate," Chicago Police Intelligence Division, 1981; "The Chicago Family," State of Illinois and the Chicago Crime Commission, 4 March 1983; "The Chicago Outfit," Chicago Police Department, unpublished, April 1987.

9. Chicago Crime Commission, "Chicago Outfit and Associates," unpublished, 1990, 4, 12.

10. *U.S. v. Rocco Infelise et al.*, 90 CR 00087-1.

11. *U.S. v. Nicholas W. Calabrese et al.*, 02 CR 1050.

12. Ibid.

13. IRS special agent, Interview respondent 20, Interview with author, 1992; *U. S. v. Frank Calabrese Sr. et al.*, Government's Memorandum in Opposition to Defendant's Motion for Release on Bond, No. 02 CR 1050-4, 6 June 2006.

14. Chicago Crime Commission, *Organized Crime in Chicago*, 1990, 4.

15. Chicago police detective, Interview respondent 13, Interview with author, 1992; IRS special agent, Interview respondent 20, Interview with author, 1992.

16. IRS special agent, Interview respondent 20, Interview with author, 1992; Chicago police detective, Interview respondent 17, Interview with author, 1992; Chicago police detective, Interview respondent 13, Interview with author, 1992.

17. U.S. Strike Force attorney, Interview respondent 7, Interview with author,

1989; Chicago Crime Commission investigator, Interview respondent 6, Interview with author, 1990; *U.S. v. Nicholas W. Calabrese et al.,* 02 CR 1050.

18. Chicago police detective, Interview respondent 13, Interview with author, 1992.

19. *U.S. v. Nicholas W. Calabrese et al.,* 02 CR 1050; Outfit associate, Interview respondent 15, Interview with author, 1992; Chicago Crime Commission investigator, Interview respondent 6, Interview with author, 1990; IRS special agent, Interview respondent 20, Interview with author, 1992.

20. IRS special agent, Interview respondent 20, Interview with author, 1992; *U.S. v. Frank Calabrese Sr. et al.*, Government's Memorandum in Opposition to Defendant's Motion for Release on Bond, No. 02 CR 1050-4, 6 June 2006.

21. Chicago Crime Commission, *Organized Crime in Chicago* (Chicago: Chicago Crime Commission, 1990), 4; Federal Bureau of Investigation, Debriefing of Gerald H. Scarpelli. Investigative File #CG183B-2272, 1988: 3.

22. FBI, Debriefing of Scarpelli, 3–4.

23. U.S. Strike Force attorney, Interview respondent 7, Interview with author, 1989.

24. FBI, Debriefing of Scarpelli, 5, 16, 23, 24; U.S. Strike Force attorney, Interview respondent 7, Interview with author, 1989.

25. U.S. Strike Force attorney, Interview respondent 7, Interview with author, 1989.

26. Chicago bookie, Interview respondent 1, Interview with author, 1987; Chicago police detective, Interview with author, Respondent 13, 1992.

27. Chicago police detective, Interview respondent 13, Interview with author, 1992; Sam Giancana and Chuck Giancana, *Double Cross: The Explosive, Inside Story of the Mobster Who Controlled America* (New York: Warner Books, 1992), 242; IRS special agent, Interview respondent 20, Interview with author, 1992.

28. Outfit guy, Interview respondent 21, Interview with author, 1993; Chicago police detective, Interview respondent 5, Interview with author, 1988.

29. Chicago bookie, Interview respondent 13, Interview with author, 1992; Giancana and Giancana, *Double Cross*, 243; Chicago bookie, Interview respondent 12, Interview with author, 1992; Chicago gambler, Interview respondent 3, Interview with author, 1988.

30. Chicago Police Department Intelligence Division, unpublished, Chicago Outfit Associates, 1960; Chicago Police Department Intelligence Division, unpublished, Chicago Outfit Associates, 1992.

31. Office of the Independent Hearing Officer, Laborer's International Union of North America, In Re. Trusteeship Proceeding of Local 1001 (Chicago, Illinois), Complaint for Trusteeship, 24 September 2003.

32. Chicago gambler, Interview respondent 3, Interview with author, 1988.

33. Ibid.

34. Ibid.; Chicago bookie, Interview respondent 1, Interview with author, 1987; U.S. Strike Force attorney, Interview respondent 7, Interview with author, 1989.

35. Chicago bookie, Interview respondent 14, Interview with author, 1992; Chicago gambler, Interview respondent 3, Interview with author, 1988.

36. IRS special agent, Interview respondent 20, Interview with author, 1992; Chicago gambler, Interview respondent 3, Interview with author, 1988.

37. Chicago police detective, Interview respondent 17, Interview with author, 1992.

38. Outfit associate, Interview respondent 15, Interview with author, 1992; Chicago police detective, Interview respondent 6, Interview with author, 1990.

39. Penny Levin, "Mob Informer Cullotta's Early Linkup with Spilotro," *Las Vegas Sun,* 10–20 April 1983.

40. Michael Goodman, "Spilotro Graduates to the Mob: Tough Grows into Vicious," *Los Angeles Times*, 20 February 1983.

41. U.S. Strike Force attorney, Interview respondent 7, Interview with author, 1989; Michael Goodman, "Spilotro Slips Up, Makes War with Cop," *Los Angeles Times*, 28 February 1983.

42. *U.S. v. Mario Rainone et al.,* 91 CR 727, U.S. District Court for the Northern District of Illinois.

43. Ibid.

44. U.S. Attorney, Interview respondent 2, Interview with author, 1988.

45. Chicago police detective, Interview respondent 13, Interview with author, 1992; Chicago police detective, Interview respondent 16, Interview with author, 1992.

46. Chicago police detective, Interview respondent 11, Interview with author, 1992; IRS special agent, Interview respondent 20, Interview with author, 1992; Outfit associate, Interview respondent 15, Interview with author, 1992; Chicago bookie, Interview respondent 1, Interview with author, 1987.

47. Outfit associate, Interview respondent 18, Interview with author, 1992; Chicago bookie, Interview respondent 17, Interview with author, 1992.

48. Chicago Crime Commission investigator, Interview respondent 6, Interview with author, 1990; Chicago bookie, Interview respondent 1, Interview with author, 1987.

49. "Accardo, Guzik Run Gantlet of Jury and Police," *CDT*, 7 March 1953; "Mafia 'Rules' on Murder Told," *CDT*, 24 March 1983; Jeff Coen, *Family Secrets: The Case That Crippled the Chicago Mob* (Chicago: Chicago Review Press, 2009), 156.

50. Outfit associate, Interview respondent 15, Interview with author, 1992; Chicago bookie, Interview respondent 13, Interview with author, 1992; *U.S. v. Mario Rainone et al.,* 91 CR 727, U.S. District Court for the Northern District of Illinois.

Chapter 8. Street Crew Neighborhoods

1. Chicago Police Department internal memo, "The Chicago Outfit," April 1987; Chicago bookie, Interview respondent 12, Interview with author, 1992; Chicago

bookie, Interview respondent 3, Interview with author 1992; Chicago police detective, Interview respondent 17, Interview with author, 1992; IRS special agent, Respondent 20, Interview with author, 1992.

2. "Citizens Fight Housing Plan: Charge Deceit," *CDT*, 15 February 1940.

3. Evelyn Kitagawa and Karl Tauber, *Local Community Fact Book: Chicago Metropolitan Area* (Chicago: University of Chicago Press,1963), 75; Outfit associate, Interview respondent 18, Interview with author, 1992.

4. Agnes S. Holbrook, "Prefatory Note," *Hull House Maps and Papers* (1895; New York: Thomas Crowell, 1970), 3; Grace P. Norton, "Chicago Housing Conditions, VII: Two Italian Districts," *American Journal of Sociology* 18, no. 4 (1913): 509–42; "Foul Ewing Street," *CDT*, 30 March 1893; Jane Addams, *Twenty Years at Hull House* (New York: MacMillan, 1916), 97–100.

5. Dominick A. Pacyga and Ellen Skerrett, *Chicago: City of Neighborhoods; Histories and Tours* (Chicago: Loyola University Press, 1986), 227; "The Wickedest District in the World Where Scores of Men and Women Are Murdered Every Year," *CDT*, 11 February 1906; "Pardon for a Thug," *CDT*, 26 October 1894.

6. Natalie Walker, "Chicago Housing Conditions X: Greeks and Italians in the Neighborhood of Hull House," *American Journal of Sociology* 21, no. 3 (1915): 285–316.

7. Gerald D. Suttles, *The Social Construction of Communities* (Chicago: University of Chicago Press, 1972); Solomon Kobrin, "The Conflict of Values in Delinquency Areas," in *Juvenile Delinquency*, ed. Rose Giallombardo, 151–60 (New York: John Wiley and Sons, 1966).

8. Allen F. Davis, *Spearheads for Reform: The Social Settlements and the Progressive Movement, 1890 to 1914* (New York: Oxford University Press, 1967), 151–62; Municipal Voters League of Chicago, *The Municipal Campaign, 1898* (Chicago: Municipal Voters League, 1898), 6; Ray S. Baker, "Hull House and the Ward Boss," *Outlook* 58, no. 3 (New York: Outlook Company, 26 March 1898), 769–71; Fred D. Pasley, *Al Capone: The Biography of a Self-Made Man* (Salem, NH: Ayer Publishing, 1930), 96.

9. "Chicago Daily News Almanac and Year Book 1925," 886–91.

10. "Diamond Joe, Storm Center; His Own Story," *CDT*, 9 March 1926.

11. Ibid.

12. "Slay Diamond Joe Esposito," *CDT*, 22 March 1928; Sam Giancana and Charles Giancana, *Double Cross: The Explosive, Inside Story of the Mobster Who Controlled America* (New York: Warner Books, 1992), 18, 27, 28.

13. George Murray, *Legacy of Al Capone: Portraits and Annals of Chicago's Public Enemies* (New York: G. T. Putnam and Sons, 1975), 313.

14. Outfit associate, Interview respondent 18, Interview with author, 1992.

15. Chicago bookie, Interview respondent 12, Interview with author, 1992.

16. Kitagawa and Tauber, *Local Community Fact Book*, 62; Rudolph J. Vecoli, "Chicago's Italians Prior to World War I: A Study of Their Social and Economic Adjustment," PhD diss., University of Wisconsin, 1962.

17. Humbert S. Nelli, *The Italians in Chicago* (New York: Oxford University Press, 1970), 46; Edith Abbott, *The Tenements of Chicago, 1908–1935* (New York Arno Press, 1970), 102.

18. Frederic M. Thrasher, *The Gang: A Study of 1,313 Gangs in Chicago* (Chicago: University of Chicago Press, 1927), 18.

19. William F. Roemer, *Accardo* (New York: Fine, 1995), 23; William Brashler, *The Don: The Life and Death of Sam Giancana* (New York: Harper and Row, 1977), 20; John Kobler, *Capone: The Life and World of Al Capone* (New York: Collier Books, 1971), 145; "More Mafia," *Alton Evening Telegraph*, 17 October 1950.

20. "Seize Capone Aid and 28 Others in Tavern Raid," *CDT*, 23 December 1935; "10 of 60 Seized in Gambling Raid Freed on Bonds," *CDT*, 7 June 1944; "Raid Hoodlum Hangout, Seize 27 on West Side," *CDT*, 13 December 1952.

21. Chicago police detective, Interview respondent 11, Interview with author, 1992; "Everybody Loves Him, Lombardo Neighbor Says," *CDT*, 3 March 1983.

22. Chicago police detective, Interview respondent 13, Interview with author, 1992.

23. Kitagawa and Tauber, *Local Community Fact Book*, 94.

24. Ibid.; Vecoli, "Chicago's Italians," 178.

25. Kitagawa and Tauber, *Local Community Fact Book*, 94; "Chinatown Plans to Move Two Miles to the South," *CDT*, 24 November 1911.

26. James M. Gavin, "Multimillion Dollar Skyscrapers Rise Where Modest Irish Homes Once Stood," *CDT*, 31 July 1960.

27. Alice Hagan Rice, *Mrs. Wiggs of the Cabbage Patch* (New York: Century Co., 1901); Vecoli, "Chicago's Italians," 177.

28. Chicago police detective, Interview respondent 13, Interview with author, 1992.

29. "11 in Roti Clan Get City Jobs Thru 1st Ward," *CDT*, 29 December 1959; Tim Novak, Robert Herguth, and Steve Warmbir, "One Family's Rise, Century of Power," *CST*, 22 May 2006.

30. Matt O'Connor, " On Leong, Moy Plead Guilty to Running Longtime Casino," *CDT*, 13 February 1994; Ronald Koziol, "5 Convicted of Mob Skimming," *CDT*, 22 January 1986.

31. IRS special agent, Interview respondent 20, Interview with author, 1992.

32. Ibid.

33. "Judge May Be Target of the Outfit," *Daily Herald*, 3 February 1999; Tim Novak and Robert Herguth, "Running a Union, Ruling the Alley," *CST*, 22 May 2006.

34. "Club Keeps Neighborhood in Touch with the Old Days," *CST*, 25 April 1996; Robert Herguth, Tim Novak, and Steve Warmbir, "Alleged Mob Social Club: We Do a Lot of Good Things," *CST*, 24 May 2006. I once had a graduate student who attempted to write a term paper about the Armour Square community. Hearing that the Old Neighborhood Italian-American Club had a display on the history of the neighborhood, he made an appointment to meet the director. When he arrived at

the scheduled time, he was ushered into an office where he was promptly searched for a recording device and asked who had sent him to conduct the interview!

35. Kitagawa and Tauber, *Local Community Fact Book*, 21; "The Kilgubbin Held to Bail," *CDT*, 21 January 1861; Clayton Kirkpatrick, "Shifting Nationality Islands," *CDT*, 1 February 1951.

36. Kitagawa and Tauber, *Local Community Fact Book*, 18; "Little Hell," *CDT*, 27 November 1875; Norton, "Chicago Housing Conditions," 531; Vecoli, "Chicago's Italians," 172; Harvey W. Zorbaugh, *The Gold Coast and the Slum: A Sociological Study of Chicago's Near North Side* (Chicago: University of Chicago Press, 1929), 160.

37. Zorbaugh, *Gold Coast*, 35.

38. Ibid.,198; William F. Whyte, *Street Corner Society: The Social Structure of an Italian Slum* (Chicago: University of Chicago Press, 1942), 36.

39. Alson J. Smith, *Syndicate City: The Chicago Crime Cartel and What to Do about It* (Chicago: Henry Regnery, 1954), 77.

40. Memorandum, "Dominick Nuccio alias Dominic Nuccio, Dominic Butcchio, 'Libby' Nuccio Hoodlum and Gambler," Chicago Crime Commission, 27 June 1951; "Name Top 20 Hoodlums on Secret Police List," *CST*, 26 January 1953.

41. Art Petacque, "How Ross Prio Escaped Mob's Last Great Blow," *CDT*, 31 December 1972.

42. "Turn Spotlight on Shady Areas in Bauler Ward," *CDT*, 30 January 1953; "3 Witnesses Unable to Tell Jury of Crime," *CDT*, 9 April 1954.

43. "Turn Spotlight on Shady Areas in Bauler Ward," *CDT*, 30 January 1953.

44. John Handley, "Lie Night and Day," *CDT*, 17 March 1996.

45. Kitagawa and Tauber, *Local Community Fact Book*, 214; Robert Taylor, "Address the Future May Be a Limitless Task: At Home in Chicago Heights," *CDT*, 17 November 1990.

46. Vecoli, "Chicago's Italians," 203; Taylor, "Address the Future," 1990.

47. Marian Lanfranchi, "A Political History of Chicago Heights," unpublished paper, Chicago, Governors State University, 1976, 9, 24; Wilfrid G. Bonvouloir, *The Blacksmith's Boy: Memoirs of Growing Up in the Early Years of the Twentieth Century!* (n.p.: Western Writers Workshop Press, 1984), 109.

48. "Chicago Heights Raided by U.S.," *CDT*, 7 January 1929; Lanfranchi, "Political History," 29; "Police Chief Slain in Home," *Chicago Heights Star*, 7 December 1928.

49. "Chicago Heights Raided by U.S.," *CDT*, 7 January 1929; Lanfranchi, "Political History," 29.

50. Dominic Candeloro, "Suburban Italians: Chicago Heights, 1890–1975," in *Ethnic Chicago: A Multicultural Portrait,* ed. Peter d'A. Jones and Melvin G. Holli (Grand Rapids: Wm. Eerdmans, 1984), 204.

51. "Another Murder; Victim an Italian," *Chicago Heights Star,* 26 July 1923; "Sanfilippo Killer Produces Mystery," *CDT*, 24 April 1924; "Prohibition Blamed for

Booze Gangs' Long Reign of Guns and Terror in Chicago Heights," *CDT*, 7 January 1929; "Corruption Free," *Chicago Heights Star*, 29 June 1922.

52. "Sanfilippo Funeral," *Chicago Heights Star*, 1 May 1924; John J. Binder and Matthew J. Luzi, "Al Capone and Friends" (Chicago: Unpublished [Copyrighted] 25 September 1995), 8.

53. Candeloro, "Suburban Italians," 204; Theresa Giannetti (GIA-54), Italians in Chicago—Oral History Project, University of Illinois at Chicago, Immigration History Research Center Collection, Box 31, Folder 239, 28.

54. "Deadliest City in the Nation," *Chicago Heights Star*, 15 February 1929.

55. "South Cook, Indiana Racket Boss Frank LaPorte Is Dead," *CDT*, 1 November 1972; William Leonard, "Cal City!" *CDT*, 2 January 1955.

56. John O'Brien, "Stolen Car Racket Spurs Mob Warfare," *CDT*, 27 July 1977; George Bliss and Ray Moseley, "Auto Theft Grows into Major Racket," *CDT*, 1 August 1977; How Much Does it Cost to Build a Car from Parts? http://www.straightdope.com (accessed 28 June 2011).

57. Lauren Fitzpatrick, "Chicago Heights Mob Boss Albert Tocco Dies in Prison," *Chicago Heights Star*, 25 September 2005.

58. John O'Brien, "Indictment Names Reputed Mob Boss: 15 from Suburbs, Indiana Charges," *CDT*, 19 December 1990; "Reputed Ex-Mob Leader for South Suburbs Dies," *CDT*, 20 April 2005.

59. IRS special agent, Interview respondent 20, Interview with author, 1992; "U.S. Charges Panici Got Tocco Payoffs," *CDT*, 12 January 1993.

60. Candeloro, "Suburban Italians," 182.

61. Chicago bookie, Interview respondent 1, Interview with author, 1987; Chicago police detective, Interview respondent 11, Interview with author, 1992.

62. Made guy, Interview respondent 21, Interview with respondent, 1993; Outfit associate, Interview respondent 18, Interview with author, 1992; Outfit associate, Interview respondent 15, Interview with author, 1992; Chicago police detective, Interview respondent 5, 1989; Chicago bookie, Interview respondent 12, Interview with author, 1992.

63. Chicago police detective, Interview respondent 11, Interview with author, 1992.

64. Made guy, Interview respondent 21, Interview with author, 1993.

65. Chicago police detective, Interview respondent 11, Interview with author, 1992; Chicago police detective, Interview respondent 13, Interview with author, 1992; Chicago police detective, Interview respondent 17, Interview with author, 1992.

66. Chicago police detective, Interview respondent 13, Interview with author, 1992.

67. "Capone's Decade of Death," *CDT*, 9 February 1936; Chicago Police Department, 1987.

68. Chicago police detective, Interview respondent 17, Interview with author, 1992.

69. Ibid.

70. Kitagawa and Tauber, *Local Community Fact Book*, 59; Chicago police detective, Interview respondent 14, Interview with author, 1992.

71. Chicago police detective, Interview respondent 16, Interview with author, 1992; Chicago police detective, Interview respondent 11, Interview with author, 1992.

72. "How Syndicate Grabbed Policy," *CDT*, 17 January 1955.

73. Chicago gambler, Interview respondent 3, Interview with author, 1988.

74. Kitagawa and Tauber, *Local Community Fact Book*, xix.

75. Suttles, *Social Construction*, 37.

76. Chicago police officer, Interview respondent 5, Interview with author, 1989; William Granger, "A Walk on the West Side," *Chicago Tribune* 28 October 1990.

77. "Great West Side Pageant of Publicity," *West Side Times*, 8 August 1920; Suttles, *Social Construction*, 195.

78. Granger, "Walk on the West Side," 21.

79. Chicago police detective, Interview respondent 11, Interview with author, 1992;

80. Albert Hunter, *Symbolic Communities: The Persistence and Change of Chicago's Local Communities* (Chicago: University of Chicago Press, 1974), 179.

Conclusion

1. Humbert S. Nelli, "Italians and Crime in Chicago," *American Journal of Sociology* 174 (1969): 373–91.

2. Alison J. Smith, *Syndicate City: The Chicago Crime Cartel and What to Do about It* (Chicago: Henry Regnery, 1954), 260.

3. William J. Chambliss, "Vice Corruption, Bureaucracy, and Power," *Wisconsin Law Review* 4 (1971): 1150–73.

4. Daniel Bell, *The End of Ideology: On the Exhaustion of Political Ideas in the Fifties* (Glencoe: Free Press, 1964).

5. Francis A. J. Ianni, *Black Mafia: Ethnic Succession in Organized Crime* (New York: Simon and Schuster, 1974).

6. Humbert S. Nelli, *The Italians in Chicago,1880–1930: A Study in Ethnic Mobility* (New York: Oxford University Press, 1970), 152; "La Cosa Nostra," Italian Organized Crime, FBI website, http://www.fbi.gov/hq/cid/orgcrime/lcn/lcn.htm (accessed 14 July 2006).

7. Joseph Albini, *The American Mafia: Genesis of a legend* (New York: Appleton Century Crofts, 1971), 108; Henner Hess, *Mafia and Mafiosi: The Structure of Power* (New York: New York University Press, 1998), 17; Salvatore Lupo, *History of the Mafia*, (New York: Columbia University Press, 2009); United States Immigration Commission, *Reports of the Immigration Commission*, Vol. 4, *Emigration Conditions in Europe* (Washington, DC: U. S. Government Printing Office, 1911), 18.

8. Robert E. Park, Ernest W. Burgess, and Roderick E. McKenzie, *The City* (Chi-

cago: University of Chicago Press, 1967), 6; Walter E. Firey, *Land Use in Central Boston* (New York: Greenwood Press, 1947).

9. Park, Burgess, and McKenzie, *City*, 7.

10. Selwyn Raab, "A Battered and Ailing Mafia Is Losing Its Grip on America," *New York Times*, 22 October 1990, A-1.

11. Outfit associate, Interview respondent, Interview with author, 1992.

12. Chicago police officer, Interview respondent 5, Interview with author, 1988.

13. Chicago police detective, Interview respondent 14, Interview with author, 1992; Made guy, Interview respondent 21, Interview with author, 1993.

14. Albert Hunter, *Symbolic Communities* (Chicago: University of Chicago Press, 1974), 178.

15. Chicago gambler, Interview respondent 3, Interview with author, 1988.

16. Chicago police detective, Interview respondent 17, Interview with author, 1992.

17. Chicago police detective, Interview respondent 13, Interview with author, 1992; IRS special agent, Interview respondent 20, Interview with author, 1992.

18. Svend Riemer, "Hidden Dimensions of Neighborhood Planning," *Land Economics* 26 (1950): 197–201.

19. Chicago bookie, Interview respondent 12, Interview with author, 1992.

20. Taylor Street resident, Interview respondent 24, Interview with author, 1994.

21. "Court Told Lombardo Has a Good Side," *CDT*, 2 March 1983; IRS special agent, Interview respondent 20, Interview with author, 1992.

22. William Leonard and Sandy Smith, "The Capone Gang Today," *CDT*, 18 October 1959.

23. Dennis Hoffman, "Tilting at Windmills: The Chicago Crime Commission v. Organized Crime," in *Organized Crime in America: Concepts and Controversies*, ed. Timothy S. Bynum, 83–99 (New York: Willow Tree Press, 1987).

INDEX

ROBERT M. LOMBARDO is an associate professor of criminal justice at Loyola University Chicago and a former Chicago police officer. He is the author of *The Black Hand: Terror by Letter in Chicago*.

The University of Illinois Press
is a founding member of the
Association of American University Presses.

Composed in 10/13 Sabon LT Std
with Compacta display
by Barbara Evans
at the University of Illinois Press
Manufactured by Thomson-Shore, Inc.

University of Illinois Press
1325 South Oak Street
Champaign, IL 61820-6903
www.press.uillinois.edu